Washington
Montana
North Dakota
Minnesota
Lake Superior
Ottawa
Maine
Oregon
Idaho
South Dakota
Wisconsin
Michigan
Lake Huron
Niagara Falls
L. Ontario
New York
VT
NH
MA
CT
RI
Boston
Sacramento River
Minneapolis
Milwaukee
L. Michigan
Detroit
L. Erie
Wyoming
Pennsylvania
NJ
New York
Pittsburgh
Philadelphia
Sacramento
Nevada
Salt Lake City
Nebraska
Iowa
Chicago
Ohio
MD
DE
San Francisco
Denver
Illinois
Indiana
West Virginia
DC
Washington
Utah
Colorado
Kansas
St.Louis
Louisville
Virginia
Jamestown
Las Vegas
California
Missouri
Kentucky
North Carolina
Santa Fe
Nashville
Tennessee
Oklahoma City
Memphis
Arizona
Arkansas
Oklahoma
South Carolina
Los Angeles
Atlanta
New Mexico
San Diego
Phoenix
Mississippi
ATLANTIC
Dallas
Georgia
Hawaii (approx. 2000 miles)
Gulf of
Alabama
Mississippi River
Texas
OCEAN
Louisiana
Houston
New Orleans
Florida
San Antonio
Miami
Gulf of Mexico
FIC OCEAN
MEXICO
Mexico City
National Parks:
1 Denali
2 Yosemite
3 Sequoia and Kings Canyon
4 Grand Canyon
5 Mesa Verde
6 Shenandoah
7 Everglades
CT = Connecticut
DC = District of Columbia
DE = Delaware
MA = Massachusetts
MD = Maryland
NH = New Hampshire
NJ = New Jersey
RI = Rhode Island
VT = Vermont

Learning English

Red Line new 4

Unterrichtswerk für Realschulen

von

Stephanie Ashford, Claudia Finkbeiner,
Rosemary Hellyer-Jones, Marion Horner,
Peter Lampater, Michael Mattison,
Peter Pasch, Rolf W. Roth,
Klaus Stenzel, Gunther Volk
und Margaret Winck

Ernst Klett Verlag
Stuttgart Düsseldorf Leipzig

Learning English

Red Line New 4

für Klasse 8 an Realschulen

von
Stephanie Ashford B.A., Villingen-Schwenningen; Prof. Dr. Claudia Finkbeiner, Heilbronn; Rosemary Hellyer-Jones M.A., Ehingen (Donau); Marion Horner M.A., Cambridge; Peter Lampater, Ehingen (Donau); Michael Mattison B.A., Stuttgart; Prof. Dr. Peter Pasch, Tübingen; Rolf W. Roth M.A., Idar-Oberstein; Klaus Stenzel, Bopfingen; Gunther Volk, Villingen-Schwenningen; Margaret Winck B.A., Tübingen

Beratende Mitarbeit
Wolfgang Froese, Oldenburg; Christoph Kunz, Bietigheim-Bissingen; Franziska Lehmann-Lezmi, Lahr; Wolfgang Weber, Lebrade

Visuelle Gestaltung
Kenneth Huey, Seattle (Zeichnungen); Bernd Bürkle, Fellbach (Grundlayout);
Christian Dekelver, Weinstadt (Grafiken, Layout)
Veit Schütz, New York (Zeichnungen Vokabular, z. T. Grammatik)

Kassetten und CDs zu diesem Band

SB *Begleitkassette zum Schülerbuch* für zu Hause und für den Unterricht mit Unittexten, Liedern, Ausspracheübungen (Klettnummer 546448).
Die *Begleit-CD zum Schülerbuch* mit demselben Inhalt hat die Klettnummer 546488.
Lieferung durch jede Buchhandlung oder, wo dies auf Schwierigkeiten stößt, zuzüglich Portokosten per Nachnahme vom Verlag.

HV *Kassette zum Hörverstehen* für den Unterricht mit den Hörverstehenstexten aller Werkteile (Klettnummer 546449).
Die *CD zum Hörverstehen* für den Unterricht hat die Klettnummer 546489.
Lieferung direkt an Lehrerinnen und Lehrer, Schulstempel erforderlich.

Software

Passend zu diesem Band gibt es einen Grammatik- und Vokabeltrainer mit abwechslungsreichem Übungsmaterial, intelligenten Fehlerrückmeldungen, integriertem „sprechendem" Wörterbuch und Lernstatistik u. a.

1. Auflage A 1 10 9 8 | 2006 2005 2004 2003
Alle Drucke dieser Auflage können im Unterricht nebeneinander benutzt werden, sie sind untereinander unverändert.

Die letzte Zahl bezeichnet das Jahr des Druckes.

Internetadresse: http://www.klett-verlag.de

Redaktion: Roland Behnke, Joanne Popp B.A.

Herstellung: Claudia Kreipl
Umschlaggestaltung: Christian Dekelver, Weinstadt
Satz: DTP-Verlag und Lihs, Satz und Repro, Ludwigsburg
Reproduktion: maurer media + more, Tübingen
Druck: Druckerei Wirtz, Speyer
ISBN: 3-12-546440-4

9 783125 464407

Inhaltsverzeichnis

Hi there!
In diesem Band geht's in die USA. Was die Sprache angeht, wird dir vieles vertraut vorkommen, aber manches ist doch ein bisschen anders. Damit du einen reibungslosen Einstieg hast, begleiten wir dich durch dieses Buch.

Der Aufbau des Buches ist ähnlich wie in Band 3. Es gibt fünf **Units** und vier **Workshops** mit jeweils unterschiedlichen Themen.
Die *Units* sind wie in den ersten Bänden aufgebaut und enden mit einer *Let's check*-Seite.
Und die *Workshops* helfen dir, bestimmte Arbeitstechniken zu lernen oder weiter auszubauen.

Auf Seite 78 beginnt die **Extra line** mit spannenden und interessanten Lesetexten, einem *tape drama* und ab Seite 86 mit Übersetzungs- und Dolmetschübungen.

Auf Seite 90 beginnt der **Grammatikanhang.**

Das **Vokabular** beginnt auf Seite 108. Hier findest du alle neuen Wörter aus den *Units* und *Workshops*, die du lernen musst oder zumindest verstehen solltest.
In einigen Texten kommen auch Wörter vor, die für das Verständnis der Texte nicht unbedingt notwendig sind. Wenn du sie nicht aus dem Zusammenhang erschließen kannst, kannst du sie in der **alphabetischen Wortliste** am Ende des Buches nachschlagen. Dort sind natürlich auch alle anderen Wörter zu finden.

Und alle **unregelmäßigen Verben** stehen wie bisher in einer Liste auf den Seiten 171 und 172.

Du solltest aber auch noch wissen, was die **Zeichen** vor den einzelnen Texten und den Übungen bedeuten:

- SB Begleitkassette bzw. CD zum Schülerbuch
- HV Kassette bzw. CD zum Hörverstehen
- Partnerarbeit
- Gruppenarbeit
- Wiederholungsübungen
- E Mit dieser Übung kannst du dich besonders gut auf die Abschlussprüfung vorbereiten.
- Word power Wortschatzübungen
- Your turn Hier kannst du über dich, deine Familie oder Freunde sprechen.
- ⟨ ⟩ wahlfreie Aufgaben
- schwierigere Aufgaben, die wahlfrei sind
- für fächerübergreifenden Unterricht besonders geeignet

Alles klar?
Na, dann – viel Spaß!

Units/Steps	*Kommunikative Schwerpunkte Arbeitstechniken (AT)*	*Strukturen (R = Revision/Wiederholung)*	*Seite*

⟨Extra line⟩

Grammar

Vocabulary

Hello America!

Step A

You'll like Issaquah, Daniel

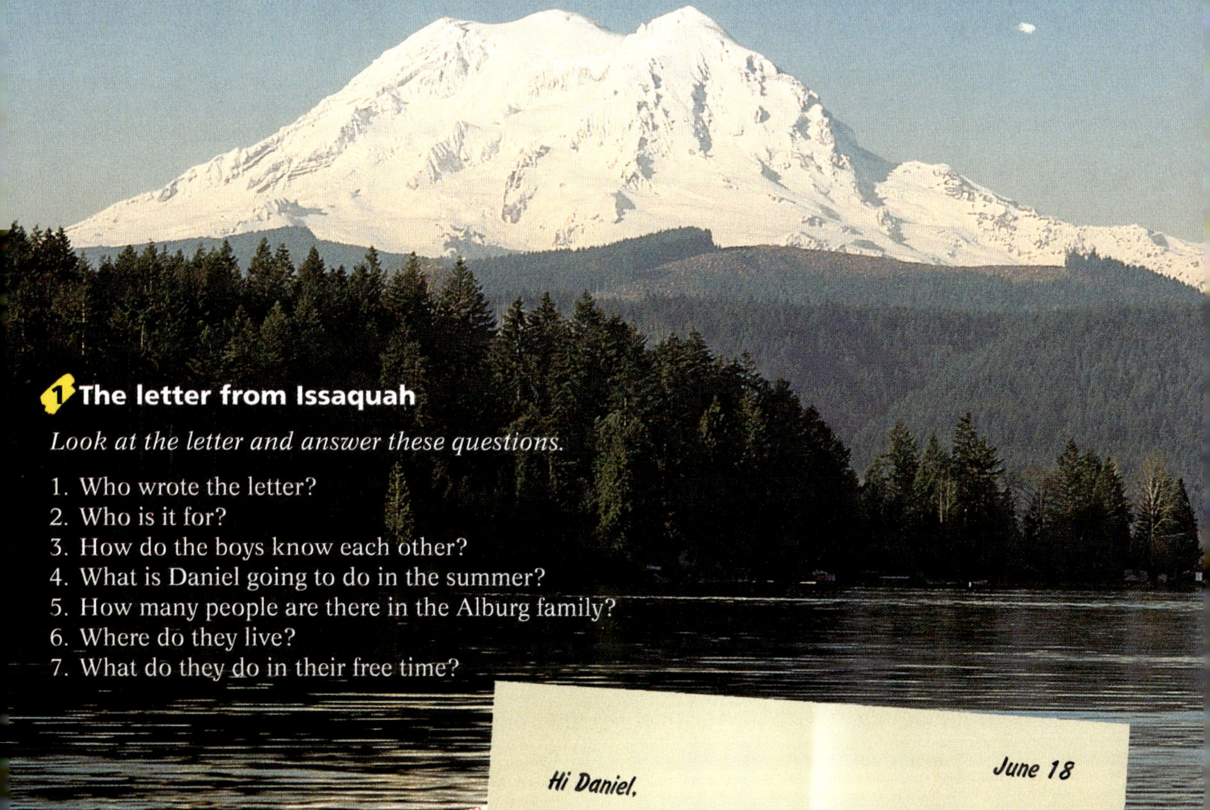

1 The letter from Issaquah

Look at the letter and answer these questions.

1. Who wrote the letter?
2. Who is it for?
3. How do the boys know each other?
4. What is Daniel going to do in the summer?
5. How many people are there in the Alburg family?
6. Where do they live?
7. What do they do in their free time?

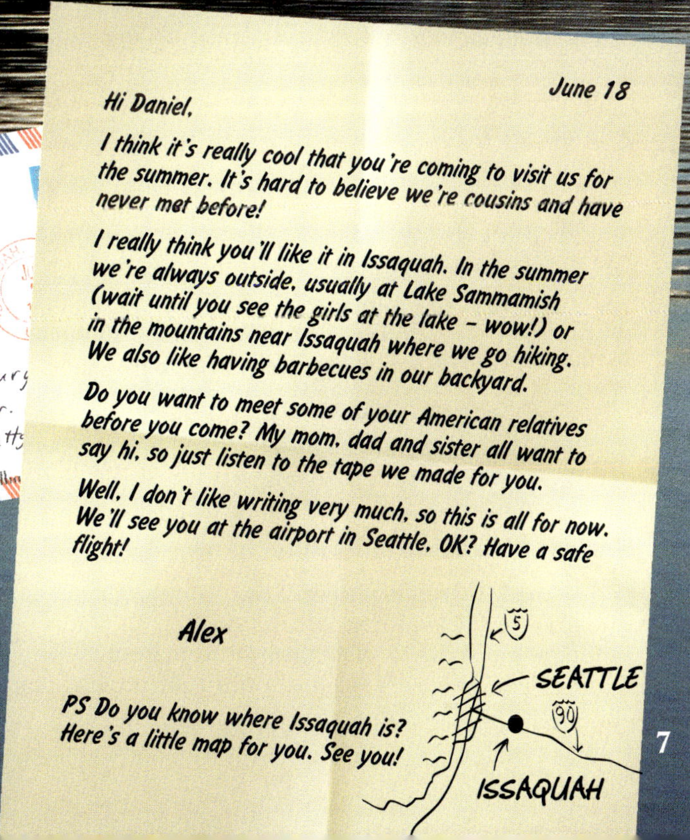

June 18

Hi Daniel,

I think it's really cool that you're coming to visit us for the summer. It's hard to believe we're cousins and have never met before!

I really think you'll like it in Issaquah. In the summer we're always outside, usually at Lake Sammamish (wait until you see the girls at the lake – wow!) or in the mountains near Issaquah where we go hiking. We also like having barbecues in our backyard.

Do you want to meet some of your American relatives before you come? My mom, dad and sister all want to say hi, so just listen to the tape we made for you.

Well, I don't like writing very much, so this is all for now. We'll see you at the airport in Seattle, OK? Have a safe flight!

Alex

PS Do you know where Issaquah is? Here's a little map for you. See you!

Step A

The Alburgs' hometown

2 →E Meet the family

a) *First read these sentences. Then listen to the messages from Alex's family. Is the information here right or wrong?*

1. Tori got her driver's license a long time ago.
2. Tori has a part-time job at a gym.
3. Lynn Alburg wants to hear about Stuttgart.
4. Daniel is going to arrive in America in June.
5. Bruce Alburg has met Daniel before.
6. Alex is 14 years old.
7. Alex's favorite Seattle music is on the tape.

b) *Listen to the recording again. What else do the Alburgs say?*

3 Hi! – Bye!

You can say "hi" when you meet someone, and when you leave again you can say "bye", but there are many other words and phrases you can use.

a) All these words and phrases are from the Alburgs' messages.
Put them in a "hi list" and in a "bye list".

Bye-bye! ***How are you?*** ***What's up?***
How are you doing? ***See you!*** ***Hi there!***

Hi!	Bye!
Hi there!	

b) *Can you add more words and phrases to your lists?*

4 A small town: A nice place to live?

Daniel is from the city, so when he arrives in Issaquah, he wants to know about life in a small town.

a) *Work in groups. Look at the pictures on the opposite page. What do you think life is like in a small town like Issaquah?*

Make notes about **people traffic noise shopping things to do in your free time …**, *then tell the class about your ideas.*

b) *Now listen to what the Alburgs say about Issaquah. Were you right?*

5 A great weekend in your town

Your turn Two young Americans, a 14-year-old girl and her 15-year-old brother, are going to stay at your house for the weekend.
What are you going to show them in your town?
Work with a partner. Make notes and tell the class about your ideas.

The Village Theatre

Hiking in the forests

A shop at Gilman Village

Issaquah's main street

At the bowling alley

At a drive-in restaurant

On Lake Sammamish

Step B

An American barbecue

1 At the barbecue

Daniel is having a barbecue with his cousins and some friends.
Listen to two short dialogues and take notes. Answer these questions.

1. What is Tori drinking?
2. What does she say about her drink?
3. How long has Daniel been in Issaquah?
4. What does he say to Tori about the food?
5. What does Alex burn?
6. How long has the food been on the barbecue?

2 I haven't been to a barbecue for ages

Can you complete these sentences? For some sentences there is more than one possible answer.

1. I haven't been to a barbecue
2. Bruce hasn't had a headache
3. Alex, come here and do your homework! You've been on the phone
4. Tori has driven to many places
5. She hasn't swum
6. Alex hasn't gone hiking
7. The fish has been on the barbecue
8. Wow, you look so different! I haven't seen you

since she got her driver's license on June 10th.
since you were three.
for 45 minutes.
for a long time/for ages.
since his last flight in April.
for a few months.
since last week at Lake Sammamish.
since he was at Mt. Rainier last month.

3 Looking at English

I have only been here	**since** Tuesday.
The fish has been on the barbecue	**for** 45 minutes.

When do we use for, *and when* since *with the present perfect? Look at the barbecue scene and at the sentences in exercise 2. Can you find a rule?*

4 Your turn How long has it been since ...?

I haven't been to

the beach / the library / my grandpa's / the zoo / an Italian restaurant / ...

for / since

last week. / Dad's birthday. / 10 months. / Christmas. / two years. / March. / ...

Can you pick up some flour, Tori?

After the barbecue Daniel, Tori, Alex and their friends are starting a game of basketball. And they're listening to some music ...

Tori: Can you turn up the music, Alex?
Alex: That horrible song? Forget it!
Tori: Come on, it's my favorite song and you're standing right next to the radio. Now can you turn it up, or not?!
Alex: OK, OK ...

Lynn Alburg is coming out of the kitchen.

Lynn: Tori honey, can you pick up some flour at the store? I need some for an apple pie.
Tori: Mom, we're in the middle of a game.
Lynn: Come on Tori. You've had your license since June, and you only see the fun side of it: shopping, going to the lake, going places with your friends – I think you could help us from time to time, too, OK? Oh, and turn down that music, please. We want to stay friends with the neighbors.
Alex: All right, Mom – that was great! Tori thinks she's so special now with her car and her license!
Lynn: Careful, young man, I've got a job for you, too. Can you clean up the backyard and take the garbage out when you're finished with your game?
Alex: OK, OK ...
Lynn: Well thank you – what a nice young man!

5 Can you please ...?

Can you **turn up** the music?
Can you **take** the garbage **out**?

Can you **turn** it **up**?
Can you **take** it **out?**

§ 2

Can you write new questions with it *or* them?
Example:

1. Can you please **pick up** some hot dogs at the store?
   Can you **pick them up** at the store?
2. Can you turn up the radio, please?
3. Could you throw away these paper plates?
4. Can you take the steaks off, please? They're burning, too!
5. Could you clean up the backyard a little before our friends get here, please?
6. Can you take the potato salad out into the backyard? Everyone's waiting for it.
7. Could you put your coke float down and watch the hot dogs, please?
8. Can you write down this recipe for me, please?

6 ⟨A recipe⟩

A real American coke float

Would you like to enjoy a real American barbecue drink?
Then just make a coke float for you, your friends and your family.
All you need is:
- *a large glass*
- *a straw*
- *a spoon*
- *vanilla ice cream*
- *coke*

Put some vanilla ice cream in a glass 3/4 full of coke and enjoy.

BIG NIGHT IN A SMALL TOWN

"Let's go to the bowling alley," Tori suggested. "Everyone in Issaquah will be there – Daniel can meet them all."

"No, no – not *again*!" Alex protested. "This town is so boring! The bowling alley is the only thing I've seen for the last six Fridays! Isn't there anything else to do?"

"I think that bowling sounds very nice," Daniel said.

"Well I have a better idea: Snoqualmie Falls!" Alex said with a proud smile.

"Forget it, Alex," Tori told her brother with an angry look. "You know Mom and Dad told us not to go up there at night, and it will be dark in an hour."

"Snoqualmie Falls? What's that?" Daniel wanted to know.

"It's a really big waterfall out in the forest – 250 feet high!" Alex explained.

"Oh yes, I would like that!" Daniel said.

"Come on, Tori – forget the bowling alley! Let's go!"

"OK, OK, but I hope Mom and Dad don't find out – they won't be happy," Tori said.

"Just get in the car, turn on some music, and drive, Tori," was Alex's answer. "Snoqualmie, here we come!"

20 minutes and a few songs later ...

"OK, we're here!" Tori told the two boys.

"Great, let's walk down the trail to the rocks," Alex suggested. "That's where you can really see how big the waterfall is, Daniel."

"Wait a minute," Tori started. "There's a phone booth – I have to call Cindy."

"Cindy? Why?" Alex didn't understand.

"Because she thinks we'll be at the bowling alley, and I forgot to call and tell her we won't be there," Tori told him. "Wait here, I'll be back in a minute, OK?"

Tori came back and the three teenagers walked down the steep forest trail to the rocks.

Suddenly Tori screamed.

"Oh no!" Alex shouted. "Tori fell into the bushes."

"Tori, are you OK?" Daniel asked.

"Yeah, I'm fine," Tori said. "But we've got to be careful here – it's not easy to see."

"Wow, look at all that water!" Daniel had to say when they reached the bottom of the trail.

"Yeah, it's really something," Tori agreed as she smiled at him.

Step C

"Your parents don't want us to come here, right?" Daniel asked. "But it's so beautiful!"

"They think it's too dangerous at night. They think we'll fall 250 feet. But you know how parents are."

The kids laughed, sang, talked, jumped from rock to rock, and listened to the sound of the water.

"Oh, I'm glad we came up here," Tori said. "Good idea, little brother. But it's time to go now."

"What? We've only been here for 20 minutes," Alex protested.

"Yeah, I forgot to tell you: we're going to the bowling alley to meet Cindy and the others now!"

"But you called Cindy when we got here!" Alex protested again.

"Yeah. She says it's too boring at the bowling alley without us. And we can't stay here all night anyway, so let's go."

The kids drove back to Issaquah, walked into the bowling alley, and got in line at the counter to rent bowling balls and shoes.

"Hey!" Tori said in an angry voice to an older boy. "Watch where you're going."

"Oh, excuse me, I didn't mean to bump into you," the boy explained and then walked off.

"Some people are so rude," Tori said to Alex and Daniel.

"Shoes and balls for three? That'll be $18.75, please," said the woman behind the counter.

Tori reached for her bag.

"The zipper is open. How long has *that* been open?" Tori said. She looked worried now.

"Oh my God, my wallet's gone – and my money and my driver's license!" Tori shouted. She was shocked.

"But ... how did you lose it?" Daniel asked.

Tori didn't answer. "How am I going to get a new license?" she asked. "What are we going to tell Mom and Dad? Let's go home."

At home 10 minutes later ...

"Hi kids, how was Snoqualmie Falls?" Lynn asked.

"What?!" was the look on the teenagers' faces.

They were shocked. And Bruce and Lynn didn't look happy ...

1 What happens next?

Work in groups. Talk about how the story will end for the kids.

1. How did Bruce and Lynn find out that the kids had been to Snoqualmie Falls?
2. What are Bruce and Lynn going to do?
3. Will Tori get her wallet back?

Make notes about your ideas and tell the class about your ending.

HV 2 → E Hi kids, how was Snoqualmie Falls?

a) *Listen to what happens to Tori, Alex and Daniel at home. Was your group right about the ending ?*

b) *Now read these questions, listen to the recording again and take notes. Can you answer the questions?*

1. Where did Tori leave her wallet?
2. Who found Tori's wallet?
3. When will Tori get her wallet back?
4. What did Bruce and Lynn do with Tori's money?
5. What will happen after Daniel goes back to Germany?
6. What were the two mistakes Tori made?

3 Role play: It isn't easy being a parent!

Work in groups. One group plays the role of the kids, the other group the role of the parents.

Maybe these phrases will help you.

"Parents"	"Kids"
You're in big trouble …	We can explain everything …
What were you kids thinking?	It's not as bad as you think …
Thank goodness you didn't have an accident.	Please don't be angry …
	We just wanted to show Daniel …

4 The Alburgs

Make sentences with the present perfect and for *or* since.

Example: 1. The Alburgs (live) in Issaquah … 1983.
1. The Alburgs **have lived** in Issaquah **since** 1983.

2. The kids (be) at the waterfall … 20 minutes now.
3. Tori (know) Cindy … April last year.
4. Daniel (be) in Issaquah … two weeks now.
5. The Alburgs (not/be) to Seattle … the last weekend in May.
6. Daniel (make) himself a lot of coke floats … he had his first one at the barbecue.
7. Tori (have) her driver's license … June.
8. Daniel (learn) a lot of new American words … he arrived in Issaquah.
9. Alex (not/buy) a CD of his favorite Seattle band … the last six months.

SB 5 ⟨A song: Friday on my mind⟩

Vanda/Young © LINE Music GmbH.

Monday morning feel so bad,
Everybody seems to nag me.
Comin' Tuesday I feel better.
Even my old man looks good.
Wednesday just don't go,
Thursday goes too slow,
I've got Friday on my mind.

Tonight I'll spend my bread.
Tonight I'll lose my head.
Tonight I've got to get
Tonight …
Monday I have Friday on my mind.

Chorus:
Gonna have fun in the city.
Be with my girl, she's so pretty.
She looks fine tonight.
She is out of sight to me.

Do the five-day's night once more,
No, I've nothing else that bugs me
More than working for the rich man,
Hey, I'll change that scene one day.
Tonight I might be mad,
Tomorrow I'll be glad
'Cause I've got Friday on my mind.

(Chorus)

Step D

Let's check

1 Be careful!

Change for *to* since *and* since *to* for *in these sentences.*
But be careful: You have to change more than just since *or* for! *(Take today's date.)*

Example: 1. I haven't seen Cindy since Monday last week.
I haven't seen Cindy **for … days**.

2. We have lived in this house for 12 years.
3. Bruce hasn't been to Germany for 20 years.
4. Tori has had her driver's license since June.
5. Alex and Tori have only known Daniel for three months.
6. Daniel has lived in Stuttgart since he was seven.

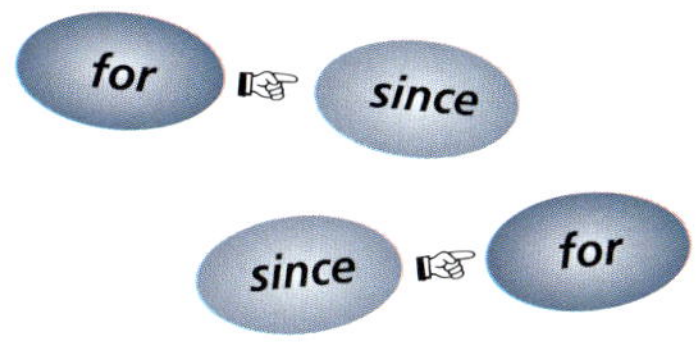

2 → E After the barbecue

Can you put these sentences in the right order?

Example: 1. Alex, these bottles shouldn't be here. You/can/please/out/them/take?
Alex, these bottles shouldn't be here. Can you take them out, please?

2. Yuck, this fish is a week old! Away/it/throw!
3. Tori, your brother and Daniel are waiting at the lake. Them/you/please/up/can/pick?
4. The backyard looks terrible! Boys/you/tidy/up/it/please/can?
5. Up/oh,/turn/it/, that's my favorite song!
6. Tori, your car is so dirty inside! Can/up/you/little/a/it/clean?

3 Word power Words that go together

a) In each group of words, one word isn't like the others.
Find the word, and explain why.

Example: 1. Germany – Mexico – Pacific Northwest – the US
Pacific Northwest doesn't belong because it isn't a country.

2. tractor – car – bus – canoe
3. fantastic – horrible – cool – great
4. sea – waterfall – lake – forest
5. barbecue – potato salad – beef steak – hot dog
6. brother – mom – dad – neighbor

b) *Can you think of more words that belong to these groups of words?*

4 American and British English

What are the British English words for these American English words and phrases?

WORKING WITH WORDS

1 Understanding new words

A
6 p.m.
Hi kids,
Dinner's in the **fridge**, just put it in the **microwave**. We've got a **neighborhood watch** meeting tonight, so we won't be back **till** late.
See you, Mom and Dad

B
Hi there, again, 6:10 p.m.
Good news, kids – Uncle Fred just called. We're **definitely** going to Colorado for his birthday party. We're taking the **red-eye flight** to Denver on Friday around **midnight**.
M & D

C
6:50 p.m.
Hi Daniel and Alex,
I'm off to the gym. Uncle Fred called again. He wants to **tour around** Colorado with us in his **motorhome** next week. Cool! Maybe we can do some **river-rafting** there. Tori

D
Hi Daniel, 4:30 p.m.
I'm **over** at Cindy's. She wants to **install** some new **software** on her computer and I'm going to **give her a hand.** Why don't you come and join us for pizza and a **movie** later? Alex

1 Can you guess?

When Daniel comes home one evening he finds these messages on the fridge. He can guess most of the words he doesn't know – what about you?

> **tip** **Understanding new words:**
> 1. Sometimes you already know parts of a word, so you can guess the meaning of it as a whole.
> 2. …

a) You can guess "microwave" because you know "wave", and "micro" is like the German. You can guess the meaning of most of the other new words, too. *Talk about how you found out what they mean. What do you do when you can't guess the meaning of a word? Try to write down more tips for the tip box.*

b) *Work out what's going on. Where are the Alburgs? Why are they going to Denver? Why are they going by plane? What do you think a red-eye flight is? (Think of what the Alburgs will look like when they arrive in Denver.)*

2 Working with your dictionary

1 Warming up

Sometimes you can't guess a word or you want to check if you have guessed correctly. Then you have to use a dictionary.

Put the words on the right in alphabetical order as quickly as possible. Compare your list with your partner's. If your list is different – who is right?

ask – annoyed – anything – alphabet – across – awful – animal – address – airport – ambulance

imagine – industry – interesting – Italian – important – inside – introduce – interview – invite – information

2 Your dictionary

a) *Look at these tips. They will help you to find the right words and meanings more easily.*

In a dictionary words are in groups under a **headword.** Look for the headword first.

A dictionary tells you how to **pronounce** a word.

Many words have more than one **meaning.** You find them under the headword. There is a number for each meaning.

A dictionary also tells you if something is **American English**.

tour [tʊə(r)] I *s* **1.** Tour *f*; Reise, Fahrt *f*; *(im Gebäude)* Rundgang *m*; **2.** Führung *f*; Rundfahrt *f*; **3.** (~ *of inspection)* Runde *f*, Rundgang *m*; 4. *theat sport* Tournee *f*; ▸ **go on a ~ of France** eine Reise durch Frankreich machen; **make a ~ of the building** einen Rundgang durchs Gebäude machen; **on ~** auf Tournee; **guided ~** Führung *f*; **coach ~** Busreise *f*; II *itr* **1.** eine Reise machen; **2.** *theat sport* eine Tournee machen; auf Tournee sein; III *tr* **1.** bereisen, reisen durch; **2.** einen Rundgang machen durch; besichtigen; **3.** *theat sport* eine Tournee machen durch.
tourism [ˈtʊərɪzəm] Fremdenverkehr, Tourismus *m*; **tourist** [ˈtʊərɪst] Tourist(in) *m (f)*; ▸ **travel ~** in der Touristenklasse reisen; **tourist agency, office,** *Am* **bureau** Reisebüro *n*; **tourist class** Touristenklasse *f*; **tourist guide 1.** *(Buch)* Reiseführer *m*; **2.** *(Person)* Fremdenführer(in) *m (f)*; **tourist industry** Fremdenverkehr(sindustrie *f*) *m*; **tourist season** Reisezeit *f*; **tourist ticket** Rundreise(fahr)karte *f*.

These abbreviations *(Abkürzungen)* tell you if the word is a **noun**, a **verb**, an **adjective** etc. Look for the list of abbreviations in your dictionary!

You also find **useful phrases** after the headword.

A dictionary also gives you **related words** – words of the same word family.

Often there is a list of **compound words** (headword + another word) after the headword or as a separate entry *(eigener Eintrag)*.

Dictionary entry: PONS Schülerwörterbuch

b) *Now use the dictionary entry to translate these sentences into good German.*

1. Uncle Fred wants to go on a **tour of Colorado** with us.
2. We're starting with a **guided tour** of Old Denver.
3. That'll be great. I read about it in a **tourist guide**.
4. Hey! My favorite rock group **is touring** Colorado at the moment.
5. So are a lot of other people. There's one **tourist season** in Colorado – the whole year!
6. Yeah, the **tourist industry** is very important there.

3 One word in German – different words in English

You will find that one word in German can have two or more meanings in English.
Example: **fahren** can be **drive** (a car); **ride** (a bike); **go** (by bus); **sail** (a boat); etc.

Look up **laufen** *and complete these sentences with the correct English word:*

1. We missed the bus, so we had to … all the way home.
2. He … the 100 m race in the fastest time.
3. This river … from east to west.
4. I have to get a new CD player. This one doesn't … any more.
5. The English test we did today … very well.
6. I've got a cold, my nose … all the time.
7. I'd like to go out tonight. What … at the movies?
8. Part of this trail … through the forest.

3 Using your skills

tip Remember: You don't have to understand every word to get the information you need.

1 Understanding a difficult text

On their tour of Colorado Alex, Tori and Daniel want to go whitewater rafting.
Look at the leaflet on the opposite page and try to answer these questions:

1. Is there a trip that is especially exciting?
2. What do you have to bring?
3. Can you rent any equipment?
4. Is it a good idea to make reservations or can you go on a trip right away?
5. When do you have to pay for the trip?

You will probably have to look up the marked words in your dictionary. Be careful to find the right meaning for the context.

2 Word building

You know that you can make adjectives from other adjectives or nouns with the beginning **un-** or with the endings **-less** or **-ful** (think of **un**happy, help**less**, or use**ful**, for example).
You can also make adjectives from some verbs if you put **-able** at the end (there are some examples in the leaflet: enjoy**able**, suit**able**, reason**able**, etc.).
For each sentence make a word of two or three parts.

un-	wash ✔ drink believ(e) chang(e) forget(t) reason	-able

Example: You've got some tomato on your new jacket. – That's no problem, it's wash**able.**

1. This water from your water bottle tastes strange. Are you sure it's …?
2. This rafting trip doesn't cost very much, the price is quite …
3. Some of the rapids are so rough, it's really …
4. What a great trip – this is an … experience.
5. What will the weather be like tomorrow? – I don't know, it's quite … at the moment.

3 Making more words

Find more nouns with these endings in the text and look up the words they come from in your dictionary. Make sentences with each noun.

-ment
involvement (→ to involve)

-ation
information (→ to inform)

-ing
training (→ to train)

4 Compound words

Put the words in the box together to make new words. Check your dictionary to see if your words exist.

tip You can write most compound words as one word or as two words. Don't worry too much about hyphens.

sun light out over back burn glasses door night weight

Whitewater Rafting and the Arkansas River

River-rafting is one of the most exciting free time activities in Colorado.
Colorado has lots of suitable rivers and enjoyable runs of all levels, from easy to difficult, for young and old, for individuals and groups.

Why go with us?

In the past 10 years the number of companies which run tours on the Arkansas River has gone from just a handful to over 80. We were part of the original handful so we have years of experience and personal involvement.
We use high quality equipment.
Our guides get excellent training, including navigation, emergency river rescue, team management and geology.
We give great trips at a reasonable price.

Information and Reservations

It's best to make reservations for half-day and full-day trips. We require a 50 % deposit when you book and the rest of your payment fifteen days before the trip. (Full payment if you book later than fifteen days before your trip.)

What to bring

Half to one day trips: Wear clothes that dry quickly – shorts and tennis shoes (lightweight pants and long sleeve cotton shirts if you sunburn easily). Bring sunglasses with strap, sunscreen, sweater or jacket, raingear, and a change of dry clothes and dry shoes.

Overnight trips: You will get a packing list and information about available rental equipment on payment of your deposit. Sleeping bags MUST be of the lightweight, compact, backpacking type.

Royal Gorge

An unforgettable overnight trip for experienced rafters. You must be in good physical condition and able to swim. You should wear a wetsuit. We start upstream of the Gorge. As we go downstream the rapids will get more and more difficult. Conditions may force us to walk around some areas.

Other trips: Contact us for information on other rafting trips and for backpacking, mountaineering, ski touring and other outdoor adventures.

A patchwork quilt

Step A

A land of immigrants

The high school students who made this patchwork quilt are not 'foreigners' in America. Although they have different origins, they are all citizens of the United States.

1 Origins

a) *What countries do you think the teenagers' families might be from?*

b) *How many of you have families who came to Germany as immigrants? Why did they come here? What was difficult for them at first?*

2 Different reasons, different journeys

You can think of America as a patchwork quilt. When you look at it closely, you don't see the quilt as a whole. You see the pieces themselves, the different groups of people who have come to settle from all over the world. Some of the pieces are old, and some are new. There are big pieces and little pieces, and each one has its own story to tell.

a) *Read about the different groups of immigrants in the United States. Which is the right order for the pictures and texts?*

A **The first Blacks arrived in America as slaves in 1619. They came from Africa and had to work for rich Virginia farmers.**

B **The first settlers probably came from Asia 35,000 years ago: the Native Americans. They were looking for better areas for hunting. They walked all the way from Siberia to Alaska and settled all over the United States.**

C At the beginning of the 17th century the English started colonies on the East Coast. Life was hard for the settlers, so why did they leave England?

D The biggest wave of immigrants came from Europe between 1800 and 1920. Some were looking for freedom. Others were poor and wanted a better life. They hoped to find work in the cities, and maybe even get rich.

E The number of immigrants from Asia and Latin America is growing fast. America is still a dream country for many people. Most immigrants are allowed to come, and after a while they become citizens. But there are some who try to get into the country illegally.

b) *Collect the reasons why the different groups of people came to the United States. Do foreigners come to Germany for the same reasons?*

3 More about the immigrants

Which texts could these sentences be from? Choose the best place for them in the texts.

1. This was possible because there was a bridge of land between Asia and North America.
2. Some arrive in small, often unsafe boats, and others come – usually on foot or in the back of a truck at night – from Mexico.
3. Their journey from England took two months, and many people died on the way.
4. When they arrived they probably learned English from the farmers.
5. There are many Native American languages, but they are slowly disappearing.
6. In those days people traveled to America by ship in 11 to 14 days, and paid less than $15.

HV 4 → E Listening practice: Origins

The patchwork quilt of America won a prize in a competition. Soo, Daryl, Isi, Josh and Anna are talking to a reporter who is collecting information about immigrants.

a) *Listen and take notes. Find out:*
- which three students answer the questions,
- where each one is from,
- why their parents are in Seattle.

Name	Where from?	Why?

b) *Work in groups of three or four. Talk about what the other two students might perhaps tell the reporter, and write the rest of the interview.*

A look at Seattle

5 Daniel's travel diary

Daniel wrote a travel diary during his stay in America, and added photos and other information.

Which text describes which photo? What makes you think so? Would you like to visit any of these places? Say why or why not.

1 *The Space Needle. Great views from the top. I tried not to think about earthquakes.*

2 *This is the International District, the part of town where Soo and her family live. Mr. Chung drove me and Alex around in his new car.*

3 *The Sonics are playing against the Sacramento Kings. Seattle is basketball crazy.*

4 *The "old" city in Pioneer Square. (Ha, ha, "old" in Seattle means about 1900!)*

5 *There are all kinds of food stalls at Pike Place Market. You could eat your way around for hours!*

6 ⟨Project: Living together⟩

Do a project about different nationalities at your school or in your town. Try to answer these questions.

- How many people with different nationalities are there? Where are they from? Think about how you can show the information. On a chart? On a map?
- Why do they live in Germany?
- What problems do they or their families have?
- How do they make our country a better place?

Tricky situations

Daniel, Cindy, Tori and Alex have just watched "Tricky Situations", a TV game show. They are talking about what they would do in the same situations as on the show.

Barbecued snake – yuck! I'd say 'No, thanks, I don't eat meat', or something like that. I wouldn't eat it just to be polite. If I did, I'd probably be sick in front of everyone, and that would be really bad!

That happened to someone I know! They offered her nice clothes, so she joined. She has no idea how dangerous gangs are. They just want to fight each other. I wouldn't become a member for a million dollars.

I'd give the change back right away. If I didn't, the manager would think the cashier stole the money. And anyway, I'd feel bad, as if I was a thief. I wouldn't be able to show my face in the store again.

I'd press the alarm and wait. I wouldn't go crazy and try to climb out of the elevator. That would be too dangerous. I wouldn't get scared, I'd just get bored. It wouldn't be so bad if there was a nice girl with me …

1 Tricky situations

Can you guess the situations? Example: Tori's situation: The cashier gave her too much change.

2 →E If it happened to me, …

I'd = I would

§ 3

Match the parts to make sentences.

1. If a man in the street asked me for money,
2. If big green spots appeared all over my body,
3. If I found a dead beetle in my lunchbox,
4. If I came face to face with a bear,
5. If someone stole my bike,
6. If someone offered me a role in a movie,

- I'd tell the police.
- I'd throw it out of the window.
- I'd run away as fast as I could.
- I'd feel very lucky.
- I wouldn't give him any.
- I'd go to the doctor.

If I **was** in Seattle, I **would go** to a Sonics game.
If someone **stole** my bike, I **would tell** the police.
past tense — would + infinitive

3 Only if …

§ 3

a) *Work in small groups. Would you ever do these things? In what situations would you do them?*

tell lies to someone — try bungee-jumping — read someone's diary — learn Japanese — paint yourself green — go to an expensive restaurant — play with teddy bears — travel without a ticket

Example: I would only try bungee-jumping if someone gave me a lot of money.

b) Your turn *What would you do if the situations in the game show "Tricky situations" and in exercise 1 happened to you?*
Example: If someone offered me barbecued snake, I'd say …

4 →E A difficult problem

Soo is talking to her cousin Cindy on the phone. *Put the verbs into the past tense or add* would.

... But don't tell anyone, OK? ... If my parents **found out** (find out) I'm going out with him, they **would go** (go) crazy! It was bad enough when my Korean friends found out ... Well, one girl won't even speak to me any more ... She thinks Daryl might be a gang member ... No, Cindy, he is not! ... I know, but if I (tell) Mom and Dad, they (not let) me see him again ... Yeah, of course it's because he's black, but they (never say so). ... Sure, they (not mind) so much if he (be) Korean, but they think I'm too young for boyfriends anyway ... Huh? ... Well, they want me to concentrate on school. ... Yeah, parents! ... Anyway, Daryl has asked me to go with him to see a Sonics game tomorrow. He has bought the tickets already, so I have to go with him ... You see, I offered to help the Korean Club get ready for the Worldfest on Saturday. Mom wants me to translate 13 recipes into English, but I've got to go to the game. If I (not go) Daryl (give) my ticket to someone else – and I can't let that happen, can I?

What is Soo's problem?

5 ⟨The Melting Pot⟩

Some people have described America as a 'melting pot' which mixes people of different nationalities into one nation. This poem shows that the melting pot idea doesn't always work.

There is a magic melting pot
where any girl or man
can step in Czech or Greek or Scot,
step out American.

Johann and *Jan* and *Jean* and *Juan*,
Giovanni and *Ivan*
step in and then step out again
all freshly christened *John*.

Sam, watching, said "Why, I was here
even before they came,"
and stepped in, too, but was tossed out
before he passed the brim.

And every time Sam tried that pot
they threw him out again.
"Keep out. This is our private pot.
We don't want your black stain."

At last, thrown out a thousand times,
Sam said, "I don't give a damn.
Shove your old pot. You can like it or not,
but I'll be just what I am."

By Dudley Randall

a) *Who is Sam? What happens when he tries to get into the melting pot? Why does it happen?*

b) *Look at the names in lines 5, 6 and 8. What countries do you think they are from?*

c) *How does Sam feel about the melting pot at the end?*

At the Worldfest

It is Sunday afternoon. Soo and Daryl are eating some Korean food at the Worldfest.

Soo: What's wrong with it? Don't you like it? Mom made it herself. It's very popular in Korea.
Daryl: It's great! I'm always interested in trying new things. It's just that I'm not used to eating with chopsticks.
Soo: Here, use a fork or we'll be here all day. I want to watch the African dancers.
Daryl: Me, too. Hey, wait! Where are you going?
Soo: Uh – oh! Mom and Dad are here. I only hope they didn't see us together. Quick – this way!
Daryl: Oh, Soo. I'm tired of hiding all the time. Why don't you tell them about us?
Soo: Well, I'm just not looking forward to telling them, that's all.
Daryl: What are you worried about? I'm not scared of meeting them. I'm proud of who I am.
Soo: Have you told your friends about me yet?
Daryl: My friends? Well, no, not yet. Tomorrow. I'll tell them tomorrow.

6 Soo and Daryl

Which sentences are wrong? Can you say what is wrong about them?

1. Daryl is eating slowly because he doesn't like Korean food.
2. Soo gives Daryl a fork because she's tired of waiting for him.
3. Daryl isn't interested in watching dance shows.
4. Soo is tired of hiding from her parents.
5. Daryl doesn't want to meet Soo's parents. He's scared.
6. Daryl isn't happy about being African-American.

Daryl is **tired of** hid**ing** all the time.

I'm not very **good at** eat**ing** with chopsticks.

§ 4

7 Your turn What are you interested in?

a) *Finish the sentences and write down your answers. Use* -ing-forms *after the prepositions.*

Example: I'm not interested in watching stupid shows on TV.

1. I'm crazy about …
2. I'm not interested in …
3. I'm good at …
4. I'm terrible at …
5. I'm looking forward to …
6. I'm not scared of …

b) *Work in groups of four or five. Make dialogues.*

Examples:

What are you crazy about?	I'm crazy about going to pop concerts.
Me, too./Are you? I'm not.	

What are you not interested in?	I'm not interested in watching football.
Me neither./Aren't you? But I am.	

The fortune cookie

Mrs. Chung looked at her husband. "Did you see what I just saw?" "I did," he answered, "and I don't like it."

"You wouldn't mind so much if he were Korean, would you?" said Mrs. Chung. "But don't worry. He's probably just one of her friends from school."

Mr. Chung wasn't so sure. "You saw the way they were looking at each other! Why did they run off like that? They didn't want us to see them! Soo is hiding something from us!"

"He's right," thought Mrs. Chung. Sometimes she felt she didn't know her own daughter anymore. In the past Soo had told her everything. Now she didn't.

"Did you notice his clothes?" asked Mr. Chung. "He was wearing red and black. Those are the colors of that gang, the Jackals. They hate people like us."

It was time to leave. Mr. and Mrs. Chung walked to the car with heavy hearts. Soo was waiting for them and saw from their faces that something was wrong. Mr. Chung spoke first. "Who was that young man you were with, Soo?"

Soo looked down at her feet. It was time for the truth. Slowly she told them about Daryl. They listened quietly and Soo felt better at the end. Her parents looked at each other. "Soo, we're worried about you," said Mrs. Chung. "It might be dangerous."

"Oh, you think he's a gang member, huh? That's crazy!" cried Soo. "Why do you always think the worst? You haven't even met Daryl! I guess it's because he's black, right?"

"I don't want you to see him again, do you hear?" said Mr. Chung. "I've read about those gangs."

Soo tried not to cry. She looked at her mother. Whose side would her mother take?

Mrs. Chung put her arms around Soo. "We just want the best for you, honey," she said.

The Chungs drove home to their small apartment above the store. Soo ran upstairs to her bedroom where Pugwacket, her dog, was waiting for her. She sat down next to him and told him her worries. What if Mom and Dad were right? What if Daryl really was a gang member? That would explain why he hadn't told his friends about her yet. If they found out, they would throw him out of the gang – or worse! Soo reached in her pocket for something to dry her eyes with. Something fell out. It was a fortune cookie someone had given her at the Chinese stall. She took off the paper and read the message inside the cookie.

What could it mean?

While Soo was thinking about the fortune cookie, Daryl was thinking about the Jackals. Some of his friends were in this gang and he had thought about joining them, too. He was getting tired of delivering pizza in the evening, a job he did three times a week. If he joined the Jackals there would be easier ways to make money. But then he had met Soo. Somehow this girl had changed him. Now he felt differently. Not only about the gang and the things they did, but about the Asians, too.

The next day Soo and her parents drove to Issaquah to see the Cho family. Soo was happy to see Cindy again. Everything went fine until Mr. Cho turned on the TV for the Seattle news. The first pictures they saw were live from the International District. Flames were coming out of buildings, and there was smoke everywhere. Suddenly they saw their store!

"Come on – let's go!" Mr. Chung wasn't just frightened. He was angry. "Those damn Jackals!"
"Wait! Look!" cried his wife. "Someone is stealing something from the store!" They looked more closely. They saw a young man with something in his arms. Soo was shocked. It was Daryl!
When they got back the fire was out. The Chungs' store didn't look too bad, but there were TV cameras everywhere. Daryl was in the middle of it all, and he was still holding something!

"I was delivering some pizzas when I saw the smoke," he was telling reporters. "This is where my girlfriend's family live. They're away at the moment. Then I suddenly remembered their dog Pugwacket. My girlfriend, Soo, had told me about Pug. His favorite place is on her bed. The fire wasn't bad at that point, so I broke a window and went in. I knew Soo would go crazy if Pug got trapped inside!"

Then Daryl noticed Soo in the crowd. He ran past the reporters and gave her Pugwacket. "He is just fine." Soo gave her dog a big kiss. "What about me?" asked Daryl.
Suddenly Mr. and Mrs. Chung appeared next to Soo. "I don't think we've met," said Mr. Chung. He held out his hand to Daryl. "Maybe," thought Soo, "the fortune cookie was right after all."

1 → E Understanding the story

1. Who do the Chungs see at the Worldfest?
2. Who does Mr. Chung think Daryl is?
3. Why is Mrs. Chung disappointed with Soo?
4. Why is Daryl thinking about joining the Jackals?
5. Why doesn't he join them?
6. Why does Mr. Chung think the Jackals started the fire?
7. Why is the story called 'The Fortune Cookie'?

2 A happy or a sad ending?

Work in groups. How do you think Soo, her parents and Daryl feel about each other at the end? Talk about what they might say to each other, and write an ending for the story.

3 Listening practice: How the fire started

A reporter is interviewing a firefighter. *Find out how the fire started. What other fires does the firefighter talk about?*

Step C

Not only hot dogs

4 Different interests

Daniel and Tori are at the Worldfest. They are in front of the Suquamish stall.
Put in the prepositions and the -ing-forms.

learn
do walk eat
see miss

at about in ✓
to of to

Tori: Come on, Daniel. Let's have a look at this stall.
Daniel: Why don't we get something from one of the food stalls first?
Tori: Aren't you interested (**in**/…-**ing**) about Native Americans?
Daniel: Of course I am. But I'm hungry!
Tori: Don't tell me you're worried (…/…) lunch! We can have something later.
Daniel: I know, but I'm not used (…/…) around hungry.
Tori: Hey, look, Daniel! They're getting things ready for the dance show. It's really fun to watch the Native American dancers. They're really good (…/…) rain dances.
Daniel: I need to eat first, Tori.
Tori: Oh, come on! The show starts in a minute. I've been looking forward (…/…) this all day!
Daniel: Well, let me just get a hot dog first. Can I get you one, too?
Tori: Daniel, you can't eat hot dogs at an international festival like this! They're boring!
Daniel: But hot dogs *are* international. Anyway, I won't ever get tired (…/…) them.

5 Sound practice

First copy this chart into your exercise book. Then listen and say each word a few times. Put the words into the different groups.

Mexico Jamaica Hispanic Poland American
Italian Japan African Italy Switzerland
Japanese Spanish British Scotland Caribbean

•●	●•	•●•	●••	••●	•●••
		Jamaica (Jamaica)	Mexico (Mexico)		

6 ⟨A Song: Americanos⟩

Holly Johnson © Neue Welt Musikverlag GmbH, München

There's a place where a kid without a cent
He can grow up to be president
Magic Kingdom filled with Barbie dolls
If you've got the time, we can make it a good time

Chorus
Americanos – blue jeans and chinos
Got Pepsi and Oreos
Americanos – movies and heroes
Land of the free, be what you want to be

Know how to advertise
Sell you anything at any price
Need it or not, that's what you got
Take no bull from anyone
We just want to have some fun
Got the Queen of Soul
Created rock'n'roll

Chorus
Americanos – blue jeans and chinos
Got Pepsi and Oreos
Americanos – low-riding Chicanos
Land of the free, be what you want to be

Satellite stations across the nation
That's cable TV for you and me
I'm cleaning kitchens
Washing pots and pans
Everything's organized
From crime to leisure time
High schools and swimming pools
Kings, sharks and fools

Chorus

Step D

Let's check

1 Who they are and what they speak

Copy the lists and put in the missing words. Can you add any more words to the list?

The People	Country	Nationality	Main language
...	United States	...	...
Mexicans	...	...	Spanish
English	...	British	...
Swiss	...	Swiss	German/...
Dutch	The Netherlands	...	...
French	...	...	...
Japanese	Japan	Japanese	...
...	...	British	Welsh/...

2 →E Daniel's questions

Here are some questions Daniel asked the Alburgs. *Put in the right form of the verb.*

1. Bruce, what (will/would) you do if there was an earthquake in the middle of the night?
2. Tori, how would you get around if you (don't/didn't) have a car?
3. What would you do if you (win/won) $1,000,000, Bruce?
4. If you lived in Germany, Alex, what American things (will/would) you miss?
5. Lynn, if I (buy/would buy/bought) some coke and ice cream, could we make some more coke floats?
6. If you (was/were/are) a star, Alex, what kind of star would you like to be?
7. Bruce, would you mind if I (used/would use) your phone to call one of my friends in Germany?
8. If you had the chance to spend a year in Europe, Tori, where (do/would) you like to live?

How do you think each person answered Daniel's questions?

3 Heroes

Complete the sentences.

1. Asterix is famous **for being** very clever. (be)
2. Lois Lane always looks forward ... with Superman. (fly)
3. Spiderman is good ... walls. (climb)
4. Bugs Bunny never gets tired ... carrots. (eat)
5. Charlie Brown is more interested ... baseball than ... to school. (play, go)
6. Kermit is crazy ... songs to Miss Piggy. (sing)
7. Batman isn't frightened ... the Joker. (meet)
8. James Bond is used ... out of planes. (jump)

Unit 2

⟨Revision 1⟩

You **have to** go.
You **don't have to** go.
Do you **have to** go?

He **has to** go.
He **doesn't have to** go.
Does he **have to** go?

1 Daniel and his cousins

Put in the right forms of 'have to'. Use the present tense.

1. Daniel is lucky to have relatives in the US. So when he visits them, his parents … pay for his stay. They just … pay for his flight to Seattle.
2. Daniel has trouble understanding American English at first. So he often … ask Alex and the others to speak more slowly.
3. He is surprised that Tori already has a driver's license. "In Germany," he tells her, you … be 18." – "Well, I guess your parents still … drive you around a lot, Daniel," Tori says. "My mom and dad are quite glad they … take me everywhere now. And I often drive Alex to places, too. So he … ask Mom and Dad. But he … ask **me** very nicely!"
4. "Can you watch those steaks on the barbecue, Daniel?" – "OK, Alex. What … I … do?" – "You just … turn them before they start to burn, that's all!"
5. "Can you put chocolate ice cream in a coke float? Or … it … be vanilla?" – "Well, a **real** coke float … be with vanilla ice cream. And the coke … be really cold!"

2 Signs you often see

Look at these signs. Explain what they mean. Use forms of 'be allowed to'.

Example: 1. You **aren't allowed** to take your dog in here./ Dogs **aren't allowed** to go in.

3 Where there's a will, there's a way

Say what they can't do now, but what they will be able to do if …

Example:
1. He **can't** buy a CD because he doesn't have enough money. But if he saves his pocket money, he'**ll be able to** buy one.

4 Making excuses

Example: – I didn't see you at the barbecue on Saturday. Why weren't you there?
– Sorry, but we had visitors, so I couldn't come.

– My party was great!	Why didn't you come?	Sorry, but	it was my Grandma's birthday, so …	I had to …
– I didn't see you at the barbecue on Saturday.	Why weren't you there?		I was ill/tired, so …	I wasn't allowed to …
– We had so much washing-up after the party.	Why didn't you help?		we had visitors, so …	I couldn't …
– You knew about the photo club meeting last night, didn't you?			I had a lot of homework, so …	
– We worked on the patchwork quilt again yesterday.			I missed the bus, so …	
– Didn't anyone tell you about our concert?			my parents needed me in the store (…), so …	
– The youth club backpacking trip was fantastic!			I was visiting my cousin (…), so …	

5 Life in the future

Vacation on the moon
Book now for the trip of your life!

Private music lessons with 'interactive video'
Teacher and student can hear and see each other, although they live in different parts of the world.

Travel back in time
– take a trip back to the 17th century, or earlier!

Cars without drivers!
Let your robot drive – faster and safer than you ever thought possible!

Stay young forever!
Climb mountains when you're 120 – or older!
Just take one SUPER-YOUTH pill every day!

a) *Say what you think. Talk to a partner – or in small groups.*

Example: – Vacation on the moon? That's a crazy idea! I'm sure we'll never be able to go to the moon on vacation!
– Why not? I think people will soon be able to do that. People have already traveled to the moon. So why not go there on vacation?
– It'll be too expensive. And …

b) *What other things do you think people on this earth will (or won't!) be able to do in the future? Write down your ideas. Then talk about what you think.*

sports? vacation? energy? transportation? …

⟨Revision 1⟩

LISTENING AND SPEAKING

1 Understanding and explaining

Issaquah High School started before Daniel flew back to Germany. So he went to school with Alex and Tori for a few days.

1 Listening for gist

First look at the material below. Then listen to the scenes on the recording. Can you say which scene goes with which picture/ lesson/activity?

tip If you don't understand every word in a conversation listen for key words. Try to get at least a rough idea of what is going on.

1

2

Schedule: Monday to Friday

Periods	Subjects
① 7:27 – 8:21	English
② 8:26 – 9:22	Math
9:22 – 9:37	Break
③ 9:37 – 10:31	Computer Science
10:31 – 11:11	Lunch
④ 11:11 – 12:05	Science
⑤ 12:10 – 1:04	History
⑥ 1:09 – 2:03	P.E.
Time for activities	

4

3

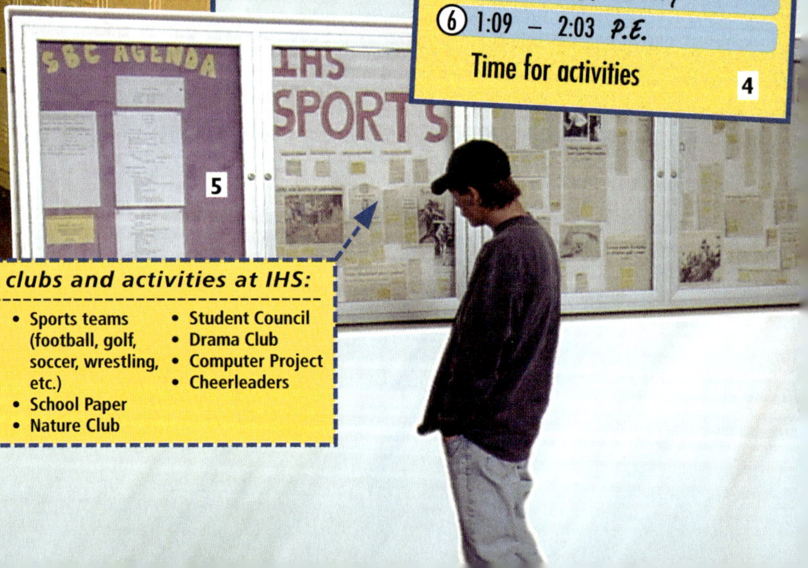

5

Some of the clubs and activities at IHS:

- Yearbook
- Chess Club
- 5 different choirs
- Music groups (band, orchestra, jazz band, etc.)
- Sports teams (football, golf, soccer, wrestling, etc.)
- School Paper
- Nature Club
- Student Council
- Drama Club
- Computer Project
- Cheerleaders

tip If you don't know the exact word for something, try to say it in another way.

2 Your turn Talking about your school

a) *Compare Issaquah High School with your school.*
Do you have the same lessons? Could you do the same activities?
What's the difference between Tori's schedule and yours?

b) *How would you explain these words in English?*

Klassensprecher **SMV** **Wanderklasse** **Schullandheim** **Nachhilfestunde**

Klassenlehrer **beweglicher Ferientag** **Aula** **Wandertag**

You can use these phrases: A … is someone who …/something which …/a place where … .
A … is a kind of … .

3 Giving advice

At Issaquah High School Daniel has met a girl named Rachel. Now he is talking to Alex.

a) *Listen to the recording and find out:* What's Daniel's problem? What does Alex tell him to do?

b) *What advice can you give a friend in these situations?*

1. Your friend wants to buy a very expensive computer but has no money.
2. Your friend has borrowed someone's camera and now has lost it.
3. Someone is very unhappy because his girlfriend/her boyfriend has gone out with someone else.
4. Your friend's parents won't let him/her go out because he/she has bad grades.

You can use these phrases: If I were you, I would … Should I …? You ought to … You shouldn't …

4 Going out

a) *What phrases does Rachel use when she doesn't understand Daniel?*

b) *How do you know that Daniel is nervous?*

2 Discussing and making suggestions

Tori is on the yearbook staff. *Look at the picture and try to explain what a yearbook is.*

1 Understanding announcements

There is an announcement about the yearbook staff meeting on the P.A. system. *Listen and write down the important details.*

tip A mind map with question words might help.

who? — WH — what?
where? — WH — when?

2 Making suggestions

a) Mr. Bell and the students are talking about the yearbook. *Find out what they decide about sports/the campus/food places.*

b) *Listen again. What phrases do they use* 1. to make suggestions 2. to agree 3. to disagree? *Make a list.*

making suggestions	agreeing	disagreeing
Let's …	You're right.	I don't think we should …
…	…	

c) *Work in groups of four. Imagine you are in these situations and make suggestions. Use the phrases you collected in b).*

1. You are making plans for Saturday night.
2. You are looking for a present for a friend.
3. You want to have a class party.
4. You want to put up some posters in your classroom.

Example: "Let's go to the bowling alley."
"Oh no, I'd rather go … ."
"Great … . And then we could … ."

3 ⟨Project: Make your own yearbook⟩

Start a yearbook for your class. Collect photos, postcards, tickets, etc. and write texts to go with them.

3 Listening to a story

Claudia Kishi isn't very good at Math. With the help of her sister Janine she has worked very hard for an important test, so she hopes she will get a good grade. When she gets an A- she is very happy, but then at the end of the lesson, Mr. Zorzi, the Math teacher, calls Claudia and Shawna, another student, up to his desk ...

First read this extract from the text, then listen to Claudia on the recording.

"I'd like both of you to take out your test papers," he said. I didn't have to look far – I hadn't even put mine away. I had been planning to show it off to all my friends. Shawna pulled hers out of her notebook.

"Put them side by side," said Mr. Zorzi, "and tell me if you notice something." I saw it right away. We'd both gotten the same exact grade – ninety-four percent. I said so to Mr. Zorzi.
"But there is something else."

Mr. Zorzi went over our tests with us. We'd each only gotten three problems wrong, but we'd each done them wrong in the same way. I still didn't understand what Mr. Zorzi was getting at, though. Maybe he thought we should have private lessons together or something.

"Girls," he said, "the probability of this happening is almost zero." He looked at each of us in turn. "Do you know what this suggests to me?"

I turned to Shawna. For just a second, I saw something like fear in her eyes. Confused, I looked back at Mr. Zorzi.

"One of you must have copied from the other," he said. He was looking straight at me. ... I felt hot all over, and I'm sure my face became bright red. I couldn't believe what Mr. Zorzi was saying.

Shawna spoke up right away. "Mr. Zorzi, you're not my regular teacher, so you don't know me that well." I turned to look at her. I felt like I was in the middle of a dream. Shawna went on. "If you did, you'd know that I would never cheat on a test." She sounded so sure of herself.

Mr. Zorzi looked closely at her and then nodded. "You can go, Shawna," he said. She got her books together and left the room without looking at me.

a) *What does Mr. Zorzi think about Claudia's good test results?*

b) *What could Claudia say to defend herself?*

The principal calls Claudia's parents about her cheating. They are angry at first. But then her sister Janine and her parents offer to help her. Claudia tells them she will take care of everything herself. The next day at school she is very unhappy. She doesn't know what to do. But then ...

Now listen to find out what happens next.
What do you think Claudia says to Shawna?
How do you think the story goes on?

tip Concentrate on the main events. What leads to what?

If you want to know more, read the rest of Claudia's story in the Reading Corner on page 78.

America's national parks

Step A

A *Grand Canyon National Park*

B *Mesa Verde National Park*

C *Shenandoah National Park*

All kinds of places

Mountains and valleys, rivers and canyons, forests and swamplands – nature has given America all kinds of landscape. Making an area into a national park helps to protect the most beautiful places, or places with a special history.

1 Key words

These short descriptions are from a travel book about the United States. *Match them with the pictures of the national parks on these pages. Which are the key words that help you?*

1. Important cliff houses; early Native American history
2. Hiking country: mountains; waterfalls; giant redwood trees
3. Part of the Alaska Range; open May to September
4. Mainly forest; best views from the Skyline Drive
5. Swampland area; famous for its alligators
6. Fantastic mile-deep canyon, 217 miles long

2 Listening practice: Favorite parks

a) *Before you listen, make a grid to organize your notes. Put in the names of the parks in the pictures – and any other information you already know.*

Name of park	Landscape	What you can do or see there
Shenandoah	forests	

b) *Now listen and collect more information in your grid. You can listen more than once, of course.*

c) *Use the notes in your grid to write a sentence about each national park. Don't give the name of the park. Can your partner guess which parks your sentences are about?*

D Yosemite National Park

E *Everglades National Park*

F Denali National Park

3 ⟨Project: A brochure⟩

Work with a partner and make a brochure for a national park in the US. You can choose one of the parks here, or a different park if you prefer.

Find out as much as you can about the park.

You can:
- look in magazines and books
- go to a travel agent's
- use CD-ROMS or the Internet
- ask your geography teacher, too.

places to stay? **how to get there?** **sights?** **landscape?** **history?** **weather?** **activities?**

Try to make your brochure interesting.
Think how you can 'sell' your national park to tourists.

Remember, the present tense has two forms.
– When you describe what's happening at the moment, use the present progressive.
– When you say what usually/often/never happens, use the simple present.

4 Vacation dialogues

Finish these dialogues. Use the ideas on the right. Use the correct present tense. Some of the phrases have signal words which help – but not all.

Example: 1. 'Mm – smell our neighbors' barbecue.'
– 'Yes, they **are cooking** something good this evening.'

1. 'Mm – smell our neighbors' barbecue.' – 'Yes, they ...'
2. 'No luck on your fishing trip, Dad?' – 'No, I ...'
3. 'What a lot of people!' – 'I know. The park ...'
4. 'Hey, look at that big alligator!'
   – 'Yes, it – Help! It ...'
5. 'Is that man in the red shirt a ranger?'
   – 'Of course not. Rangers ...'
6. 'Can you understand those people?'
   – 'No, I can't. I think they ...'

- (swim) towards us now
- (speak) German
- never (catch) anything
- always (wear) a uniform
- (cook) something good this evening
- often (get) full in summer

5 I've done it all

Some people have done everything.
At least that is what they say!

*Work with a partner. Now **you** have done everything. Use these ideas or find your own ideas. Don't forget to say where and when you did these things.*

see an alligator
go rafting
visit an Indian village
do bungee jumping
be in a hurricane
meet a famous person
...

6 → E A tall story

a) *Read the example on the right. What do you think a 'tall story' is?*

b) *Now write your own tall story. Maybe these words will help you to start your story, and to connect the ideas in it.*

My story happened when I was in ...
One day I decided/wanted to ...
Suddenly ...
So/But ...
After that ...

A walk on the beach

I want to tell you what happened when I was on vacation in California. One day I wanted to go for a walk on the beach. It was a beautiful hot day, but suddenly I felt a strong wind around me. The wind picked me up and I flew high into the air, then out over the sea, far from land.

After a time I saw a strange cloud around me. A door opened in the cloud and I saw a 'thing' with a terrible face. That was enough for me! I fought against the wind that was taking me to this thing, and I dived down into the sea.

Now I was in the water many miles from the coast. But I didn't give up. I swam for hours and hours. Then, just when I was getting tired, I saw a dolphin and it carried me back to the beach.

Step B

Parks and people

Careless people do a lot of damage in national parks. A park ranger is talking to a group of visitors who have just arrived in Yosemite.

'Hi. I'm Dee – I'm also called the Red Ranger! – and I'd like to say welcome to Yosemite. I hope you'll enjoy your time here. I also hope you'll help us to protect this beautiful place. Damage is done so easily.

Of course some kinds of damage are easy to avoid. There's no excuse when pictures are drawn on the rocks – or when names are cut into the trees. And we've put garbage cans and recycling bins all over the park – but you'd be surprised. Garbage is still left around, or it's thrown into the rivers.

But sometimes damage is done because people don't understand nature. It's important to stay on the trails, for example. When short cuts are taken, new trails are cut – and so more and more land is lost. Often rare plants are destroyed like that, too.

And then there's another problem. Many visitors come to Yosemite to see the birds and the animals. But they go too near, and the animals get frightened.

So that's why we have to have some rules for visitors ...'

1 Damage in the park

Look again at what Dee says. Which words explain what damage is done in the park? You can start: Pictures are drawn on the rocks. – Names are ... *Go on.*

2 Why are they called that?

a) *Look at Dee. Why do you think she is called the Red Ranger?*

b) Some of the other rangers are called funny names, too. *Say why you think they are called these names. (There is no right or wrong answer.)*

Mal/the Giant
Pam/Laugh-a-Minute
Leo/the Lion
Karen/Queen of the Mountains
Jim/the Chief
Bill/the Hat

Example: 'I think Mal **is called** the Giant because he is very big.'
– 'Maybe it's a joke. Someone who **is called** the Giant might be very small.'

3 Recycling bins

Look at this garbage and say which recycling bin the things should go in – A, B or C? Explain why.

Start: 1. The toy spade should go in bin C because it **is made of** plastic.

4 ⟨A group game⟩

Think of things in your classroom which are made of different materials (plastic, wood, paper, leather, ...). The others ask questions to find out what the thing is. You can only answer with "yes" or "no". The person who gets the right answer goes on with the next thing.

Example: *You:* I'm thinking of something that is made of leather. What is it?
Another player: Can you wear it?

A newspaper report

MONSTER SEEN IN EVERGLADES

A giant water monster was seen in Everglades National Park yesterday. Two German tourists were in a remote part of the park when their boat was hit by something huge under the water.

'We couldn't see it very clearly,' said Jutta Werner from Hamburg. 'But we're sure it wasn't an alligator. It was many meters long, and it was a darker color than an alligator.'

Jutta and her friend Thomas Klein were badly frightened by the experience. Then, because the engine was damaged, they had to leave their boat and try to find their way back on dry land.

'It was terrible. We didn't know where we were, and we were cut off by water everywhere,' Thomas told our reporter. 'We were very glad when a ranger found us and brought us back in his boat.'

The ranger could not explain what the tourists had seen. 'I was born in this area, and I've lived and worked here all my life,' he said. 'But even I don't know everything about the Everglades.'

1 What happened?

a) *Check what the report in the newspaper says. Then put the right parts of the sentences together. Start like this:*
1. A monster was seen by two tourists.

1. A monster was seen …
2. Their boat was hit …
3. The tourists were frightened …
4. Their way back was cut off …
5. They were found …
6. They were all interviewed …

BY

a reporter.
the experience.
something huge.
a ranger.
two tourists.
water.

b) *Did the tourists really see a monster? Say what you think.*

2 → E Listening practice: A radio program

a) *Listen to part of a talk-radio program. You will hear the host and three other people who are named Trudi, Sam and Patricia. Take notes about what each of them says.*

b) *Use your notes about the host. What is wrong here?*
1. Many years ago the swamplands in Florida were smaller.
2. The farmland is used for summer fruit.
3. There are a lot of new buildings in the Everglades.
4. Trees are taken from the Everglades.

c) *Now say who thinks these things, and why.*
1. The Everglades aren't so important.
2. It isn't possible to protect the Everglades.
3. We must protect the Everglades right away.

d) *Which person do you agree with and why?*

3 [Another news story]

a) Tourists like Florida because the weather is usually good. But sometimes Florida is hit by hurricanes, too. The picture shows a scene after a hurricane. *Describe what damage was done. Use passive forms.*

Example:
Trees were brought down.

b) *Write a newspaper report about the hurricane. Try to use the sentences you made in a). Maybe you can add more details, or what people said about the hurricane. Don't forget a headline for your report.*

The auxiliaries (was/were) are often left out in headlines. See §6 in the grammar section.

HV 4 Listening practice: American and British English

a) *Listen to these people. Are they American or British?*

b) These words are all spelled in the American way.

center – mom – color – program – favorite – meter – neighbor

How would you spell them in British English? Can you find any rules when you compare the spelling?

You can use American or British English – it doesn't matter which. But try not to use both together. It sounds and looks a bit strange!

c) Sometimes Americans use different words.
What would Americans say instead of these British words?

holiday – queue – rubbish – back garden – lift

(If you can't remember, listen to the recording again!)

5 A quiz

Do you know who these people are and when they were born?

James Cook
Christopher Columbus
Walt Disney
William the Conqueror
John Lennon and Ringo Starr
Guy Fawkes

was
were

born in

1446. 1728. 1570. 1940. 1901. 1027.

Step C

A bear problem

"The General Grant Tree? Oh no, Mom!" – "Who wants to see another big tree?" It was only the second day of the Gibsons' vacation, and already there were problems. Rick and Debbie were not interested in the nature walk their parents were planning. They were city kids from Pittsburgh. Malibu and exciting beach parties with wild music were their idea of a summer vacation in California – not the quiet mountains and forests of Kings Canyon National Park. The family argument was stopped by the arrival of Ed Moreno, one of their neighbors in the campground.

"Hi. We didn't have a chance to talk yesterday evening. Did you have a good day?" Ed asked.

"Wonderful," Mike Gibson told him. "We're just – er – discussing what we want to do today."

"Well, wherever you decide to go, watch out for that bear," Ed laughed.

"What bear?" asked Debbie.

"Oh, haven't you heard? It attacked a hiker last week," Ed told them. "We were told about it when we arrived. It's a big ugly thing – half of its right ear is missing. The rangers want to hear from anyone who sees it. When they find it, they'll kill it. Don't worry," he went on when he saw Helen Gibson's worried face. "Nobody else has seen the bear. Ha, ha – I think it's heard the bad news and it's hiding!"

Debbie and Rick stayed in the campground while their parents went to see the General Grant Tree. For a while they played cards, but the time seemed to go very slowly. Then Debbie had an idea.

"Remember what that guy said, Rick? Let's look for the big bad bear."

"You're crazy. Bears are dangerous. What will we do if we see it?" Rick asked.

"We'll stay close together, shout and make noises, and throw things at it. See? I know all the rules – I once saw a TV program about bears. Anyway, we don't have any real chance of seeing it. It's just something to do. Come on. Let's take some food with us and hit the trail."

Debbie and Rick had been on the trail for more than an hour.

"Well, you were right – there's no bear here," said Rick.

"I know – but those deer we saw were beautiful. Maybe this place isn't so bad," smiled Debbie.

They walked on for a time. Suddenly Debbie gave a little scream. Rick grabbed her arm nervously. "What is it? The bear?"

"Ha, ha," Debbie laughed. "It isn't anything. I just wanted to make things a bit more exciting for you."

"Very funny, Debbie. – Well, I'm hungry. Let's sit down on those rocks over there and eat our food."

Rick took off his backpack and took out their food. They ate without talking.

Debbie was looking into the forest behind Rick. She was hoping to see some more deer.

"Rick," she whispered suddenly. "The – the bear."

"A joke is funny the first time, Debbie. It is *not* funny the second time," Rick told her.

"This isn't a joke." Her voice really sounded frightened.

Rick turned around slowly – and saw the bear, not very far away. It was a large black bear. Half of its right ear was missing, and its eyes were black and angry.

Unit 3

Debbie stood up and took a step back. Rick ran several steps back. Then the bear made a strange noise and started to move towards them.
"Oh no, it's going to attack us!" Debbie took another step back and fell over the backpack on the ground. She found a stone in her hand. Without thinking she threw the stone as hard as she could at the bear. She was lucky. It hit the animal on the nose. The bear stopped.
Then it turned and disappeared back into the forest.
Debbie and Rick were still shaking when they arrived back at the campground …

1 A summary

Make a summary of what happened. Write one or two sentences for each part of the story – in your own words. You can finish these sentences and use them for your story but you will have to put them in the right order.

Start like this: The Gibsons …

- But the bear found them and …
- A neighbor told them …
- Debbie threw … and the bear …
- The Gibsons were on vacation in …
- Debbie and Rick decided to …

2 → E The bear

a) *What information does the story give about the bear? Collect all the details, and explain where you found the information.* *Example:* The bear is big and ugly. That is in line 20.

b) *What should you do if you meet a bear? What rules did Debbie learn from the TV program? Discuss what Debbie and Rick do when they see the bear. (Do they do the right or the wrong thing? Why do you think they react in this way?)*

c) *Which of these questions does the story* ***not*** *answer?*
- What does the bear look like?
- What did it do?
- Why does it attack people?
- What will happen when the rangers find it?

3 Don't be bear careless!

a) *Read this article from the 'Yosemite Guide'. The new words are in the Alphabetical Word List, but try to guess as many of them as you can. Part b) will help you.*

b) *Find phrases in the article which mean:*
1. because people are so careless
2. bears don't start the problem
3. they do what their noses tell them
4. they go on looking for it
5. they are no longer scared of people
6. food is put away in the right places

c) *Think back to the question you couldn't answer in exercise 2c). Can you answer the question now?*

d) *Do you think that 'A bear problem' is a good title for the story – or how would you change it?*

DON'T FEED THE BEARS!

Each year black bears are killed in Yosemite, Sequoia and Kings Canyon national parks as a direct result of human carelessness. We call it a bear problem, but bears are not to blame.

Driven by their powerful sense of smell, black bears are drawn to human food. Once bears get this food, they continue to seek it out – from backpacks, picnic tables, and even visitors' cars. Their natural fear of people fades and they may become aggressive. When the bears become too aggressive, they often have to be killed.

The only way to stop this is to make sure that all food items are stored properly.

4 ⟨Project: A beautiful place in your country⟩

a) *Collect words about nature in* ***your*** *country. Use your dictionary. Organize them in different groups.*

landscape	animals	plants	weather
	Reh – deer	Eiche – oak (tree)	

b) *Make a wall display about beautiful places in your country.*
- *Use pictures and written information. The words you collected in a) will help you.*
- *Think how you can put the different parts of your display together. (On a big map, maybe? Or in alphabetical order?)*

5 ⟨A song: The bare necessities⟩

Look for the bare necessities,
The simple bare necessities;
Forget about your worries and your strife.
I mean the bare necessities,
Old Mother Nature's recipes
That bring the bare necessities of life.

Wherever I wander, wherever I roam,
I couldn't be fonder of my big home.
The bees are buzzin' in the tree
To make some honey just for me.
When you look under the rocks and plants
And take a glance at the fancy ants,
Then maybe try a few,
The bare necessities of life will come to you,
They'll come to you!

Look for the bare necessities,
The simple bare necessities;
Forget about your worries and your strife.
I mean the bare necessities,
That's why a bear can rest at ease
With just the bare necessities of life.

Now when you pick a paw-paw or a prickly pear,
And you prick a raw paw, next time beware.
Don't pick the prickly pear by the paw,
When you pick a pear, try to use the claw.
But you don't need to use the claw
When you pick a pear of the big paw-paw,
Have I given you a clue?
The bare necessities of life will come to you,
They'll come to you!

Look for the bare necessities …

So just try to relax, yeah cool it.
Fall apart in my backyard
'Cause let me tell you something, little britches
If you act like that bee acts uh uh,
You're workin' too hard.
And don't spend your time lookin' around
For something you want that can't be found.
When you find out you can live without it
And go along not thinkin' about it,
I'll tell you something true,
The bare necessities of life will come to you.

Step D

Let's check

1 Where were they made?

This family on vacation in Yosemite has things from all over the world.

1. The boy's headphones **were made** in Korea.
2. The father's guitar **was** … 3. The girl's …

Go on.

2 Word power A word countdown

Can you write down these words within two minutes? Look at your watch to check what time you start and what time you finish.

- 5 kinds of landscape
- 4 different materials
- 3 wild animals you read about in this unit
- 2 places where you can put garbage
- 1 place where you can put a caravan in a national park

3 [Newspaper reports]

What happened yesterday? Use the headlines – and one extra piece of information from the box.

shoot/ranger hit/lightning rescue/ranger feel/thousands of people save/mother

Example: 1. A tourist was attacked by an alligator. He was rescued by a ranger.

TOURIST ATTACKED BY ALLIGATOR

Two Children Rescued After Rafting Accident

GIANT REDWOODS DAMAGED IN THUNDERSTORM

DANGEROUS BEAR KILLED IN SEQUOIA

Earthquake reported in California

⟨Revision 2⟩

1 Tips for young drivers

These tips were in a little book Tori got when she was learning to drive. *Find the right word – and put in the correct adverb form. (Sometimes more than one answer is correct.)*

early careful late slow dangerous quick correct safe fast

- Always drive carefully/... when you are near schools or playgrounds. Sometimes you have to stop ...!
- Check the mirror ... before you start.
- If you want to turn left, remember to give your signal ... . If you give a signal too ..., other drivers won't know what you're planning.
- Always drive ..., even when you see no other cars on the road.
- Even if you're in a hurry, never drive too ... . The important thing is to arrive ...!
- Young people sometimes think driving ... is cool. It isn't! Dangerous driving costs lives.

2 Drive-in movie theaters

Put in the right forms. Sometimes you will need an adjective, sometimes an adverb.

1. Richard Milton Hollingshead had a ... *(great)* idea. It was a ... *(big)* surprise for his friends and neighbors when they ... *(sudden)* saw what he was doing. He was sitting ... *(quiet)* in his car – in front of his garage at home. A movie was on, and he was watching it ... *(happy)*. The picture was projected onto the garage door.

2. It was a ... *(clever)* idea, and – like most ... *(bright)* ideas – it was ... *(simple)*, and it worked ... *(good)*. In 1933 Hollingshead opened the ... *(first)* drive-in movie theater in the world – in Camden, New Jersey. At once it was a ... *(huge)* success. The number of drive-in movie theaters grew ... *(quick)*. By 1946 there were 300, and by 1958 the number had reached 4,700!

3. A visit to a drive-in was always ... *(enjoyable)*. In the car, you could always see the screen ... *(good)*. You and your friends could talk in ... *(loud)* voices, and you could laugh, eat and drink as ... *(noisy)* as you liked. For teenage dates it was ... *(ideal)*, too! Young people ... *(definite)* loved it!

4. But in the 1960s things began to change – ... *(slow)* but ... *(sure)*. Young people preferred going to ... *(big)* open-air concerts to see their ... *(favorite)* stars, and now that everyone had a TV, people ... *(natural)* chose to watch movies on the ... *(small)* screen at home. But the "drive-in" idea ... *(quick)* became ... *(popular)* for other things, too. Drive-in restaurants, banks and churches are ... *(typical)* examples.

5. Today there are only about 900 drive-in theaters in the US. A ... *(large)* number of them have six or eight ... *(different)* screens. In ... *(remote)* country areas, most drive-ins have closed. Many of them were losing money ... *(bad)*, and so they became too ... *(expensive)* to run.

3 Wow! That's a long time!

Ask questions with 'How long ...?' Can your partner give the answer?

Example: 1. The Alburgs' neighbors have a cat. His name is Smokey, and he is very old. They got him eighteen years ago. (have?)
– How long have they had their cat?
– They've had him for 18 years./They've had him since 19.. .

2. Uncle Fred moved to Colorado in 1989 and got a new job there. (be?)
3. Rick Gibson lives in Pittsburgh. He and his family moved there in 1997. (live?)
4. Soo's parents first met in Korea. That was twenty years ago. (know each other?)
5. The Chungs' store is in the International District in Seattle. They bought the store in 1993. (have?)
6. Alaska belongs to the USA. It became a US state in 1959. (be?)

4 Can you explain?

Imagine you are Daniel. Can you explain who – or what – these people, things and places are – or were? (Sometimes you need to know the meaning of a word, and sometimes you need to remember Daniel's experiences! You can use some of the words and phrases more than once).

Example: 1. What's a coke float?
Daniel: It's a drink that you make with coke and vanilla ice cream.

2. What's Snoqualmie Falls?
3. Who are the Sacramento Kings?
4. What are chopsticks?
5. What's a ranger?
6. What's a redwood?
7. What's a hiker?
8. What's a wetsuit?
9. What's apple pie?
10. Who is Rachel?
11. Who is Uncle Fred?
12. What's an illegal immigrant?
13. Who were the 'first Americans'?

tree people relative person team girl drink ✔ waterfall kind of cake thing(s)

that ... who ... which ...

... meet at ... ... make with ... ... go ... ... use when you eat ... ... be 250 feet high! ... play for ... ... try to ... ... grow in ... ... probably come from ... ... wear when ... ... look after ... ... live in ...

5 Word power Building adjectives

a) *Explain the meaning of the words – with relative clauses. The examples show you how!*

Examples: 1. an **unforgettable** adventure? – That's an adventure that you'll never **forget**!
2. an **enjoyable** holiday? – That's a holiday that you **enjoy**.

3. an **unanswerable** question? 4. a **washable** anorak? 5. an **uninteresting** tennis match? 6. a **helpful** map? 7. a **useless** pen? 8. an **unimaginable** experience?

b) *Now find the right words. Look at the example.*

Example: 1. a glass that you **can't break**? – That's an **unbreakable** glass.

2. a story that you **can't believe**? 3. a number that **isn't lucky**? 4. an evening that you **didn't enjoy**? 5. a tip that you **can use**? 6. a room that **isn't tidy**? 7. weather that quickly **changes**?

READING AND UNDERSTANDING

1 Starting off

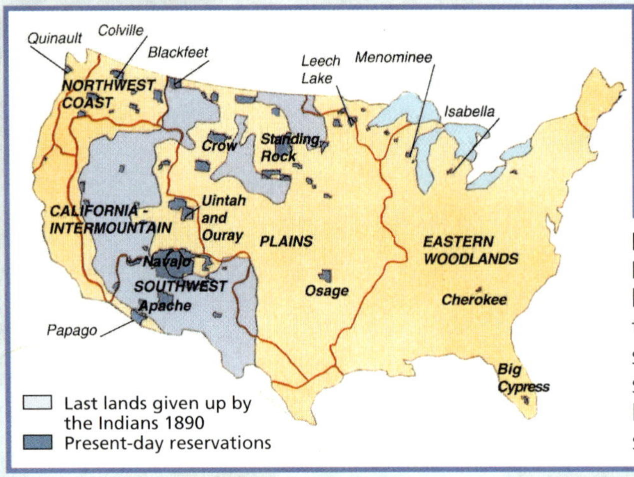

1 *"We did not ask you white men to come here. The Great Spirit gave us this country as a home. You had yours. We did not interfere with you. But you have come here; you are taking my land from me ... You say, why do you not become civilized? We do not want*

Before the Europeans arrived, the Indians occupied most of what later became the United States. The tribes were roughly grouped into six geographical regions. European settlement gradually forced the Indians to the west and southwest, so that by 1890 they were living on 2

3 Oh, do you remember sweet Betsy from Pike, Who crossed the wide prairies with her lover Ike?

1 The subject

The texts on these two pages are not complete – they are just the beginnings of texts.

tip Remember: When you look at a text, think first:
- What is it about?
- What do you already know about this subject?

Look at them carefully, then think ...

1. What are the texts about?
   Try to give the main idea of each text in one sentence.

   Text 1 is about the white people who came to ...
2. Can you find a good heading for each text?
3. What do you already know about the American Indians? About the 'Wild West'?
4. What do you think of stories/movies about the 'Wild West'?
   Why do you think they are so popular?
5. Look at texts 1 and 5 again. How do you think they go on?
   Choose one of them, and add a few more sentences.

2 More information

It isn't only from words that you can get information.
Look at the other material on these two pages. What new information can you find?

Example:
"The map on page 49 is interesting. It shows how the settlers moved west in covered wagons."

CT-4178A SEATTLE, WASHINGTON
Seattle blushes during this summer sunset.
© Photo by David S. Curran

4 Hi, Darren!
We're having a great holiday! Today we visited an open air Indian museum near Seattle. The Indians here didn't live in teepees like the Sioux. They lived in longhouses.

5 White in the face, she stood in the door of her cabin with a shotgun in her hands. Beside the door was a Winchester, and on the table inside the house were two Walker Colts. Her heart beat heavily. Outside the cabin were twelve Apaches on ponies, and one of the Indians had lifted his hand. The

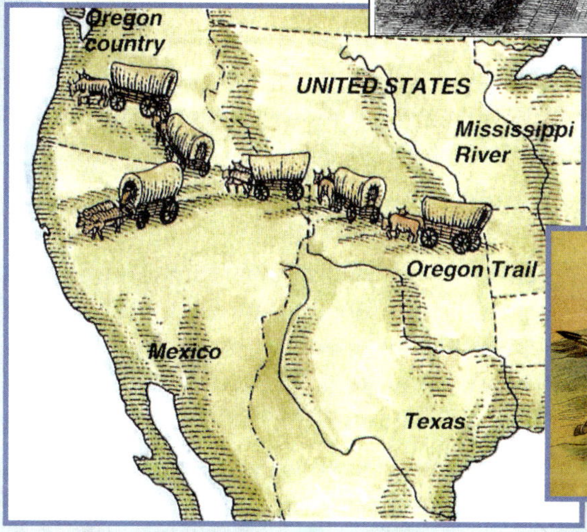

HUNTING BUFFALOES

3 Facts

What do you find out on these two pages about the Indians – and about white people in America? *Make a list of facts.*

Indians	*white people*
– *were in America before the whites*	– *took the land from the Indians*

4 Different kinds of text

First think of all the different kinds of text you know. Then look at each text again.

1. What kind of text is this? Or where could it be from? speech history book …
2. What do you expect when you read this kind of text?

When I see a …, I expect to	find out … read …	facts (about …) something about … an exciting story. interesting things about … about someone's experiences/…

A …	often usually	has … gives …	jokes/funny pictures. rhymes. details about … …

3. What do you like (or *not* like) about different kinds of texts?

Example:	I	like / don't like	poems because	the rhymes sound nice. / they are often difficult.

2 Finding out more

1 → E Checking what you already know

Which of these statements are true? Say what you think.
(Try to remember what you know from books you've read or movies you've seen.)

?
1. Most people who went west were hoping to find gold and get rich quickly.
2. Most people traveled all the way in wagon trains. It was dangerous to travel alone.
3. The Indians didn't like the white settlers, and often attacked them.
4. The whites took all the land for themselves.

Now read the text – to check if you were right and to find out more.

tip Think about what you already know:
- Is it right according to the text?
- What else would you like to know?
- Can you find this out from the text?

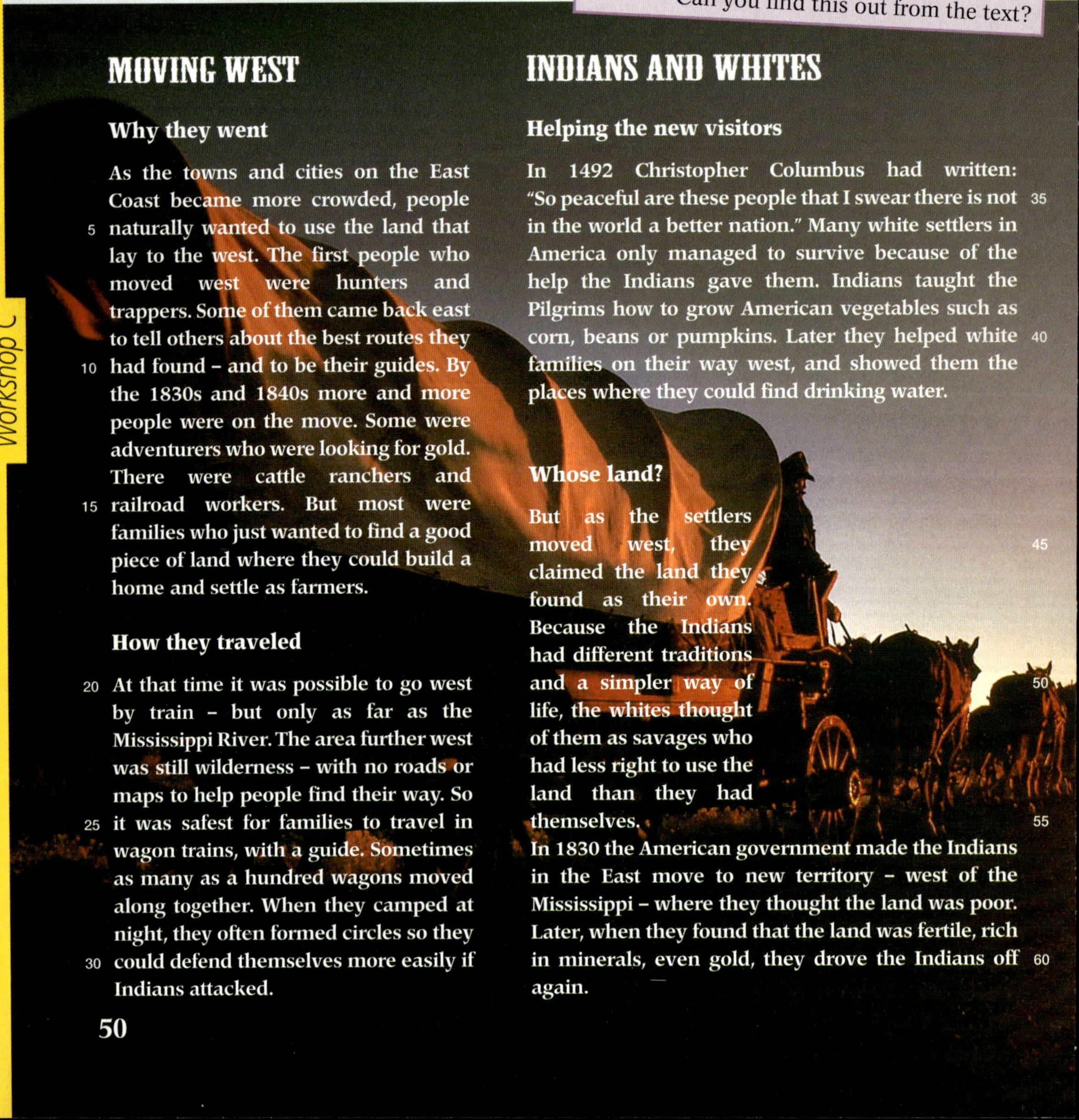

MOVING WEST

Why they went

As the towns and cities on the East Coast became more crowded, people naturally wanted to use the land that lay to the west. The first people who moved west were hunters and trappers. Some of them came back east to tell others about the best routes they had found – and to be their guides. By the 1830s and 1840s more and more people were on the move. Some were adventurers who were looking for gold. There were cattle ranchers and railroad workers. But most were families who just wanted to find a good piece of land where they could build a home and settle as farmers.

How they traveled

At that time it was possible to go west by train – but only as far as the Mississippi River. The area further west was still wilderness – with no roads or maps to help people find their way. So it was safest for families to travel in wagon trains, with a guide. Sometimes as many as a hundred wagons moved along together. When they camped at night, they often formed circles so they could defend themselves more easily if Indians attacked.

INDIANS AND WHITES

Helping the new visitors

In 1492 Christopher Columbus had written: "So peaceful are these people that I swear there is not in the world a better nation." Many white settlers in America only managed to survive because of the help the Indians gave them. Indians taught the Pilgrims how to grow American vegetables such as corn, beans or pumpkins. Later they helped white families on their way west, and showed them the places where they could find drinking water.

Whose land?

But as the settlers moved west, they claimed the land they found as their own. Because the Indians had different traditions and a simpler way of life, the whites thought of them as savages who had less right to use the land than they had themselves.
In 1830 the American government made the Indians in the East move to new territory – west of the Mississippi – where they thought the land was poor. Later, when they found that the land was fertile, rich in minerals, even gold, they drove the Indians off again.

2 What you found out

Now think again about what you knew before you read the text.
Pick out words and sentences in the text that tell you if your information was right.

Example: It's true that some of the people who went west were hoping …
But there were others who had different reasons. (In line … it says: …)

tip When you're looking for information,
- headings
- the beginnings of paragraphs
- pictures

can be very helpful.

On the warpath

Many Indians now began to see the whites as their enemies, and some tribes decided to fight for their land. But more and more whites came. In 1869 the railroad between the East and West Coasts was finished. For the Indians, this was the beginning of the end. The Indians had no chance against all the whites who came into their land now. By 1890 many thousands of Indians had died in the battles against the American army. Thousands of others had died of disease and starvation – many on long journeys to the reservations on lands the whites had chosen for them.

3 Looking for information

Look at this information from a brochure about the Native Americans.
Find out which page (or pages) you should read if you want to know these things:

1. How many different tribes were there, and where did they live?
2. Did the tribes sometimes fight against each other?
3. What was Indian life like?
4. What kind of religion did the Indians have?
5. How were tribes with different languages able to understand each other?
6. Why was the buffalo so important to Indian life?

Can you explain how you found out?

Example: "I saw the word '…'.
That's a bit like '…'./I know the noun '…'."

3 Reacting to a text

HOME ON THE INDIAN TRAIL

Now the sun was warm, but there was a feeling of autumn in the air. Indians came riding on the path that passed so close to the house. They went by as though it were not there.

Jack, the dog, hated Indians, and Ma said she didn't blame him.

She said, "Indians are getting so thick around here that I can't look up without seeing one."

As she spoke she looked up, and there stood an Indian. He stood in the doorway, looking at them, and they had not heard a sound.

"Goodness!" Ma gasped.

Silently Jack jumped at the Indian. Pa caught him by the collar, just in time.

The Indian hadn't moved; he stood as still as if Jack hadn't been there at all.

"How!" he said to Pa.

Pa held on to Jack and replied, "How!" He dragged Jack to the bedpost and tied him there.

While he was doing it, the Indian came in and squatted down by the fire.

Then Pa squatted down by the Indian, and they sat there, friendly but not saying a word, while Ma finished cooking dinner.

Ma gave Pa and the Indian their dinners on two tin plates, and they ate silently.

Then Pa gave the Indian some tobacco for his pipe. They filled their pipes, and they lighted the tobacco with coals from the fire, and they silently smoked until the pipes were empty.

All this time nobody had said anything. But now the Indian said something to Pa.

Pa shook his head and said, "No speak."

A while longer they all sat silent. Then the Indian rose up and went away without a sound. Laura and Mary ran to the window. They saw the Indian's straight back, riding away on a pony. He held a gun across his knees.

"Let Indians keep themselves to themselves," said Ma, "and we will do the same. I don't like Indians around."

Pa told her not to worry.

"That Indian was perfectly friendly," he said. "And their camps are peaceable enough. If we treat them well and watch Jack, we won't have any trouble."

The next morning, when Pa opened the door to go to the stable, Laura saw Jack standing in the Indian trail. He stood stiff, and all his teeth showed. Before him in the path, the tall Indian sat on his pony. Indian and pony were still as still. Jack was telling them plainly that he would spring if they moved.

Only the eagle feathers that stood up from the Indian's scalplock were waving in the wind. When the Indian saw Pa, he lifted his gun and pointed it straight at Jack.
Laura ran to the door, but Pa was quicker. He stepped between Jack and that gun, and he reached down and grabbed Jack by the collar. He dragged Jack out of the Indian's way, and the Indian rode on, along the trail.
Pa stood and watched the Indian riding farther and farther away across the prairie.
"That was darned close!" Pa said. "Well, it's his path. An Indian trail, long before we came."

One evening Laura asked, "Will the government make the Indians go west?"
"Yes," Pa said. "When white settlers come into a country, the Indians have to move on. The government is going to move these Indians farther west, any time now. That's why we're here, Laura. White people are going to settle all this country, and we get the best land because we get here first and take our pick. Do you understand?"
"Yes, Pa," Laura said. "But Pa, I thought this was Indian Territory. Won't it make the Indians mad to have to –"
"No more questions, Laura," Pa said firmly. "Go to sleep."

(L.I. Wilder)

1 Looking at the characters

a) How do Ma and Pa feel about Indians?
- *Look at the text and find out what they say and do.*
- *Then try to explain what the examples show about their feelings.*
- Do they feel the same way about Indians? *Give reasons for your opinion.*

Ma
- *Jack hated Indians, and Ma said she didn't blame him.*
- *"Indians are ..."*

This shows that she doesn't like Indians.

b) *What impression do you get of the Indian in the story? Look for examples of how he moves and acts.*

c) *What do you think about Indians? Do you agree with Ma? Or Pa?*

2 Reading between the lines

When you read a text, there are sometimes places where you want to stop and think:

What does the author mean here?
Can I read between the lines?

tip A story and a report about facts are not the same kind of text.
In a story you often have to "read between the lines" to find out:
- how the characters in the story feel
- what the author wants to tell you.

1. They went by as though it were not there. (line 2) Try to imagine why the Indians take no notice of the house at first.
2. Jack hated Indians. (line 3) Can you think why?
3. He held a gun across his knees. (line 22) What do you imagine Laura thinks when she sees this?
4. When the Indian saw Pa, he lifted his gun. (line 47) Why does the Indian wait until Pa comes out before he lifts the gun?
5. "No more questions." (line 60) Can you imagine why Pa doesn't want to answer?

New York, New York

Step A

The Big Apple

This is part of a TV program about New York City.

My real name is Jerry Mikhailovich, but I call myself Jerry Reynolds. I'm a courier. If a business wants to send something to somebody – a letter or a package, they call my agency and *they* call me on my phone. And then I use my bike to deliver it. That's faster than anything – the mail, the subway, a cab or whatever. The traffic is really crazy here. But I don't stop for red lights or anything and I know lots of tricks and short cuts.

I'm from Nebraska. I came to New York City a year ago because I want to be an actor and a singer. So I try out for parts all the time. There's a role in a new musical on Broadway now that would be perfect for me …

For now being a courier is OK. It's dangerous work, but I make good money – especially with tips. And I'm outside all day. I love it here in Manhattan. It's the greatest place on earth.

My favorite place is Broadway. Can you guess why? And Times Square, too, with all its billboards and neon signs. When I have a little time, I go to one of the cafés there.

Some people say Manhattan's greatest attraction is Central Park. You can do almost anything there – play games like basketball, skate, go to the zoo, take a boat out, jog or just lie on the grass. I often wait in the park between jobs.

And I really love all those skyscrapers – not just the Empire State Building or the World Trade Center. I mean all of them. It's like being in another world.

Of course New York City isn't just Manhattan. There are four other boroughs – the Bronx, Queens, Brooklyn and Staten Island – but Manhattan is where all the action is.

I love the international atmosphere of places like Chinatown, Little Italy and Little Ukraine – the food, the languages you hear. There really are people from everywhere in the Big Apple. From all over the world. It's multi-cultural, multi-ethnic, multi-everything here.

And last but not least there's Manhattan's most interesting neighborhood – my neighborhood, Greenwich Village. No wonder I love living here, with all the artists, galleries, cafés and clubs – like the Hard Rock Café. Yeah, I've seen a few stars in the Hard Rock. Too bad I'm not one of them – yet!

1 →E Looking at the text

a) Who is Jerry?

b) What did you find out about New York in the text? What else do you know about the "Big Apple"? *Make a mind map.*

c) *Look at the map at the back of the book and try to find all the places Jerry talks about.*

d) *Explain what Jerry means by multi-everything.*

e) *Try to compare New York with European cities (think what you know about London, for example). What's different, what's the same?*

Step A

Times Square

The Empire State Building

Central Park

Chinatown

A Broadway theater

2 Listening practice: Pablo García

Pablo García is a cab driver in New York City.

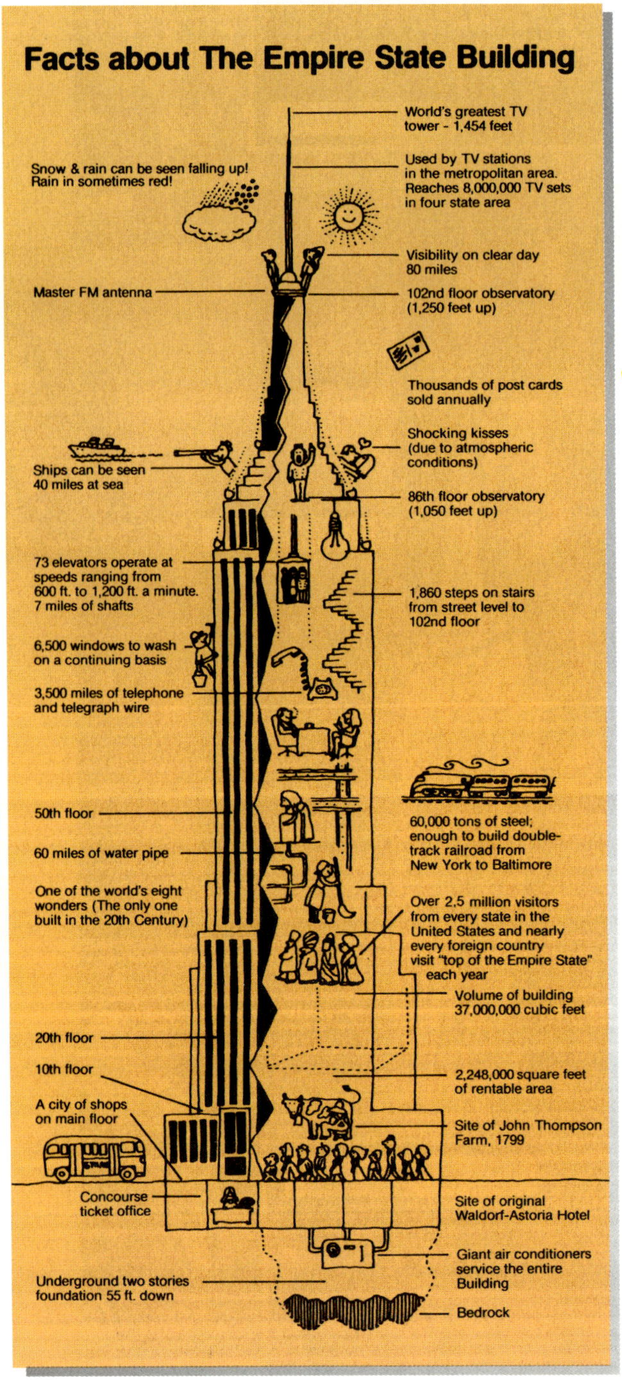

a) *Listen to what he says about himself. Take notes. Then write a short report on him.*

Pablo comes from Puerto Rico. He is …

b) Pablo's next passenger has been to the Empire State Building.
First study the leaflet on the left. Don't worry about new words, you will understand the important bits. (Think of the tips in Workshop A!) Now listen to the recording. What does Pablo's passenger get wrong?

3 →E The way to Chinatown

Julia is a fourteen-year-old girl from Germany. She is visiting New York City with her parents. A German lady at her hotel wants to talk to the man at the reception. Julia is helping them.

What must she say?

Lady: Kannst du ihn mal fragen, wie ich nach Chinatown komme?
⇐**Julia**⇒ This lady would like to know the way to …
Man: All you have to do is follow Fifth Avenue south. It's right after Greenwich Village. Little Italy is down there, too.
⇐**Julia**⇒ *Sie müssen …*
Lady: Ja, aber wo ist denn diese Fifth Avenue? ⇐**Julia**⇒
Man: That's easy. It's the east side of Central Park. ⇐**Julia**⇒
Lady: Ach ja, da sind doch die vielen Geschäfte, oder? ⇐**Julia**⇒
Man: That's right. There are lots of shops there – expensive ones. ⇐**Julia**⇒
Lady: Gut, und was ich noch wissen wollte: kann ich von hier aus nach Chinatown laufen oder ist es zu weit? ⇐**Julia**⇒
Man: It's really far from here. It's better to take a cab or the subway. ⇐**Julia**⇒
Lady: Vielen Dank – euch beiden. ⇐**Julia**⇒

Unit 4

Step B

Jerry – in a hurry

– If Jerry **had stopped,** this **wouldn't have happened.**
– This **wouldn't have happened** if Jerry **had stopped.**

§ 7

1 If Jerry hadn't been in such a hurry ...

Put the parts of the sentences together.

If	
Jerry hadn't been in a hurry,	Jerry would have hit her.
Pablo hadn't stopped,	there would have been an accident.
Jerry had stopped,	he would have stopped.
the lady hadn't jumped out of the way,	there wouldn't have been any trouble.

	if
The old man wouldn't have fallen down	he hadn't fallen down.
He wouldn't have knocked over the table	it hadn't run off.
The police officer would have warned Jerry	she had seen him earlier.
Jerry would have hit the dog	the lady hadn't dropped her bag.

2 The tastes of New York City

Find out how to pronounce these words in the vocabulary section on page 108. Then read the dialogue and listen to the recording to check if you were right.

['beɪglz]

['su:ʃɪ]

The Braddocks, two tourists from Kansas, are looking for something to eat.

Daisy: They've got all kinds of food around here. Look, **bagels** – and over there they've got **sushi**. We could try that.
Herbert: I don't know, honey. I think that's raw fish. How about some Mexican food?
Daisy: But we can get **burritos** and **nachos** everywhere, dear.
Herbert: Or Chinese food, honey?
Daisy: We have **chopsuey** in Kansas all the time. I want to try a hot **pastrami** sandwich.
Herbert: OK, why not. We could have it with **sauerkraut**.
Daisy: Right, and a chocolate **sundae** for **dessert**.

[bəˈri:təʊz]

['sʌndeɪ]

['saʊəkraʊt]

['nʌtʃəʊz]

[ˌtʃɒp'su:ɪ]

[pə'strɑ:mɪ]

[dɪ'zɜ:t]

Graffiti Girl: a true success story

New York City: Graffiti Girl is not her real name, but it's the only one she wants. A lot of guys spray graffiti – and now there's a girl, too – and she's good at it.

What's good about graffiti? Since the City decided to concentrate on the creative rather than on the criminal side of graffiti, we've seen some really great works of art – and artists out there. Graffiti Girl is one of them.

Last year the city offered her a wall, and in Graffiti Girl's words, "I sprayed a crazy picture on it, and then they sent me a letter. They really liked it. They even gave me a prize. They gave it to me at a dinner party with all kinds of people there. Now everybody calls my friends and me about walls. They offer them to us and they pay us. Crazy. A big company has even promised us a deal for a book. I mean, they want to make a picture book with our stuff in it. And, hey, if you're ever in the Big Apple, look me up. I'll show you the best stuff."

A true American success story – and thanks for those great works of art, Graffiti Girl.

3 Looking at the text

1. Who is Graffiti Girl? What does she do?
2. What is different for Graffiti Girl and her friends now? Why?

I sent **my friend/him** a postcard.
I sent a postcard **to my friend/to him.**
it **to my best friend/to him.**

§ 8

4 Tourists

Say it with 'to'.

1. You mean they give **those kids** money?
   – You mean, they give money **to** …?
2. I'm going to send **my friends** some photos of this.
3. Can you lend **my husband** a pen? He wants to write **our children** a postcard.
4. We promised **our neighbors** a postcard, too.
5. What? They want to give **that girl** another prize?

5 More opinions

Put these sentences in the right order.

1. They shouldn't give **the money** to them. They should give/it/me/to.
2. I can show you **some better graffiti.** Come on, I'll show/to/you/it/right away.
3. There are **some terrible stories about this girl**. A friend told/to/them/me.
4. Your sister would like **a book about Graffiti Girl**? OK, let's buy one and send/her/to/it.
5. These posters of **Graffiti Girl's paintings** are great. Can you sell us/to/them?

6 → E Listening practice: Voices

WFMU, one of New York City's 117 radio stations, has a program called 'Voices'. It gives New Yorkers and tourists a chance to talk about themselves and the Big Apple.

a) *First copy the grid into your exercise book. Then listen to these people and take notes on what they say about:*

☆ their jobs or activities ☆ where they live ☆ their opinion on New York City

Who?	the Braddocks	Shelley Grant	Anne Ross	Michael O'Reilly
Jobs:	'tourists'			
They live in	Kansas			
New York City	...			

b) *What did you learn about New York City from the people? Make a list of good and bad things about the Big Apple. Add other information from earlier in this unit, too.*

7 ⟨A song: New York, New York⟩

Fred Ebb/John Kander © BMI Warner Bros. Rec.

Start spreading the news.
I'm leaving today.
I want to be a part of it:
New York, New York.

These vagabond shoes are longing to stray,
right through the very heart of it:
New York, New York.

I want to wake up in a city that doesn't sleep
and find I'm king of the hill, top of the heap.
These little town blues are melting away.
I'll make a brand new start of it in old New York.
If I can make it there, I'll make it anywhere.
It's up to you, New York, New York.

New York, New York!
I want to wake up in a city that never sleeps
and find I'm A-number-1, top of the list,
king of the hill, A-number-1.

These little town blues are melting away.
I'm gonna make a brand new
start of it in old New York.
And if I can make it there,
I'm gonna make it anywhere.
It's up to you, New York,
New York.

Step C

All in a day's work

"This is George M. Crane's office at Lincoln Square," a voice said. "Can you pick up a passport at our Madison Avenue office and get it to Lincoln Square fast? Mr. Crane has to fly to Europe. The helicopter for the airport will be here in 15 minutes."

The agency receptionist knew the company. They were good customers.

"OK," she said. "Passport for Crane from Madison to Lincoln. We're on the way."

Jerry was in Central Park in the southeast corner across the street from the Plaza Hotel. It was one of his favorite places in Manhattan – and a good central point to wait for the next job. He looked at all the activity around him – the cars, the yellow cabs, a red double-decker Apple Tours bus, a limo and the people everywhere – all kinds of people in all kinds of clothes. He smiled. Yes, he liked it here in New York City.

His phone rang and Jerry reached for it right away. He was proud of his speed. He was the fastest. Everybody knew that. Nothing could stop him. That's why he had enough work – as a courier. What he needed was a chance to get a job as a singer and actor.

"Job for you," the voice from the agency said. "Passport for Crane. From Madison to Lincoln," it said. "15 minutes. Life or death!"

"I'm on the way," Jerry said. He was already riding his bike north on 5th Avenue. On East 76th he cut over to Madison and was at the office in a few minutes.

At the office he picked up the passport, and was off again.

On 5th Avenue Jerry nearly crashed into a limo. Several people jumped out of the way as he raced into the park. "Damn idiot!" someone shouted after him as Jerry raced towards the lake.

A man with a baby suddenly appeared in front of him and he had to go across the grass to miss them. He raced towards the bushes now and saw a young woman walking towards the lake. And then he saw the two guys and knew what was going to happen. Best to avoid the whole scene. Cycle around it. It would take a minute longer – maybe two – but he didn't want any trouble now.

He moved to the side fast – away from the woman – and heard her scream as he did. God, the crime in this city! There were other people there. Somebody else would help her. He went faster. The woman screamed again – louder. Damn!

Jerry braked hard and he almost fell but caught himself at the last minute – he saw the woman by the lake now. She was fighting with the two muggers – was she crazy? Jerry turned his bike and raced to the scene.

One of the guys had a knife and was coming at her. Jerry put on more speed and raced right towards him. When the guy saw him, it was too late. Jerry had hit him and they both went flying into the water.

Jerry stood up first and saw the other boy. He was trying to take the woman's bag. Jerry shouted and moved towards him, and both of the muggers ran away.

Jerry didn't follow them. He went to the woman. She was shocked but not hurt and thanked him, but Jerry didn't listen.

A few people came over now, and when he was sure she was OK, he said, "Can you look after her?" and got his bike. He'd lost several minutes – and the passport in his bag was wet, too.

He jumped on his bike and rode off. Damn! The crash had bent his front wheel, but he went on and tried not to think about anything as he hurried to the west side of the park.

He went across Central Park West as fast as he could and was nearly hit by a car. On 68th West he went against the traffic and made it to Lincoln Square in a minute.

Jerry checked his watch as he pulled his bike into the building. Inside, he took off the front wheel and went to the elevator with it. ... Damn! Two were on other floors and one was broken. He pressed the buttons, waited a minute, then raced for the stairs.

Ten minutes later and very tired, he entered the office on the 35th floor with the wheel and the wet passport.

"You're too late. Damn you!" Crane shouted at him. "And what's this? Look at my passport! This is going to cost you your job!"

"Sorry, there was somc trouble," is all Jerry said.

"Damn right there's trouble. I just missed my flight, you idiot!"

"Maybe you can get the next one, sir," the clerk said.

"With this damn passport," Crane held it up. "Get his agency on the phone right now!"

Jerry left then. He knew he was in trouble – but perhaps he could try to explain everything at the agency. Maybe things would still be OK.

When he arrived there, the receptionist tried to smile at him. "There've been two calls about you," she said. "One from Mr. George M. Crane."

"What did he say?"

"He was really angry, and he wanted to talk to the manager. I wouldn't go in there now if I were you," she said.

Jerry nodded and sat down on a hard chair. He was sure he would lose his job now.

"Oh, and the other call," the receptionist said, "was from a William Weston. Over on Broadway, I think. He wants to see you."

"William Weston?" Jerry repeated. Not *the* William Weston?

"He said you saved his daughter Mary in the park. When did you do that, Jerry?" she asked.

But Jerry wasn't listening. William Weston was a famous producer – and he had a fantastic new musical on Broadway.

1 → E Understanding the text

1. How does Jerry feel when the story begins? How do we know? (On the one hand … On the other …)
2. What exactly is Mr. Crane's problem?
3. The 'voice' from the agency only says a few words to Jerry. Say it in normal sentences.
4. Why doesn't Jerry go and help the woman right away?
5. What problems are there for Jerry after he has helped the woman?
6. Why does it take Jerry so long to get up to the office?
7. Why does Mr. Crane ask the clerk to call Jerry's agency?
8. What do you think will happen now? Say why you think so.

2 Reporting the story

How would you report the incident in the park on TV or in a newspaper?

1. *Write a text. You can use these sentences:*

Yesterday afternoon Jerry Reynolds, a bicycle courier, rescued Mary Weston, daughter of the famous musical producer William Weston, in Central Park. Mary Weston was walking … when two muggers …

Jerry acted like a hero, but he might lose his job because of this: He was on his way across Central Park because he had to …

But Jerry isn't too worried about this. He says: "I've always wanted to be … and maybe …"

or

2. *Write an interview between Jerry and a reporter. Start like this:*

Reporter: OK, Jerry, can you tell us how it all happened?
Jerry: Well, I was standing near the Plaza Hotel when my phone rang. It was my agency …

3 ⟨A cartoon⟩

Ros Chast, © The New Yorker

Step D

Let's check

1 **Word power**

a) *Divide these 16 words into 4 groups.*

sundae | courier | limo | Broadway | subway | cab | the Empire State Building | burrito | sauerkraut | actor | Chinatown | Times Square | bagel | cab driver | bus | singer

b) *Find a title for each group.*

3 After the rescue

Say it with 'to' and put the sentences in the right order.

1. "Sorry, I can't get Jerry on the phone at the moment." – "Well, that's too bad. Could you give him a message?" – "Sure, I'll give (him/it) when he comes in this afternoon."
2. "Hi, Jerry, this is Nick from Radio WMFU. Could you tell us the whole story of that fight in the park?" – "No problem, I've already told (it/some newspapers)."
3. "Are you going to send this article about the rescue to your parents, Jerry?" – "No, I'm going to send (Mr. Crane/it). Then he'll know why I was so late!"
4. "Are you going to offer Jerry a part in a musical, Dad?" – "Don't worry, Mary, I've already offered (him/it)."
5. "Wow, Jerry, you're going to get a part in that new musical? Are you sure?" – "Of course, Mom, Mr. Weston promised (me/it)."

2 More graffiti

Say it with 'to'.

1. A big company wrote Graffiti Girl a letter.
2. They sent her and her friends an invitation.
3. They showed the graffiti artists their buildings.
4. They 'gave' the kids all the walls.
5. They are going to give the artists money.

4 ⟨A cartoon: The streets of New York⟩

© McLachlan, Punch

"No one, but no one, is safe on New York's streets these days!"

Unit 4

WRITING LETTERS

1 Looking at model letters

- The Superbowl football game at the end of January is watched on TV all over the country.
- Valentine's Day, February 14th, is a chance to send a card to someone you love.
- Halloween, on October 31st, is when kids put on crazy costumes and go trick-or-treating in the neighborhood.
- Thanksgiving is always on the last Thursday in November. Family members come together for a turkey dinner and give thanks for the Pilgrims' first harvest.
- Independence Day, or 'the Fourth of July', is a big festival with parades, fireworks, barbecues and picnics. It celebrates the day when the colonies became free from England in 1776.

23 Lakeview Drive
Issaquah, WA 98027
March 6th

Dear Daniel,

I'm sorry I haven't written for so long, but I haven't forgotten you!

Thanks for that sweet Valentine's card. Did you get my postcard from Florida? We flew there for a weekend to see my grandpa. It was a long way to go for such a short stay, but Grandpa got us tickets for the Superbowl! He and Dad are crazy about football. For them the Superbowl is more important than the Fourth of July, or even Thanksgiving! I bought a Superbowl T-shirt for you. I hope you like it.

What special days do you celebrate? We're doing a project at school about festivals and holidays in other countries, and I chose to do Germany. Could you tell me something about them in your next letter? It would help me a lot! I'm sending you something I wrote about our special days as it might be useful in YOUR English lessons.

It was nice of you to invite me to Stuttgart this summer. Too bad, my parents think I'm too young to go on my own, although I'm allowed to go to camp this summer! I hope I can come next year.

I miss you, too, Daniel. Write back soon!

Love and kisses,

Rachel

1 Special days

a) *Read Rachel's letter.* Why does she write to Daniel?
b) *Describe the pictures. Which events in the box do they go with?* Are any of those events celebrated in Germany, too?

23 Lakeview Drive
Issaquah, WA 98027

Tennis Camps
P.O. Box 123
Spokane, WA 99204

April 2nd 1997

Dear Sir or Madam,

I saw your advertisement about tennis camps in the Teen Camp Guide. Please send me your brochure as soon as possible so that I can book early. I look forward to hearing from you.

Sincerely,

Rachel Baker

Rachel Baker

23 Lakeview Drive
Issaquah, WA 98027

AAC
2245 Cropstone Way
Golden, Colorado
80401-8524

April 23rd 1997

Dear Mr. Abbott,

Thank you for sending me your brochure. I would like to take part in your Wilderness Basics Camp, and enclose my application form.

Sincerely,

Rachel Baker

Rachel Baker

TENNIS CAMPS

Summer camps for young people aged 11–18, June, July, August

Improve your tennis skills with experienced coaches!

Write to:
Tennis Camps
P.O. Box 123
Spokane 99204

American Adventure Camps

Have the greatest summer of your life. Choose from rock climbing, mountain biking, rafting, horseback riding, sailing, wilderness camping, backpacking, and a whole lot more.
For details, contact Tony Abbott at:

AA Camps
2245 Cropstone Way
Golden, CO 80401-8524

Tennis Camps
P.O. Box 123
Spokane, WA 99204

Dear Rachel,

Thank you for your letter of April 2nd. We are sorry to tell you that our tennis camps are already full for the summer. If there are any cancellations, we will let you know.

Sincerely yours,

Peter Walker,
Program Manager

2 Looking at formal letters

When Rachel was planning her summer vacation, she compared different camps.
Read the advertisements and letters and find out which camp she chose in the end.

3 Finding useful phrases

Copy the checklist into your exercise book and put in phrases from the letters. You can add your own phrases, too. (Don't write the whole sentence – just the phrase.)

Beginning	Dear Sir or Madam, Dear …	Asking for something	Please would you …? …
Saying why you're writing	I am writing to ask you … I would like to tell you about …	A friendly ending	I look forward to hearing from you. I hope to hear from you soon. …
Thanking	Thank you for … (-ing) …	Sending something with the letter	…
Saying you're sorry	…		
Giving good or bad news	I am happy to tell you … I'm glad/sad to say … …	Before you sign your name	Sincerely, … …

2 Using your skills

1 Connecting ideas

When Fred and Wilma moved into their new house, all the neighbors came round with pies. Apple pies, pumpkin pies, every kind of pie you could think of, and enough to feed an army. They couldn't possibly eat all the pies, but they didn't want to throw them away either.

That evening Wilma was putting out the garbage when she noticed some strange figures in the street. She ran inside and screamed, "They're here!"

"Who?" asked Fred as he followed her into the kitchen. "What's going on?" Then the bell rang.

Fred went to the door and opened it nervously. As soon as he saw the little band of ghosts he remembered that it was Halloween.

"Trick or treat!" they cried. Then Fred had a terrible thought. They didn't have any candy! He felt in his pockets for some money, but they were empty. What could he do? Fortunately, Wilma rescued him. She appeared from the kitchen with a huge stack of pies and gave the kids a piece each.

"They won't play any tricks on us now!" said Wilma proudly. It wasn't long before the next hopeful gang of monsters arrived.

Complete the sentences.

1. The neighbors arrived with pies **as soon as** …
2. **Although** there were too many pies to eat, …
3. Wilma saw some strange figures **as** …
4. She didn't want them to see her, **so** …
5. Fred remembered it was Halloween **when** …
6. Fred couldn't give them any money **as** …
7. Wilma gave away the pies **so that** …
8. **After** one group of kids had left, …

tip Use connecting words (e. g. because, so that, etc.). They connect your ideas and make your text flow better.

so (that) = damit
so = daher, deshalb
as = da, während
when = als

2 Rules and tips

Some of these rules are wrong. Can you find and correct them?
If you aren't sure about a rule, check the model letters.

1. The address of the person you're writing to goes in the top right hand corner of the letter.
2. Start the main part of the letter (after 'Dear …') with a capital letter.
3. You shouldn't write 'Dear …' in the middle of the page. Always write it on the left.
4. Never put a comma after 'Sincerely' or 'Sincerely yours'.
5. Always use an -ing-form after 'I look forward to …'. Don't use an infinitive.
6. Don't use paragraphs in a letter to a friend.
7. If you start with 'Dear Sir or Madam', you finish with 'Love and kisses'.

tip Sometimes exam questions tell you how many words to write, for example 'about 120 words'. Try to get a rough idea of what this looks like in your handwriting.

3 Writing a formal letter

You are interested in going to a summer camp in the United States.
Write a letter to American Adventure Camps and follow these points:
• *Write the addresses, the date and the beginning with 'Dear …'.*
• *Explain how you got the address. (Make up a reason, e. g. an advertisement in a magazine, or a friend recommended the organization to you.)* • *Ask for their brochure with information about the camps, dates and prices.* • *Say which camp(s) you are especially interested in. Ask if you need to have experience and if you should bring your own equipment.* • *Finish with a friendly sentence.* • *Sign the letter.*

4 →E Writing to a friend

a) *Write Daniel's letter to Rachel. Follow this plan in your letter. Check your list of useful phrases.*
- Bedanke dich bei Rachel für ihren Brief und das Superbowl-Hemd, das sie dir geschickt hat.
- Sag, dass die Informationen über amerikanische 'special days' interessant und nützlich waren. Stell eine Frage zu etwas, worüber du mehr wissen möchtest.
- Sag, dass du einige Informationen über deutsche 'special days' beilegst. Entschuldige dich, dass du es nicht früher gemacht hast.
- Sag ihr, dass du dich darauf freust sie wiederzusehen.
- Bitte sie bald wieder zu schreiben.
- Beende deinen Brief.

b) *Check your letter for mistakes. Then find a partner and suggest ways to improve each other's letters. Write your letter again before you show it to your teacher.*

5 ⟨Project: Special days in Germany⟩

Work in groups. Write a report on special days in Germany. Choose events you think would interest an American friend. Collect information and pictures.
Make notes and organize the points under headings before you write your report.

tip Think first about what your reader might want to know or will find interesting.

6 ⟨Just for fun: Halloween⟩

7 ⟨Guess the rhymes⟩

Can you guess the missing words of these poems?

God made the bees,
The bees make the (...).
The students do the work
And the (...) get the money.

Roses are red,
Cabbages are (...),
My face is a laugh,
But yours is a scream.

Trick or treat! Smell my (...)!
Give me something good to eat!

⟨Revision 3⟩

1 What if …?

When Soo tells her mother about her plans to go to Issaquah with Daryl at the weekend and go hiking with Cindy and her friends, Mrs. Chung starts to worry.
What does she say? What does Soo answer?

Example: *Mrs. Chung:* What if the weather is bad?
Soo: It won't be! But cheer up, Mom. If that **happens,** we'**ll stay** in Issaquah.

weather – bad? ✔
one of you – get – ill?
get lost – mountains?
there – thunderstorm?
have – accident on – road to Issaquah?
…?

stay – Issaquah ✔
get – wet
someone – find us
come back home
call – police – ambulance
…

2 If only …!

Daniel is back in Germany. But he's still thinking a lot about America. Dreaming a lot, too!
Put the verbs in the right form.

Example: 1. If only we … *(live)* in Issaquah, I … *(see)* Alex and the others every day!
If only we **lived** in Issaquah, I'**d** (I **would**) **see** Alex and the others every day!

2. If only my parents … *(have)* more money, I … *(fly)* to Seattle every summer!
3. I … *(feel)* so happy if I … *(can)* see Rachel all the time!
4. If only telephone calls to America … *(not cost)* so much, I … *(call)* her every week.
5. Life … *(be)* so much easier if only America … *(not be)* so far away.
6. If only I … *(be)* a few years older, I … *(move)* to the US right away!

3 Your turn What would you do?

Imagine these situations. What would you do if they happened to you?

Example: 1. After a friend's party, you miss the last bus – and it's a very long walk back home!
– If that **happened** to me, I'**d call** my parents and ask them to collect me.
– If I **missed** the last bus, I'**d go** back to my friend's house.
– Well, I don't really know! I think I'**d stay** the night with my friend.
I definitely **wouldn't walk** home!

2. A child stops you in the street and asks you for some money.
3. You look in the mirror one morning and see hundreds of horrible spots on your face.
4. Your neighbors are away on vacation, but you hear noises in their apartment.
5. Someone in a department store steals a CD. You are the only person who sees it!
6. All the lights go out one evening, so you can't finish your homework.
7. A friend lends you her sunglasses. You drop them – and break them!
8. Your parents have guests in the living-room. You want to watch a video.

4 The right job for the right person

Read what these people say about their jobs. Who is speaking?

A I like helping other people. But working in the emergency ward isn't always easy. And I must say I'm not crazy about working at night!

B In my job you have to be good at getting to places – fast! And you can't be afraid of cycling in city traffic!

C I like my job. I really enjoy being on the road all day. Driving in heavy traffic is no problem, I'm used to it!

D My job is just right for me, because I like being out in the open air. And I never get tired of talking to the visitors.

truck driver | ranger | courier
firefighter | travel agent | nurse

E At first I was scared of getting stuck in a burning building. But you get used to being in tricky situations.

F I love working with other people. But sitting at the computer makes my eyes tired!

Your turn *Say what **you** think of these jobs. What would – or wouldn't – you enjoy?*

Example: I wouldn't **enjoy being** a truck driver. I'd **hate being** on the road all day! **Driving** in heavy traffic must be horrible!

5 Word power Verbs with prepositions

UP	AWAY	OFF	ON
clean	give	get	leave
look	put	take	put
pick	take	throw	try
put	throw	turn	switch

a) *Can you find the right verb – with the right preposition?*
1. Grandpa has dropped his keys. Can you **pick** them **up**? 2. Are you cold? … a sweatshirt …, then! 3. We don't need these old newspapers. Let's … them … . 4. It's so cold today. I think we'll have to … the heating … . 5. What does this word mean? Let's … it … in the dictionary. 6. The TV was on all night. Didn't you … it …? 7. The kitchen's so untidy! Please … those plates and glasses … in the cupboard. 8. You're wearing **my** scarf! Please … it …!

b) *Now try to make more sentences with the verbs you haven't used yet. If you aren't quite sure what they mean, check in the Alphabetical Word List.*

Communication and Technology

Step A

Ways to communicate

1 Different forms of communication

a) *Look at the picture. How many different forms of communication can you see? Use your ideas to make a 'word map'. Do you know any more ways to communicate?*

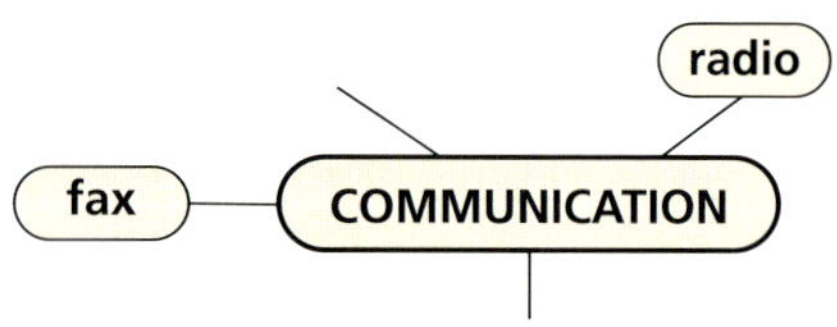

b) Your turn *When or in what situations do you use different forms of communication?*

Example: When I want to find out the latest sports news I switch on the TV and look at the teletext.

c) *Imagine you want to communicate from where you live with one of the people in this house in the US. Which form of communication would you choose, and why?*

Example: I would make a telephone call – because it's easy.

fun? easy? cheap? quick? ...?

2 Understanding instructions

a) *Read the text on the right. It is part of the instructions for a TV. Try to guess as many of the new words as you can.*

b) Word power 'Technology' words are sometimes different from the words you usually use. *Match the words on the right with these 'technology' words. (It will help if you check how the new words are used in the text.)*

1. operation
2. select
3. view
4. display
5. input
6. digit
7. error

see — mistake — number — show — way of working — choose — put in

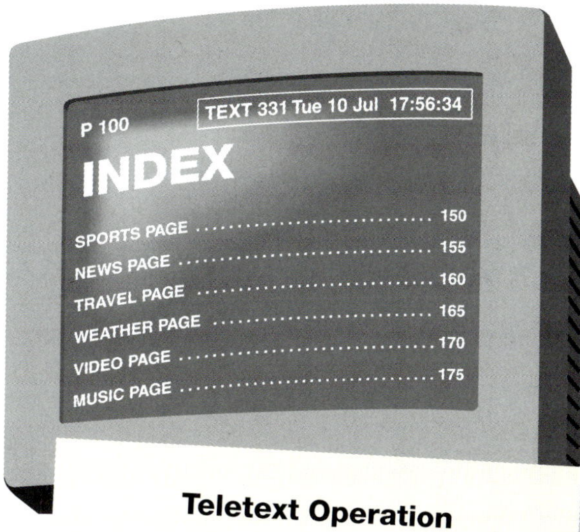

Teletext Operation

TV stations broadcast teletext programs via the TV channels. For basic operation of teletext, use the remote control.

Basic Teletext Operation

Switching Teletext on and off

1 **Select the channel which carries the teletext service you wish to view.**

2 **Press [11] to display Teletext.** If no teletext signal is broadcast, the indication P100 is displayed on a black screen.

3 **Input three digits for the page number using the number buttons [4].** The numbers are displayed on the screen and the requested page appears in a few seconds. Note: If you make a mistake, type in any three digits, then re-enter the correct page number.

4 **Press [3] once or [11] twice to return to the TV mode.**

Note: To change the teletext channels, first press [3] to return to the TV mode, then repeat steps 1 to 3.

Note: If the signal of a TV channel is weak, teletext errors may occur.

c) *What would you say to this person? (He/she has the remote control and you have the instructions.)*

1. "I want page 150, but I pressed 1 twice. What do I do now?"
2. "Look, there are some mistakes in the text. Why is that?"
3. "I want to change the teletext channel. Do I just press the number of the channel?"
4. "Now I want to watch TV again. I pressed the button with the lines on it once, but the text still stayed on the screen."

3 → E Listening practice: Teachers or computers?

Some high school students have to write about the advantages and disadvantages of teachers and computers. Before they start, their English teacher lets them discuss their ideas in groups.

a) *Listen to one group of students.*
When you listen the first time, don't write anything. Just try to follow what they say.
While you listen the second time, take notes. First think how you can organize your notes.

b) *What is* ***your*** *opinion about teachers and computers? If you like, you can use the ideas you collected in your notes. But maybe you have got other ideas, too.*

c) *Now talk about computers and books. What can you say for or against them?*

more fun — eyes/get tired — cheaper — read in bed — ...

Step B

Telephone talk

Lynn Alburg is opening the mail while the family are having breakfast …

Tori: … so I can't take you to school by car today, Alex. You'll have to –

Lynn: Oh, my God! I don't need a shock like this at breakfast!

Bruce: What is it, Lynn?

Lynn: We never had such a huge telephone bill. Look at all these calls to Germany.

Bruce: Let's see. – Well, Tori? Alex? Why are you so quiet? Who made the calls?

Alex: I – I guess I sometimes call Daniel. But only about – er – once a week.

Bruce: Two or three times a week, you mean. Look – and one call was over half an hour.

Alex: That can't be right.

Tori: Oh yes, it can, little brother. You're always on the hotline to Germany. I heard you again on Monday.

Alex: Thank you, Tori! Well, while we're telling stories, who drove at over seventy miles an hour through –

Lynn: That's enough, you two! Don't scowl, Alex. It's quite clear. The bill shows the time you spent on the phone.

Bruce: Yes – and it's very expensive.

Tori: How much does it cost a minute to call Germany?

Bruce: A lot more than calling another place in the US. – I'm an engineer, you know, Alex. I'm not a millionaire.

Alex: I'm sorry. I guess I – well, you see, poor Daniel misses us all. So I have to give him all our news and tell him about the guys at school and everything.

Lynn: But you can tell him all that in a letter, or an e-mail.

Alex: I know. It's just – it takes quite a long time to write everything down.

Lynn: Well, it'll be a very long time before you use the telephone again!

1 Phrases from the dialogue

Find phrases in the dialogue which answer the questions.
Then write the phrases down.

a/an … | … an hour | quite a … | such a … | … a week

1. Why is the telephone bill a shock for Lynn?
   – 'We never had **such a** …' Lynn says this in line 8.
2. How often did Alex call Daniel? (What does Alex say, and what does the bill show?)
3. How long was the longest call to Germany?
4. How fast did Tori drive?
5. What is Bruce's job? And what does he say he is *not*?
6. Why doesn't Alex like writing letters or e-mails to Daniel?

2 Looking at English: The indefinite article

English and German don't always use the indefinite article ('a/an') in the same way.

Look again at the phrases you wrote down in exercise 1.
Think how you would put these ideas into German.
(Do you need the indefinite article? Does it go in the same place?
Do you use different words in place of the indefinite article?)

3 An e-mail from Alex

Write an e-mail from Alex to Daniel. Use the ideas on the right, and put in the indefinite article where it is needed.

Start like this: Hi, Daniel!
A huge phone bill arrived …
There were … so …
Go on.

huge phone bill – arrived few days ago –
lot of calls to you on it – so argument –
with Mom and Dad – (Dad says – not millionaire!) –
now only allowed to call – once – month – that's why –
writing e-mail – want to tell you – latest news about Cathy –
(remember her? – one of cheerleaders) – but –
not only cheerleader now – also singer in new band! –
has just recorded song – not hit yet – but quite good song –
will send you tape

4 Names

Daniel saw or heard all these names while he was in the US. You know the names, too.
Put them into two groups. (If you aren't sure which names need 'the', look back in your book.)

1. Names with 'the'
   the United States, the …
2. Names without 'the'
   Colorado, …

United States   Colorado   New York City
Empire State Building   Central Park   Chicago Bulls
International District   Chungs   Issaquah High School
Arkansas River   Lake Sammamish

Can you add more names to these lists?

5 Looking at English: The definite article

You don't always need the definite article ('the') in English where you use it in German.
Look back at the dialogue and find examples of this. These clues will help you.

a place where you learn things   a kind of transport
a meal   a day of the week   a name with an adjective

Example: a place where you learn things – In line 3 Tori says 'to school'.
There is no definite article in English, but you would need it in German.

6 Bits and pieces

Complete what Alex and Daniel say on the telephone. Use the same word twice – once with 'the', and once without 'the'. Choose from the words on the right.

money   music   life   time   technology

1. *Alex:* Mom says I must limit … I spend on the phone.
   The trouble is, … goes so fast when I'm talking to you.
2. *Alex:* I can't stand … my sister listens to. I mean, for me that just isn't …!
3. *Daniel:* We're doing a project on … at school.
   My group has to imagine what changes … of the next fifty years will bring.
4. *Daniel:* … seems a bit boring now. I prefer … you guys have over there in the US.
5. *Alex:* Why is … always such a problem? I already spent all … I got for my birthday.

A future world

1 Before you read the text

a) *Find the texts that go with these pictures of a city in the future.*

A There are no gardens where plants can grow normally. But there are 'Hydroponic Facilities' where trees grow in special bags.

B The different parts of the city are on different levels. You have to use an elevator to get from one level to another.

C The housing units have Factcenters which display information you need. If you dial Adscan, you can choose things to buy.

D There are no cars. You get around each level on walkways. It never rains there because even the walkways are not outside in the open air.

b) *Think about the information in a). What are the good points of a city like this? Is there anything which isn't so good?*

2 Captain Courage

"I'm going to Beowulf's," Lance said to Arty. "He got a cool toy, an autogram, for his birthday. D'you want to come?"

Arty followed his brother onto the walkway. He and Lance walked for about twenty minutes along the walkway, around the Hydroponic Facility. Beowulf lived on the other side of the Hydro.

When they went in Beowulf was looking angrily at a small control module.

"Hello, it's us," Lance said. "Where's the autogram, then?"

Beowulf hit the control module against his knee. "You tell me. I can't get it out."

"Let's have a look," Lance said.

"It doesn't work. Looking at it won't help."

Arty went over to the Factcenter and dialled first Adscan, then Autograms. On the screen appeared a picture of an autogram. This was followed by a list of models: People from Living History, like a cave man, a Roman soldier, a Nineteenth-Century Granny and a Twentieth-Century Commando. There history ended. "Which one have you got?" Arty asked.

"Twentieth-Century Commando," Beowulf said. "Captain Courage." At the same moment Lance managed to press the correct buttons. In the corner of the room, life-sized, the autogram appeared. It still wasn't working properly. It moved about, one leg shorter than the other.

"What's it meant to do?" Arty asked.

"It's meant to talk," Beowulf said, grabbing back the control module from Lance.

"What's your name?" Arty asked it.

"It should only respond to my voice," Beowulf said. "It's personalized. What-is-your-name?" he said to the autogram, as if he were speaking to an idiot. It turned its head. "Wha-a-at?"

"Your name!" Beowulf shouted.

Captain Courage bent down, holding his gun. "Kitty-kitty. Nice kitty. Come to Gran."

There was silence after this. "What's it meant to say?" Lance asked, in the end.

Beowulf scowled. "Drop your gun or I'll blow you away."

"Who's a pretty boy, then?" said Captain Courage.

"That's the Granny," Arty said. "They've programed it with the wrong voice."

Beowulf played with the buttons and Captain Courage danced wildly, but did not go away. "It's stuck," Beowulf said. "I can't switch it off."

"How are your cabbages coming along?" Captain Courage asked.

"Damn this," Beowulf said. "I'm going out. You don't catch me stuck here all day with Grandma Courage." He went into the fast food area. Captain Courage lurched after him.

"We're going out," Beowulf said to his mother. He put the control module on a shelf.

"It's a very fine morning," said Captain Courage.

"Get that thing out of here," Beowulf's mother said.

"It's stuck at 'on'," Beowulf said.

"I don't care where it's stuck as long as it's not stuck here. Take it with you."

The three of them went onto the walkway and the door slammed shut behind them. After a moment Captain Courage followed them out, through the door.

"I don't want anyone to see me with that," Beowulf said.

"Where did I leave my umbrella?" the Captain responded.

They were passing the Hydroponic Facility. Beowulf threw the control module in between the trees. Captain Courage lurched after it. "Here, kitty-kitty-kitty."

"Quick, before it notices," Beowulf said, and started to move away.

"Don't be silly," Lance said, "it doesn't know anything." But he quickly joined Beowulf and Arty. A shout stopped them.

"You! Come back here." An angry Senior Citizen was coming along the walkway, waving the control module. Behind him came Captain Courage.

"Nothing to do with us," Beowulf said.

"Cabbabbabbabbages!" responded Captain Courage.

"I saw you throw it in," the Senior Citizen shouted. "Take it away."

They went on down the walkway.

"Let's go down to Level Ten," Arty said.

"There's an idea," said Lance. "Perhaps we could leave it in the elevator." But when they reached the elevator area a large sign informed them: ELEVATORS OUT OF ACTION.

They walked on. Captain Courage followed, a few steps behind.

"When we get to the next corner," Beowulf promised, "we'll lose it."

"If you get me the wool, I'll knit one for you," the Captain said.

"It's good fun, really," Arty said. It was like having a crazy but harmless adult with them.

Beowulf pushed the control module into his hands. "You look after it then, if you think so much of it. If anyone asks, it's your autogram." He went ahead, with Lance, and Arty walked behind, trying different buttons. He felt that Beowulf simply did not understand Captain Courage. If you pressed *Volume Control* the Captain went up to shoulder height, *Forward Motion* made him grab his gun and *Lateral Hold* made him throw himself to the ground. Arty kept his fingers on *Volume Control* and *Lateral Hold*, and the Captain swam along next to him, responding to Beowulf's voice when he talked to Lance.

"If you get me the wool, I'll make one." "How are your cabbages?" "Where is my umbrella?"

"What's a cabbage?" Arty asked, but the others did not answer. "What's an umbrella? What's wool?"

(From 'Captain Courage and the Rose Street Gang' by Jan Mark, adapted)

3 It doesn't work!

a) *Go through the text and find the different problems with the autogram.*
Start like this: At first Beowulf can't get the autogram out. That's in line 14.
Then the autogram appears, but … *Go on.*

b) How does Beowulf react to the autogram?
Look in the text for words or actions that show his feelings.
Example: He is angry when he can't get the autogram out.
So he hits the control module against his knee.

c) *Talk about how Arty reacts. Think about what he does when Beowulf gives him the control module and what he asks at the end of the text. What does this tell us about Arty?*

4 Your turn What about you?

a) Would you like to have Captain Courage or any other 'autogram'? *Explain why or why not.*

b) Have you ever been in a situation where something didn't work?
Explain what the situation was, how you felt, and what you did about it.

5 Things people say

a) *Find examples of what the autogram says. What other words might a Granny use?*

b) *Play a game: Choose one of the people below (or think of a different person). Write down a few things that this person might say, then read your sentences to a partner. How quickly can he/she guess which person you chose?*

Example: *You:* My person says: 'How was school today?' – 'Tidy your room!' – 'Why –'
Your partner: Oh, I know – that's a mother!

teacher | tourist | young child | football fan | doctor | police officer | …

6 ⟨A song: Space oddity⟩

David Bowie © Essex Musikvertrieb GmbH, Hamburg.

Ground Control to Major Tom
Ground Control to Major Tom
Take your protein pill and put your helmet on

Ground Control to Major Tom
Commencing countdown, engines on
Check ignition and may God's love be with you

This is Ground Control to Major Tom
You've really made the grade
And the papers want to know whose shirt
you wear
Now it's time to leave the capsule if you dare

This is Major Tom to Ground Control
I'm stepping through the door
And I'm floating in a most peculiar way
And the stars look very different today

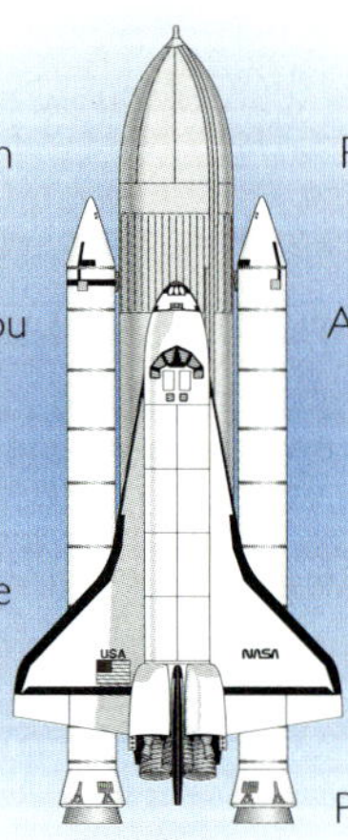

For here I am sitting in a tin can
Far above the world
Planet Earth is blue and there's nothing I can do

Though I'm past 100,000 miles
I'm feeling very still
And I think my spaceship knows which way to go
Tell my wife I love her very much, she knows

Ground Control to Major Tom
Your circuit's dead, there's something wrong
Can you hear me Major Tom?
Can you hear me Major Tom?
Can you hear me Major Tom?

… am I floating around in my tin can
Far above the moon
Planet Earth is blue and there is nothing I can do

Step D

Let's check

1 Word power Words from the unit

a) Do you remember all the new words in these phrases?
Find pairs and make sentences.
Start like this: You're pressing …

- you're pressing
- respond to my voice
- the teletext program
- let's inform everybody
- by fax
- should respond to the remote control
- I can't knit a pullover
- the wrong button
- it's meant to
- with this wool

b) *Choose one of the sentences you made in a).*
Think what the situation might be, and write a little dialogue.
Use the sentence somewhere in your dialogue.

2 Signs

Explain the information on these signs.

Start: 1. The supermarket is open 24 hours a …
2. Rooms are …
3. The speed limit is … miles …
4. Carrots cost …
5. These apples are …
6. Music Express is …

a/an: day, hour, pound, night, ride

3 A lesson in history

Some places in the text are marked with numbers.
At which numbers do you need the definite article ('the')?

I think ❶ history is very interesting. On ❷ Monday I learned about ❸ history of ❹ twentieth century. In those days there were different countries, like ❺ United States or ❻ Mexico. People went everywhere by ❼ car, but ❽ technology they had was not very good, so ❾ cars they used often had accidents. There were computers then, too. But children had to go to ⓫ school, and a lot of ⓬ time they spent there was with human teachers. – Yes, ⓭ life was very strange in ⓮ past!

⟨Extra line⟩

⟨Reading corner⟩

In the following texts you will find some words you don't know. Most of them are explained at the bottom of each page. You should be able to guess the others from the context. If not, use a dictionary.

The Middle School Mystery

continued … (after Workshop B)

Claudia has heard Shawna and two of her friends in the girls' room[1]. She knows that Shawna cheated in the test but she can't prove[2] it to Mr. Zorzi.

Claudia and her friends break into Shawna's locker. They find a note there from one of Shawna's friends:
Congratulations[3] on your A –. Who would have guessed that C.K.'s paper would have so many right answers?

Claudia realizes[4] that she can't prove that one of Shawna's friends wrote it. At home she talks to her sister Janine.

The next day when the last bell rang, I went to my locker and got my things together. Suddenly I saw Janine. I couldn't believe my eyes and ran after her. "What are you doing here?" I asked.

"I decided it was time to do something about this terrible situation," she said. "I always had a good relationship[5] with the principal when I was at Stoneybrook[6] Middle School. He might remember me."

Remember her! Teachers and principals never forget Janine. They'll hold her up as an example[7] of a model student for the next fifty years.

"I know you didn't cheat. I'm going to talk to the principal about it," she went on.

"But –," I started to protest. Then I asked her, "What are you going to tell him?"

"Don't worry," said Janine. "I'm only going to tell him how hard you studied[8]."

Janine then goes to the principal's office and talks to both the principal and Mr. Zorzi. When they call Claudia in, they tell her that they will try to think of a way for her to have a fair[9] chance … .

I arrived in math class a little early the next day, so I could find out what Mr. Zorzi and the principal had decided. When I walked into the room, Mr. Zorzi was grading[10] papers at his desk.

"Claudia," he said. "I'm glad you're here early. This is what we've decided. During class today, you're going to take the test over again[11]."

"OK," I said. "I'm ready."

"The test isn't exactly the same," Mr. Zorzi went on. "It covers[12] similar[13] material, but the questions are different." He led[14] me to a desk at the back of the room.

I sat down and looked around me. There were no other desks near it. Good! I didn't want there to be any doubt[15] in anybody's mind[16] about *this* test.

The other kids in my class were coming in by now, but they didn't speak to me. Shawna looked at me like she was *dying* to know[17] what I was doing. I started to work on the test.

This time I wasn't n<early as nervous. Again there were questions that looked harder and questions that looked easier. I just started with the easier ones and worked my way through the test. When I had finished I checked my work, walked up to Mr. Zorzi's desk and handed[18] the paper to him. There was still time left[19] in the period, so he said he'd check it right away.

I sat down at my normal desk and started to study. Once in a while[20] I looked up to see if Mr. Zorzi had finished grading my test.

Just before the bell rang, Mr. Zorzi called me to his desk. I crossed my fingers[21] as I went to the front of the room.

"You know, Claudia," said Mr. Zorzi, looking up at me as I stood in front of his

[1]girls' room ['gɜ:lz ru:m] *Mädchentoilette* – [2]to prove [pru:v] *beweisen* – [3]congratulations [kənˌgrætʃʊ'leɪʃnz] *Herzlichen Glückwunsch* – [4]to realize ['rɪəlaɪz] *sich über etwas klar werden* – [5]relationship [rɪ'leɪʃnʃɪp] *Verhältnis* – [6]Stoneybrook ['stəʊnɪbrʊk] – [7]to hold s.o. up as an example *jdn. als leuchtendes Beispiel hochhalten* – [8]to study ['stʌdɪ] *studieren, lernen* – [9]fair [feə] *gerecht, fair* – [10]to grade [greɪd] *korrigieren, benoten* – [11]over again [ˌəʊvər‿ə'gen] *noch einmal* – [12]to cover ['kʌvə] *abdecken* – [13]similar ['sɪmɪlə] *ähnlich* – [14]to lead, led, led [li:d] *führen* – [15]doubt [daʊt] *Zweifel* – [16]mind [maɪnd] *hier: Kopf* – [17]be dying to [bi: 'daɪɪŋ tə] *für sein Leben gern wollen* – [18]to hand [hænd] *überreichen* – [19]left [left] *übrig* – [20]once in a while [ˌwʌns ɪn‿ə'waɪl] *hin und wieder* – [21]to cross one's fingers: *die ersten zwei Finger über Kreuz legen = die Daumen drücken*

desk, "I believe that taking a test is like playing a game. You can either[22] win the game, or you can lose it." He looked at me to see if I understood what he was saying. "If you lose," he continued, "it just means you need more practice."

What was he trying to tell me?

"Good news, Claudia!" he said with a smile. "You've won the game this time. You did even better on this test than on the first one. You only missed two questions."

Wow! I had done it! All right!

"I must apologize[23], Claudia," said Mr. Zorzi. "I'm sorry I said you cheated. I've learned a lesson from this."

"That's OK, Mr. Zorzi," I said. "As long as you believe me now." It was fantastic that he had apologized right away.

Then the bell rang and everybody got up to go. "Just a minute," said Mr. Zorzi. "Shawna Riverson[24], please stop at my desk."

"Shawna," said Mr. Zorzi. "Claudia has just retaken[25] the test and she has passed it with flying colors[26]."

Shawna looked at me for a second, and then back at him. "Yeah?" she answered. "So what?"

"I believe she has shown that she didn't cheat on the test," said Mr Zorzi. "I'm going to ask you to prove the same thing."

Shawna turned white.

"You don't have to stay late today," he said. "You may take the test tomorrow morning during homeroom[27]."

"I – I can't!" said Shawna. Now her face was red. "I can't take it because I don't know the material. Even if I studied all night I wouldn't pass the test." Shawna looked like she was about to cry. "I did it! I copied off of Claudia's paper!"

My mouth fell open. I never expected[28] her to admit[29] it.

Mr. Zorzi's mouth was open, too. Just for a moment. "Why, Shawna?" he asked. "Why did you cheat?"

She told him the story: how she had stretched herself too thin[30] with her activities and clubs. "So I just didn't think there was any other way," she finished.

"And you led me to believe that Claudia was the one who had cheated?" Mr. Zorzi asked. "I think you should apologize to her."

Shawna looked at me and said something I couldn't hear. I didn't care[31]. I'd done it! I'd stuck this thing out[32] and with Janine's help I'd proved that I hadn't cheated. I felt like a huge weight had fallen off my shoulders. Shawna, the cheater, was in tears[33]. I almost felt sorry for her. Almost.

Mr. Zorzi sent her straight to the principal's office, and I found out later that she got suspended[34] for two days. Plus, she got an F on that test. Poor, poor Shawna.

That's what my friends said when I finished telling the story in the cafeteria.

"Poor, poor Shawna."

WENDY by Richard Warwick

[22]either ['aɪðə] *entweder* – [23]to apologize [ə'pɒlədʒaɪz] *sich entschuldigen* – [24]Riverson ['rɪvəsən] – [25]to retake [rɪ'teɪk] *noch einmal machen* – [26]to pass with flying colors ['pɑ:s wɪð ˌflaɪɪŋ 'kʌləz] *blendend bestehen* – [27]homeroom ['həʊmru:m] *Klassenstunde* – [28]to expect [ɪk'spekt] *erwarten* – [29]to admit [əd'mɪt] *zugeben* – [30]to stretch o.s. too thin ['stretʃ … tu: 'θɪn] *sich übernehmen* – [31]I didn't care ['keə] *es war mir egal* – [32]to stick s.th. out ['stɪk 'aʊt] *etw. durchhalten* – [33]to be in tears [bɪ ɪn 'tɪəz] *in Tränen aufgelöst sein* – [34]to get suspended [sə'spendɪd] *Schulverbot haben* – [35]true, truly [tru:, 'tru:lɪ] *wahr (hier: richtig), wahrhaftig*

Clementine and the miner, forty-niner

after Workshop C

Light[9] she was and like a fairy[10],
And her shoes were number nine,
Herring[11] boxes without topses[12]
Sandals[13] were for Clementine.
Chorus

Drove she ducklings[14] to the water
Ev'ry morning just at nine,
Hit her foot against a splinter[15],
Fell into the foaming brine[16].
Chorus

Ruby lips[17] above the water
Blowing bubbles[18] soft and fine,
But, alas[19], I was no swimmer,
So I lost my Clementine.
Chorus

How I missed her! How I missed her,
How I missed my Clementine,
But I kissed her little sister,
and forgot my Clementine.
Chorus

In the year 1848 California had just become part of the United States of America. It was a long way away from the eastern states of the US, but some people from the East wanted to go there because the climate was so good for farming[20]. Then news began to arrive in the East about gold in the hills of California. At first people just laughed. "Oh, the newspapers are just trying to make this new part of the US sound really good," they said. But they found out it was true[21]: there were pieces of nearly pure[22] gold in the rivers in California.

HOW DID THEY GET THERE?

It wasn't easy to get there. There was no Panama Canal[23] and no railway across North or Central America in the 1840s. Some travellers went by ship from the eastern coast of the US all round Cape Horn[24] at the southern tip[25] of South America. When they got to San Francisco Bay[26], the nearest place to the gold fields, the passengers[27] and crews[28] just left the ships where they were and went straight off[29] to look for gold. The gold rush[30] was on!

Lots of people decided to go across the country. They took a train as far as the railroad went, then they took a steamboat[31] to St. Joseph, Missouri[32]. After that, they had to walk 2000 miles across the country. They started in the spring of 1849, with

[1]cavern ['kævən] *Höhle* – [2]excavating ['ekskəveɪtɪŋ] *ausgrabend* – [3]to dwell, dwelt, dwelt ['dwel], ['dwelt] *leben, wohnen* – [4]forty-niner [ˌfɔ:tɪ 'naɪnə] *(siehe Text)* – [5]Clementine ['kleməntaɪn] – [6]darling ['dɑ:lɪŋ] *Liebling* – [7]thou art lost [ˌðaʊ ɑ:t 'lɒst] *du bist (mir) verloren* – [8]dreadful ['dredfəl] *fürchterlich* – [9]light ['laɪt] *leicht* – [10]fairy ['feərɪ] *Fee* – [11]herring ['herɪŋ] *Hering* – [12]topses = tops ['tɒpsɪz] *Deckel* – [13]sandals ['sændəlz] *Sandalen* – [14]duckling ['dʌklɪŋ] *Entlein* – [15]splinter ['splɪntə] *Splitter* – [16]foaming brine [ˌfəʊmɪŋ 'braɪn] *schäumendes Salzwasser* – [17]ruby lips [ˌru:bɪ 'lɪps] *rubinrote Lippen* – [18]bubble ['bʌbl] *Blase* – [19]alas [ə'læs] *O Weh! Aber ach!* – [20]farming ['fɑ:mɪŋ] *Landwirtschaft* – [21]true [tru:] *wahr* – [22]pure [pjʊə] *rein* – [23]Panama Canal ['pænəma: kə'næl] – [24]Cape Horn [keɪp 'hɔ:n] – [25]tip [tip] *hier: Spitze* – [26]bay [beɪ] *Bucht* – [27]passenger ['pæsɪndʒə] *Passagier* – [28]crew [kru:] *Mannschaft* – [29]to go straight off [gəʊ 'streɪt‿ˌɒf] *schnurstracks losgehen* – [30]gold rush ['gəʊld rʌʃ] *Goldrausch* – [31]steamboat ['sti:mbəʊt] *Dampfer* – [32]St. Joseph, Missouri [sənt'dʒəʊzɪf mɪ'zʊərɪ]

groups of wagons, animals to pull them, food and what they would need for a new home. They crossed the Rockies[33] in the summer, then started the long walk across Wyoming[34]. It looked flat, but it was all uphill[35] and was difficult for the animals that pulled the wagons. Soon, people started to throw away anything heavy: stoves, beds, mirrors. They moved south west across the desert[36] of Utah[37] and into what is now Nevada[38]. It was August and hot. There were no rivers, no good water and people and animals died. Then they came to 65 miles of desert with no water at all. It took 52 hours to cross it, if they could keep going[39]. People and animals went mad and died, but some got through and found rivers and trees again. However[40], they still had to cross the High Sierras[41]. They had to get through before September, after that the mountain paths were blocked[42] by snow.

At last they came down to the rich grassland of the American River and could start to look for gold. The "forty-niners" washed it out of the river mud[43] or they dug[44] into the hill and became miners. Some of them didn't even have time to build houses, but lived in caves. Many of those who came later were disappointed. The first people there found gold and became rich, but there was nothing left for the late-comers. Those who didn't find gold went on later to look for silver[45] in Nevada or to a later gold rush in Colorado[46] in 1858.

"230 egg an' chips, 150 steaks an' mash[47], 200 ham an' eggs ..."

[33]Rockies ['rɒkɪz] *Bergkette im Westen der USA* – [34]Wyoming [waɪ'əʊmɪŋ] – [35]uphill ['ʌp'hɪl] *bergauf* – [36]desert ['dezət] *Wüste* – [37]Utah ['ju:tɑ:] – [38]Nevada [nə'vɑ:də] – [39]to keep going [ki:p 'gəʊɪŋ] *weitermachen* – [40]however [haʊ'evə] aber, allerdings – [41]High Sierras [ˌhaɪ sɪ'erəz] *Bergkette westlich der Rockies* – [42]blocked [blɒkt] *blockiert* – [43]mud [mʌd] *Schlamm* – [44]to dig, dug, dug [dɪg], [dʌg] *graben* – [45]silver ['sɪlvə] *Silber* – [46]Colorado [kɒlə'rɑ:dəʊ] – [47]mash [mæʃ] *Kartoffelpüree*

A tape drama

Record this story on tape and put in the sound effects. They're marked in the story with [FX]. On the opposite page there are some ideas for making these sound effects. You could turn it into a play – with a narrator[1], and someone to play Pat[2] and the actor. In the story Pat is a boy, but the part can be played by a girl, just as the narrator can be a boy or a girl. Of course, you could do the story or play "live", too, for example as a Halloween play.

One night last fall[3] I was alone in our apartment. The Mayhews[4] upstairs had gone to Miami for two weeks. The man downstairs had gotten a new job in Chicago and moved out. There was nobody in the house but me and my cat, Benjy. Don't get the wrong idea: it was Halloween, but I don't believe in ghosts and things. It was a dark, stormy night: the wind was howling[5] *[FX: wind]* and the rain was beating against the windows *[FX: rain]*. I heard a clock strike[6] ten *[FX: clock]* and I was just going to bed when the doorbell rang *[FX: bell]*. I went to the door. "Who's there?" I called.

"Hi, it's me – Pat," said a voice. I opened the front door *[FX: buzzer[7]]* and up the stairs came my cousin Pat. *[FX: footsteps on stairs]*

"My bike just got a flat tire[8]," he said. "I was in the next street, so I thought I'd come here." He was wet and cold.

"Sure," I said. "Come in." I made the couch[9] up into a bed for Pat, then went into my bedroom. I was nearly asleep when there was a loud bang[10] *[FX: bang]*. I sat up.

"Did you close the front door when you came in?" I called to Pat.

"I think so, do you want me to look?" The couch creaked[11] *[FX: creaking couch]* as Pat sat up.

"No, it's definitely closed now!" I said. Benjy jumped onto the bed. I lay down again.

Suddenly there was the sound of a gunshot[12] *[FX: shot]* and a scream *[FX: scream]*. I jumped out of bed and ran into the room where Pat was. His face was white.

"It came from upstairs!" he said.

We went out to the stairs *[FX: door]* to listen. Nothing … silence. Then, the sound of the gunshot and the scream again *[FX: shot, scream]*. Pat and I looked at each other.

"Call the police," Pat said, but I went up the stairs *[FX: footsteps on stairs]* and knocked on the door *[FX: knocking]*.

A young man opened the door and looked at me in surprise.

"Is everything OK?" I asked.

"Yeah! Hey, I'm sorry if I scared you. I'm Bob Mayhew. My parents are away. They said I could use their apartment. I thought the house was empty. I'm just …

"Oh, only we heard a scream … ."

"Oh, that's just a tape. I'm an actor and I'm practicing for a role in a murder[13] play. I have to say my lines just when the shot comes."

"That's OK, but do you have to do it at night?" Just then a clock struck twelve. *[FX: clock]*

"Oh yes, it *is* late," he said. "I'm sorry. I'll stop now. Good night." *[FX: door shuts]*

So we didn't call the police and Pat and I went back to bed. *[FX: snoring[14]]*

[1]narrator [nəˈreɪtə] *Erzähler/in* – [2]Pat [pæt] – [3]fall [fɔ:l] *AE; BE: autumn* – [4]Mayhews [ˈmeɪhju:z] – [5]to howl [haʊl] *heulen* – [6]to strike, struck, struck [straɪk], [strʌk] *schlagen* – [7]buzzer [ˈbʌzə] *hier: Türöffner* – [8]tire [taɪə] *AE; BE: tyre* – [9]couch [kaʊtʃ] *Sofa* – [10]bang [bæŋ] *Knall* – [11]to creak [kri:k] *quietschen* – [12]gunshot [ˈgʌnʃɒt] *Schuss* – [13]murder [ˈmɜ:də] *Mord* – [14]to snore [ˈsnɔ:] *schnarchen* – [15]saucepan lid [ˌsɔ:spən ˈlɪd] *Topfdeckel* – [16]pea [pi:] *Erbse* – [17]cardboard [ˈkɑ:dbɔ:d] *Pappe, Papp-* – [18]step ladder [ˈstepˌlædə] *Stufenleiter* – [19]to breathe [bri:ð] *atmen* – [20]strip [strɪp] *Streifen, schmales Stück* – [21]wooden [ˈwʊdn] *hölzern, aus Holz* – [22]ruler [ˈru:lə] *Lineal* – [23]edge [edʒ] *Rand* – [24]microphone [ˈmaɪkrəfəʊn] *Mikrophon*

FX

Some sound effects can be made as you need them, but some should be recorded before they are needed. When you are recording "real" sounds as sound effects, be careful of extra sounds that you don't need: cars or planes going past, a radio or TV on somewhere near.

footsteps

Record the real thing, footsteps with hard shoes on a hard floor.

door

Record the real thing. Record "door opening", "door shutting", "door opening and shutting" to use at different times.

bang

Drop something onto a hard floor or piece of wood.

snoring

Heavy breathing[19], and a snore or two – not too many.

wind

One or two people blow across the top of the microphone[24].

footsteps on stairs

Record someone walking up a step-ladder[18].

creaking couch

Take a strip[20] of wood (e.g. a wooden[21] ruler[22]), hold one end on a table with half the strip over the edge[23] of the table. Press down hard on the free end, then let it go quickly.

knocking on door

Bang with your hand on a piece of wood – or a door!

clock striking

Hit a saucepan lid[15] with a spoon.

rain

Put rice or dried peas[16] in a cardboard[17] box and move the box about.

scream

Record the real thing, but tell family and neighbors first!

shot

Take a strip of wood, tie a piece of string round one end and stand on the other end (on a hard floor). Let go of the string.

bell or buzzer

Record the real thing or use an alarm clock with a bell or buzzer.

American holidays

Every country has its colorful holidays, the US too. When Americans say 'holiday', they could mean one of the special days in the calendar. And what are the main holidays in the US?

January 1
New Year's Day[1]

Many people welcome[2] the new year at midnight with funny hats, loud parties, and the song "Auld lang syne[3]" (Old Scottish for 'the good old times') which is only sung on this holiday. This is one of the few days in the American calendar on which all businesses and offices (except[4] some gas stations[5], super-markets and restaurants) are closed.

January – 3rd Monday
Martin Luther King, Jr. Day[6]

became a national holiday in 1986. This day honors[7] the great African-American civil rights[8] leader. Markets and restaurants are closed.

February – 3rd Monday
Presidents' Day[9]

is a holiday which honors all US presidents. Some states choose to have Abraham Lincoln's[10] Birthday (February 12) and/or George Washington's[11] Birthday (February 22), two holidays which honor America's two most respected[12] presidents. No state has all three of these "president holidays".

February 14
Valentine's Day[13]

is a holiday on which shops and offices are open. It's a day for lovers[14], but lovers can quickly become enemies if candy, flowers or other presents are forgotten!

March 17
St. Patrick's Day[15]

is another "fun holiday" like Valentine's Day. A quarter of all Americans have Irish blood, but it's not just for Irish-Americans. School children are told to wear green that day – the other students have the right to pinch[16] the "non-green" kids!

March – April
Easter Sunday[17]

is the next big festival in the calendar. For some people it's a religious holiday, for others just a day to look for eggs and baskets full of candy from the Easter Bunny.

May – last Monday
Memorial Day[18]

is a national holiday and was created[19] to honor American soldiers who died. Memorial Day week-end has for many years been the beginning of summer in America, and Americans use their long weekend for barbecues and boating!

July 4
Independence Day[20]

The Fourth of July is another traditional day for barbecues. On this day in 1776 the American colonists declared[21] their independence from England, and so of course this is a very patriotic[22] day of fireworks, parades, and lots of red, white and blue clothes.

September – 1st Monday
Labor Day[23]

Labor Day is the end of summer in the US. This national holiday honors workers. It means "back-to-school time" for most students – the first day of class is the next day.

[1]New Year's Day [ˌnju: jɪəz 'deɪ] *Neujahr(stag)* – [2]to welcome ['welkəm] *begrüssen, willkommen heißen* – [3]auld lang syne [ˌɔ:ld læŋ 'saɪn] – [4]except [ɪk'sept] *ausser* – [5]gas station ['gæs steɪʃn] *Tankstelle* – [6]Martin Luther King, Jr. ['mɑ:tɪn lu:θə 'kɪŋ 'dʒu:njə] *amerik. Bürgerrechtler* (1929-68) – [7]to honor ['ɒnə] *ehren* – [8]civil rights [ˌsɪvl 'raɪts] *Bürgerrechte* – [9]President's Day ['prezɪdənts ˌdeɪ] – [10]Abraham Lincoln [ˌeɪbrəhæm 'lɪnkən] *Präsident der USA (1861-65)* – [11]George Washington [ˌdʒɔ:dʒ 'wɒʃɪŋtən] *erster Präsident der USA (1789-97)* – [12]respected [rɪ'spektɪd] *angesehen* – [13]Valentine's Day ['væləntaɪnz ˌdeɪ] *Valentinstag* – [14]lover ['lʌvə] *Geliebte(r)* – [15]St. Patrick [snt 'pætrɪk] *heiliger Schutzpatron Irlands* – [16]to pinch [pɪntʃ] *kneifen, zwicken* – [17]Easter Sunday [ˌi:stə 'sʌndeɪ] *Ostersonntag*

Fourth of July Cake

1 pound (500 g) of strawberries[24]
half a pound (200-250 g) of blueberries[25]
or blackcurrants[26]
2 packets of basic cake mix[27]
1 packet of icing mix[28] or two cartons of cream[29]

Make the cake from the packets and bake it on a flat oven tray[30]. When it is cold cover[31] it with the icing or whip[32] the cream and use it to cover the cake. Make a 5 inch (12,5 cm) square section in the top left corner. Put the blueberries here, very close together. Slice[33] the strawberries and lay them in stripes[34] across the rest of the cake. Start with a stripe of strawberries at the top and make 13 stripes in all, (7 red, 6 white) so that you finish with a red line.

October 31
Halloween

American students have been in school for about two months and so are ready for a day of fun. In Celtic[35] times people put on frightening costumes to drive bad spirits[36] away, but now it's a chance to put on costumes and just have a good time at a party!

November – last Thursday
Thanksgiving

is the country's most important holiday. In November 1621 people who had left England in the *Mayflower*[37] to escape religious persecution[38], landed at Plymouth Rock[39]. The first winter killed half of the small group. Fortunately, the Indians showed them how to grow local crops[40]: pumpkins, corn and beans. The colonists were thankful and invited the Indians to a feast[41] in celebration. The idea of "thanksgiving" was born.
Thanksgiving is a quiet day to spend with the special people in one's life and it still celebrates a good harvest. No Thanksgiving table would be complete without a huge roast[42]turkey with stuffing[43] and cranberry sauce[44], but the true highlight of any Thanksgiving dinner is the dessert: a delicious[45] pumpkin pie.

December 24-25
Christmas Eve – Christmas Day

Many families have large parties on Christmas Eve but it is no holiday – stores are open until midnight for last-minute shoppers! Christmas Day is the national holiday, and the day when stockings[46] are opened and presents are exchanged[47]. But December 26th it's back to work for everyone – or back to shopping: the 26th is the biggest shopping day in America!

[18]Memorial Day [mɪ'mɔ:rɪəl ˌdeɪ] *Heldengedenktag* – [19]to create [kri:'eɪt] *ins Leben rufen* – [20]Independence Day [ˌɪndɪ'pendəns ˌdeɪ] – [21]to declare [dɪ'kleə] *erklären* – [22]patriotic [ˌpætrɪ'ɒtɪk] *patriotisch* – [23]Labor Day ['leɪbə ˌdeɪ] *Tag der Arbeit* – [24]strawberry ['strɔ:brɪ] *Erdbeere* – [25]blueberry ['blu:bərɪ] *Heidelbeere* – [26]blackcurrant [ˌblæk'kʌrənt] *schwarze Johannisbeere* – [27]basic cake mix [ˌbeɪsɪk 'keɪk ˌmɪks] *Kuchen-Fertigmischung* – [28]icing mix ['aɪsɪŋ ˌmɪks] *Glasur-Fertigmischung* – [29]carton of cream ['kɑ:tn‿əv 'kri:m] *Becher Sahne* – [30]flat oven tray ['flæt 'ʌvn ˌtreɪ] *flaches Backblech* – [31]to cover ['kʌvə] *bedecken, überziehen* – [32]to whip [wɪp] *(zu Schaum) schlagen* – [33]to slice [slaɪs] *in Scheiben schneiden* – [34]stripe [straɪp] *Streifen* – [35]Celtic ['keltik] *keltisch* – [36]spirit ['spɪrɪt] *Geist* – [37]*Mayflower* ['meɪˌflaʊə] – [38]religious persecution [rɪ'lɪdʒəs ˌpɜ:sɪ'kju:ʃn] *religiöse Verfolgung* – [39]Plymouth Rock ['plɪməθ ˌrɒk] – [40]crop [krɒp] *Feldfrucht* – [41]feast [fi:st] *Fest(mahl)* – [42]to roast/roast/roast [rəʊst] *braten* – [43]stuffing ['stʌfɪŋ] *Füllung* – [44]cranberry sauce ['krænbərɪ ˌsɔ:s] *Preiselbeer-Sauce* – [45]delicious [dɪ'lɪʃəs] *lecker* – [46]stocking ['stɒkɪŋ] *Strumpf* – [47]to exchange [ɪks'tʃeɪndʒ] *austauschen*

⟨Translation practice⟩

Tip 1
- The **word order** is often different:
  – Yesterday we were in the gym for an hour.
  – *Gestern waren wir eine Stunde lang in der Turnhalle.*

Tip 2
- You sometimes have to use **more words** in one language than in the other:
  – Daniel is staying for a long time.
  – *Daniel bleibt lange.*

Tip 3
- You often say things **in a different way** in the other language:
  – Tori is on the phone.
  – *Tori telefoniert.*

Tip 4
- There are sometimes **two or more different words** in one language for one word in the other:
  – I know Alex. – I know.
  – *Ich kenne Alex.* – *Ich weiß.*

Tip 5
- The **tense** in English isn't always the same in German:
  – I saw you yesterday.
  – *Ich habe dich gestern gesehen.*

Tip 6
- There is often **more than one 'correct' translation**:
  – They think it's too dangerous.
  – *Sie denken/glauben/sind der Meinung …*

Tip 7
- Little phrases like 'you know', 'you see', 'remember', are **fillers**[1]. Don't translate them. German fillers like 'ja', 'schon', 'nämlich' or 'halt' may be useful:
  – Tomorrow's Sunday, remember.
  – *Morgen ist ja Sonntag.*

Unit 1 The Alburgs

Try to translate what the Alburgs said into good German.

1. *Alex:* I'm sure you'll like it here, Daniel. It's really strange that we're cousins and have never met before!
2. *Tori:* Daniel has been here since Tuesday, and we haven't had a barbecue yet. Let's have one tonight. I'll pick up some fish.
3. *Lynn:* You're in big trouble, Tori. You know Dad and I told you not to go up to the Falls at night. Well, thank goodness you didn't have an accident!
4. *Bruce:* You haven't got much experience yet, Tori. You've only had your driver's license since June, remember.

Unit 2 New in New York

First read the story carefully. Then close your book and try to tell the story again – but in German! Now compare the two. Did you forget any important points?

Many years ago there was an Englishman who had heard so many wonderful stories about life in America that he decided to go and live there himself. "It's a dream country!" people had told him. "The streets in New York are all paved with gold!"
So he got on the next ship to America, and two weeks later he arrived in New York. He had had a terrible journey, the sea had been rough and stormy, and he hadn't slept well. So when he got off the ship at last, he was very tired indeed. As he was walking along the street, he looked down and saw a ten-dollar bill[2] at his feet. He bent down to pick it up, but then he thought better of it. "No," he said to himself and smiled, "why should I hurry? I'm too tired now. I'll start tomorrow!"

[1] filler *Füllwort*
[2] bill *Geldschein*

Daryl and Soo

In English there are lot of phrases with '-ing'-forms. *Find these phrases in the dialogue. How can you put them into good German?*

Soo: You remember when we were at the Worldfest? I really thought you might be in a gang!
Daryl: Well, it's no good lying to you, Soo. Only a few days ago I was seriously thinking about joining the Jackals. I was getting tired of delivering pizzas and I was – well, I was interested in trying something new. But somehow, being together with you made me different. Suddenly I just didn't feel crazy about getting into the gang any more.
Soo: Thank goodness my parents know about us now. When we first started going out, I was somehow scared of telling them about you. But now that they know you, everything's OK!
Daryl: Well, I must say, saving Pugwacket helped a bit! Everyone loves a hero.
Soo: I guess you're right. When they first saw us together, they were so worried!
Daryl: Well, they don't have to worry about seeing us together now!

How afraid are you?

Test yourself to see! Can you translate this for your school magazine? Work in groups.

1. If you read that your favorite food was very unhealthy, would you
   a) give it up at once?
   b) go on eating it and forget the report?
   c) try to eat less of it?
2. If you were standing in line and someone pushed in front of you, would you
   a) protest loudly?
   b) say nothing?
   c) say 'Excuse me, but I think ...'?
3. If you woke up in the night and heard a noise in the apartment, would you
   a) get up and see what it was?
   b) think it was probably nothing and go to sleep again?
   c) stay in bed, too scared to move?
4. If you thought your teacher had been unfair to you in a test, would you
   a) try to forget about it?
   b) tell him/her right away, in front of the whole class?
   c) try to think of a way to tell him/her about it politely?
5. If you found a hole in a new T-shirt, would you
   a) take it back and ask for a new one?
   b) mend the hole yourself?
   c) put it away and forget about it?

Check your points
1. a) 3 b) 1 c) 2
2. a) 1 b) 3 c) 2
3. a) 2 b) 1 c) 3
4. a) 3 b) 1 c) 2
5. a) 1 b) 2 c) 3

10 points or more? You would enjoy life much more if you weren't so scared!
7–9 points? You're usually OK – even in tricky situations!
Under 7 points? Maybe you're a bit too sure of yourself!

Unit 3 From the newspaper

How would you put these pieces of news into German?

1 Every year more roads are built and more of our beautiful landscape is changed. Even in our national parks damage is done by thousands of visitors.

2 Two teenagers were killed in a rafting accident on the Colorado River last week.

3 A hiker was attacked by a black bear in Yosemite National Park yesterday. Later the bear was shot by a ranger. The hiker was taken to the hospital; luckily he was not badly hurt.

GRAND CANYON HELICOPTER TOURS

Since 1975 our helicopter tours have been the great tourist attraction of the Grand Canyon. Over 100,000 people fly with us each year. No wonder our tours are so popular – we have so much to offer! Each helicopter has four to six seats, so that nearly everyone gets a window seat. This way you can really enjoy the magnificent bird's eye view of the canyon. Foreign visitors have no need to worry about their English – all information on our tours is translated into five different languages.

Fly with us and enjoy the most spectacular views of the world-famous Grand Canyon. This great canyon was cut by the Colorado River over 2 million years ago. It extends over a distance of 217 miles (349 km). At its deepest point the canyon is a mile deep (1.6 km). Trails lead down from the rim of the canyon to its floor, where the Colorado River snakes its way through the rock. A flight in one of our helicopters is an unforgettable experience. Don't miss it!

Florian Walter, 14, is on holiday in the USA with his parents and younger sister. The Walters have trouble understanding this leaflet. *How does Florian help them?*

tip When you're explaining something – or interpreting[1]:
- Just try to give the main ideas.

Frau Walter: ‚Helicopter Tours' – am Grand Canyon? Sicher gut! Ist es etwas Neues?
Florian: Nein, …
Herr Walter: Aber lohnt sich so ein Flug für uns? Mutti und ich verstehen ja so wenig Englisch!
Florian: …
Frau Walter: Dann ist Deutsch sicherlich auch dabei. – Ich sehe das Wort ‚birds'. Werden wir dann von da oben viele Vögel beobachten können?
Florian: …
Herr Walter: Da steht was von 349 km. So lang kann der Flug doch nicht sein, oder?
Florian: …
Frau Walter: Also, wenn wir schon mal da sind, möchte ich auch zu Fuß was unternehmen. Es gibt bestimmt auch Möglichkeiten zum Wandern?
Florian: …
Frau Walter: Aber schau mal: ‚snakes' sind doch Schlangen! Das hört sich weniger schön an!
Florian: …
Herr Walter: Ich möchte das Ganze am liebsten aus der Luft sehen. So was bleibt einem ja lange in Erinnerung.
Florian: Ja, die behaupten hier …

Unit 4 It could all have been different

Translate what Jerry is thinking. Be careful with the word order (Tip 1) and the tenses (Tip 5).

1. If Mr. Cohen hadn't forgotten his passport, I wouldn't have gotten that call.
2. If I'd been a minute earlier, I wouldn't have seen the woman near the lake!
3. I would have felt terrible if I hadn't gone back and helped her!
4. If nobody had stopped those muggers, they might have hurt her really badly.
5. Of course, I would have gotten to Lincoln Square in time if all this hadn't happened. But then I would never have met William Weston!

[1]to interpret *dolmetschen*

Signs in town

Philipp's American friend Rick is staying with him in Germany. One Monday afternoon they go into town. Philipp's older sister Sophie is driving.

1. *Rick:* 'Einbahnstraße'? What's that? Isn't 'Bahn' the word for 'railroad'?
   Philipp: Not here! It means ...
2. *Rick:* There's a 'No Entry' sign. But two cars just drove through.
   Philipp: The sign says ...
3. *Rick:* Look, you can park here at the station, Sophie. There's a 'P' sign.
   Sophie: Yes, but ...
4. *Rick:* I guess 'Privat' means private, so we can't park here?
   Sophie: Right! If you ...
5. *Rick:* Is it OK here? What's a 'Parkscheibe'?
   Sophie: Look, it's like a ... You ...
6. *Rick:* This looks like a nice little café. Let's go in and have a coke.
   Philipp: Oh no, it's Monday. Look, ...

Unit 5 At a German post office

When you are at the post office one afternoon, the girl in front of you needs help. She can't speak German – and the clerk behind the counter can't understand what she wants.
Can you help? (Don't try to translate everything word for word. Just try to explain.)

Clerk: Ich verstehe nicht, was die junge Dame hier sagt.
You: Vielleicht kann ich helfen. *(to the girl)* What's the problem? Can I help?
Girl: Well, I was trying to get some stamps out of that machine outside.
You: ...
Clerk: Wieviel Geld haben Sie eingeworfen?
You: ...
Girl: I think I put in five marks all in all. But the machine isn't working. There's something wrong with it.
You: ...
Clerk: Haben Sie überhaupt keine Briefmarken 'rausgekriegt?
You: ...
Girl: No! No stamps came out at all! I pressed all the buttons I could see, but nothing happened.
You: ...
Clerk: Und haben Sie auch den Knopf für Geldrückgabe gedrückt?
You: There's a special button to get ... Did you ...?
Girl: I think so. Anyway, all my small change is still in that stupid machine! So what happens now?
You: ...
Clerk: Wieviele Marken brauchen Sie?
You: ...
Girl: Enough for these postcards. – Oh, thank you so much!
Clerk: Bitte schön! Auf Wiedersehen.
Girl (to you): Thanks for your help. You were great!

Grammar

Hallo Sportsfreunde,

wie in den Bänden 1-3 ist hier noch einmal die Grammatik zusammengefasst. Inzwischen seid ihr ja keine Anfängerinnen und Anfänger mehr und wisst, dass Sprachen, so wie jedes Spiel, ihre Regeln brauchen. Viele davon habt ihr schon gelernt. Alles, was in diesem Band an Grammatik neu ist, findet ihr auf den folgenden Seiten. Wie schon im letzten Band haben wir auch diesmal ein paar kleine Aufgaben „zum Training“ für euch dazu gepackt. Damit könnt ihr gleich testen, ob auch alles richtig „sitzt“.

In der Übersicht auf Seite 104 findet ihr eine alphabetische Grammatikliste mit den deutschen und englischen Begriffen und Beispielen zu den Regeln. Hier könnt ihr nachschlagen, wenn euch etwas nicht ganz klar ist.

Und wie bisher gilt weiterhin: Wenn euch selbst Möglichkeiten einfallen, grammatische Gebiete zusammenzufassen, darzustellen oder anderen zu erklären, habt ihr bereits einen entscheidenden Schritt vorwärts gemacht.

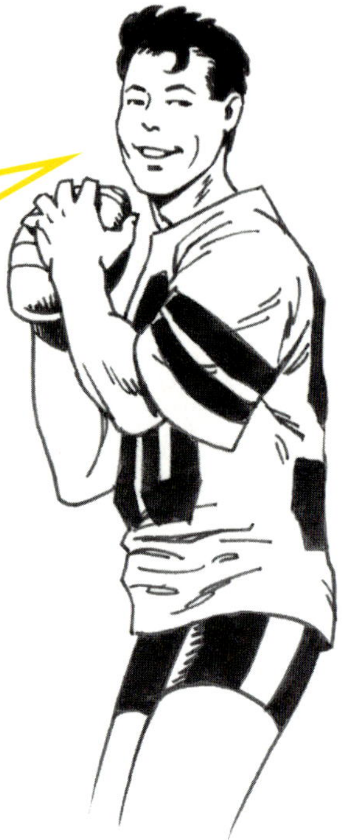

Unit 1 Step B

§ 1 Das present perfect mit ‚for' und ‚since'

Mit dem *present perfect* und *for* und *since* kannst du ausdrücken, dass ein Zustand, der in der Vergangenheit anfing, schon eine bestimmte Zeit andauert.

Since when?	
Tori **has had** her driver's license **since June.**	… hat (schon) seit Juni …
Daniel **has been** in America **since Tuesday.**	… ist (schon) seit Dienstag …
We **haven't seen** him **since he was three.**	… haben ihn (schon) seit er drei war …

Since bezieht sich auf den **Zeitpunkt,** an dem ein Zustand begann: *since 4 o'clock, since Christmas, since 1996 …*

How long?	
The Alburgs **have lived** in their house **for five years.**	… wohnen (schon) fünf Jahre lang …
Tori **has known** Daniel **for three months.**	… kennt … (schon) drei Monate lang.
Mrs. Alburg **hasn't been** to New York **for ten years.**	… ist 10 Jahre lang nicht mehr … gewesen.

For bezieht sich auf die **Dauer** eines Zustands: *for five hours, for twenty minutes, for ages …*

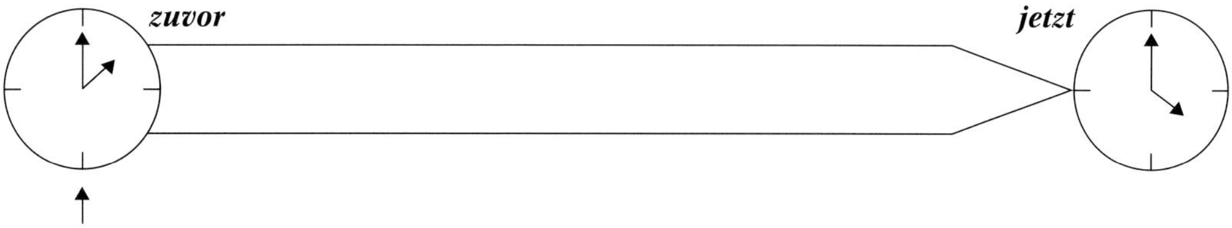

since two o'clock
Zeit**punkt** des Beginns

for two hours
Dauer des Zustands

Sei vorsichtig beim Übersetzen: Im Deutschen benutzen wir bei bejahten Sätzen in der Regel das Präsens und betonen die Dauer des Zustands mit **schon.**

Tori **has had** her part-time job for three months. — Tori **hat** ihren Teilzeitjob (schon) drei Monate lang.

§ 2 Phrasal verbs

Phrasal verbs sind Verben, die fest mit einem *short word* (einer Präposition oder einem Adverb) verbunden sind. Viele Verben können mit unterschiedlichen *short words* verbunden werden. Sie haben dann jeweils eine ganz andere Bedeutung. Du kennst schon eine ganze Reihe dieser Verbindungen, z. B.:

to look after	sich um jdn. kümmern	*to look for*	suchen
to look at	anschauen	*to look up*	nachschlagen

Bei *phrasal verbs*, die aus Verb und Adverb, also

Verb +	**in** and **out**	
	up and **down**	
	on and **off**	
	and **away**	

bestehen, kannst du das Adverb entweder direkt hinter das Verb oder an das Ende des Satzes stellen:

Subjekt	Verb	Adverb	Objekt
Tori	turned	up	the music.
Alex	took	out	the garbage.
They	have thrown	away	the papers.

Subjekt	Verb	Objekt	Adverb
Tori	turned	the music	up.
Alex	took	the garbage	out.
They	have thrown	the papers	away.

Zu welcher Wortart gehören in diesen Beispielen die Objekte *(music, garbage, papers)*?

Wenn das Objekt jedoch ein Personalpronomen *(him, her, it, them)* ist, muss das Adverb hinter dem Objekt stehen:

Subjekt	Verb	Objekt	Adverb
Tori	turned	it	up.
Alex	took	it	out.
They	have thrown	them	away.

In Fragen stehen *short words* am Ende des Satzes:

What are they waiting for ?

Versuche in diesen Fragen die richtigen *short words* zu finden:
(Bei einigen gibt es mehrere Möglichkeiten.)

1. Who are you thinking ...?
2. What are they looking ...?
3. What are you talking ...?
4. Which sweatshirt will she put ...?
5. Who are you writing ...?

Wie viele *phrasal verbs* mit *get, go, put, take* kennst du schon? Kannst du mit ihnen eine Liste aufstellen wie die mit *look* unten auf der Seite 91?

Unit 2 Step B

§ 3 Bedingungssätze Conditional sentences

Typ 1:

Du kennst schon einen Typ von Bedingungssätzen:

If the weather ***is*** *nice tomorrow, we****'ll go*** *swimming. But if it* ***rains,*** *we* ***won't go.***

In diesen Beispielen geht es um Bedingungen, die erfüllbar sind; d. h. es ist gut möglich, dass das Wetter morgen schön ist.

Typ 2:

Wenn du jedoch ausdrücken möchtest, dass eine Bedingung nur theoretisch oder auch gar nicht erfüllbar ist, musst du einen anderen Typ von Bedingungssätzen verwenden:

if-Satz *if-clause*			Hauptsatz *main clause*		
If Daryl	**found**	a wallet in the street,	he	**would take**	it to the police.
If someone	**offered**	Soo a role in a movie,	she	**'d feel**	very lucky.
If Soo's parents	**knew**	that she was going out with Daryl,	they	**wouldn't like**	it.
If Daryl	**was**	Korean,	Soo's parents	**wouldn't mind.**	
If she	**was**	older,	it	**wouldn't be**	so bad.
past tense			would + infinitive (= conditional)		

- Im *if*-Satz steht das *past tense*. Im Hauptsatz steht das *conditional (would + infinitive)*.
- Bedingungssätze können entweder (wie in den Beispielen oben) mit dem *if*-Satz oder mit dem Hauptsatz beginnen:

  If Daryl was Korean, Soo's parents wouldn't mind. =
  Soo's parents wouldn't mind if Daryl was Korean.

  (Stelle die Beispielsätze im Kasten um, so dass sie mit dem Hauptsatz beginnen.)

Im Deutschen kann man den Satz *If Daryl found a wallet, …* übersetzen mit: „Wenn Daryl eine Brieftasche fände" oder „finden würde". Im Englischen darfst du **would** im *if*-Satz jedoch **nicht** gebrauchen.

Vergleiche noch einmal die beiden Typen von Bedingungssätzen. Welche Verbformen werden im ersten und welche werden im zweiten verwendet?

Setze die jeweils richtigen Verbformen in die folgenden Bedingungssätze ein:

1. If I … Soo, I'd tell my parents.
2. If I … a bear, I'd run away.
3. If I … a lot of money, I'd fly to New York.
4. If Peter … this afternoon, I'll tell him everything.
5. We'll be late if we … .

be
see
have
call
not hurry

§ 4 Das gerund (die -ing-Form) nach Präpositionen

The gerund after prepositions

Du weißt schon, dass man das *gerund* wie ein Substantiv als Subjekt und Objekt verwenden kann:

Swimming** is fun. But I don't like **cycling.

(Kannst du erklären, wie das *gerund* gebildet wird?)

Sehr häufig steht das *gerund* nach Präpositionen:

a) verb + preposition + gerund

Soo often **thinks of telling** her parents about Daryl.	… denkt oft daran … zu erzählen.
Of course, she doesn't want to **give up seeing** him.	… aufhören ihn zu sehen.
And she **is looking forward to going** to the Sonics game tomorrow.	… freut sich darauf … zu gehen.

Careful!
The 'to' in 'look forward to' is a preposition.
You have to use a noun after it or a gerund:
Soo is looking forward to the game.
Soo is looking forward to **going** to the game.

b) adjective + preposition + gerund

Are you **tired of doing** the same things every day?	Haben Sie es satt … zu tun?
Would you be **interested in trying out** something new?	… interessiert daran … zu versuchen?
Are you **used to being** in the open air and **to sleeping** under the stars at night?	Sind Sie daran gewöhnt im Freien zu sein und … zu schlafen?
If you are **good at working** together with other people and not **afraid of getting** wet –	… gut … arbeiten können … … keine Angst haben nass zu werden – …
We've got the ideal job for you: Be a guide with us. Write to: Whitewater Rafting, Arkansas River, …	

(Wärest du an einem solchen ‚*job*' interessiert? Schreib 6 Sätze mit *-ing-forms* und sag, warum oder warum nicht. Oder: Schreib ein ähnliches *advertisement* für irgendeinen anderen ‚*job*' und verwende dabei *-ing-forms.)*

Workshop B 1

§ 5 Modale Hilfsverben und Sprechabsichten

Modal auxiliaries and speech intentions

Mit den modalen Hilfsverben *will, would, should, ought to* kannst du deine persönliche Einstellung zum Ausdruck bringen, d. h. du kannst Vorschläge machen, um etwas bitten, Ratschläge geben usw.

a) um etwas bitten/einen Wunsch ausdrücken: *will you?, would you?*

Will you shut the window, please? **Will you** give me the paper, please? **Would you** help me please, Mr. Alburg? **Would you like to** go to a movie with me, Rachel?	Machst du bitte das Fenster zu? Gibst du mir bitte die Zeitung? Würden Sie mir bitte helfen …? Möchtest du mit mir einen Film ansehen …?

- Fragesätze mit *Will you?, Would you?* drücken eine höfliche Bitte oder einen Wunsch aus.
- Fragen mit *Would you?* sind höflicher als solche mit *Will you?*.
- Mit *Would you like to …?* kann man eine Einladung aussprechen oder ein Angebot machen.

b) einen Vorschlag machen/ein Angebot machen: *shall I?, shall we?, should I?, should we?*

Shall I open the window? It's so hot in here.	Soll ich das Fenster aufmachen?
Shall we have a picnic on Sunday – or **should we** have it on Saturday?	Sollen wir …? Oder sollen wir (lieber) …?
Let's have it on Sunday. Where **shall we** go?	Wohin sollen wir/wollen wir …?

Mit *Shall I?, Shall we?* oder *Should I?, Should we?* kannst du erfragen, was jemand anderes wünscht und einen Vorschlag oder ein Angebot machen.

c) einen Rat geben/jemanden ermahnen: *should, ought to, If I were you, I would …*

You **should** ask Rachel for a date, Daniel.	Du solltest …
You **shouldn't** think twice about it.	Du solltest nicht …
And you **ought not** to worry so much.	Du solltest … nicht …
If I were you, I'd go out with her on Saturday.	Wenn ich du wäre, würde ich …
– Hm, perhaps I **ought** to call her right away.	Vielleicht sollte ich …

Was soll *should* in den folgenden Sätzen ausdrücken?

The concert should be over at ten, so we'll be able to get home by train.
The Chicago Bulls should win the game easily, they are a lot stronger than the Sonics.

Der Sprecher oder die Sprecherin will ausdrücken, dass er oder sie etwas für wahrscheinlich hält.

Unit 3

§ 6 Aktiv und Passiv Active voice and passive voice

Vergleiche einmal diese beiden Sätze:

Dies ist ein **Aktivsatz:** Dies ist ein **Passivsatz:**

active voice	passive voice
Tourists often throw garbage into this lake.	A lot of garbage **is thrown** into this lake.

Hier wird ausgesagt, **wer** etwas macht.
In diesem Satz ist *tourists* das Subjekt des Satzes und steht im Vordergrund.

Hier wird betont, **was** gemacht wird.
Die Handlung selbst steht im Mittelpunkt.
Du kannst also Passivsätze vor allem dann benutzen, wenn du nicht genau weißt oder wenn es nicht wichtig ist, wer die Handlung ausgeführt hat.

a) Simple present passive

Das *simple present passive* wird mit **am/is/are + past participle** (3. Verbform) gebildet.

A lot of damage **is done** in Yosemite.
Pictures **are drawn** on the rocks and names **are cut** into the trees.

b) Simple past passive

Last year mountains of garbage **were left** around in Yosemite and a lot of damage **was done.**

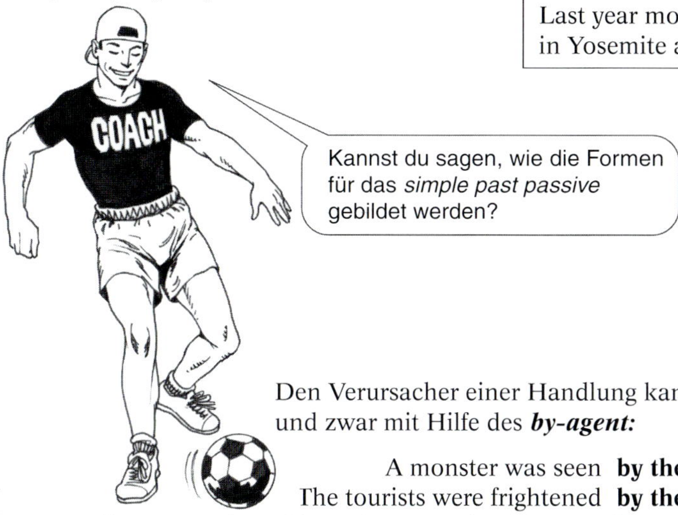

Das *simple past passive* wird mit **was/were + past participle** (3.Verbform) gebildet.

Den Verursacher einer Handlung kannst du auch im Passivsatz nennen, und zwar mit Hilfe des ***by-agent:***

A monster was seen **by the tourists.**
The tourists were frightened **by the monster.**
Every morning a Yosemite ranger is woken up **by a grizzly bear.**

TOURIST ATTACKED BY ALLIGATOR = A tourist **was attacked** by an alligator.

TREES BROUGHT DOWN BY HURRICANE = Trees **were brought down** by a hurricane.

In *headlines* von Zeitungen wird das Passiv häufig in verkürzter Form verwendet.

Unit 4

§ 7 Bedingungssätze Conditional sentences

Auf einen Blick

Du kennst schon Bedingungssätze des Typs I und des Typs II. Daneben gibt es noch einen weiteren Typ. Wie du weißt, bestehen Bedingungssätze aus einem if-Satz *(if-clause)* und einem Hauptsatz *(main clause)*.

Typ I

if-Satz *(if-clause)*	Hauptsatz *(main clause)*
If my mom **gives** me 20 dollars, Wenn meine Mutter mir 20 Dollar gibt,	**I'll** go to the pop concert. gehe ich ins Pop-Konzert.
simple present	will-future

Beim Typ I drückt das *simple present* im *if*-Satz aus, dass es tatsächlich dazu kommen kann, dass die Bedingung also erfüllbar ist. Im Hauptsatz steht das *will-future.*

Beim Typ II drückt das *past tense* aus, dass es unwahrscheinlich oder sogar unmöglich ist, die Bedingung zu erfüllen. Im Hauptsatz steht das Konditional I *(would + infinitive).*

Typ II

if-Satz *(if-clause)*	Hauptsatz *(main clause)*
If I **had** a million dollars, Wenn ich eine Million Dollar hätte,	**I'd travel** around the world. würde ich um die Welt reisen.
If I **found** a gold ring,	**I'd take** it to the police.
past tense	would + infinitive

Typ III

if-Satz *(if-clause)*	Hauptsatz *(main clause)*
If the police officer **had seen** Jerry earlier, Wenn die Polizistin Jerry eher gesehen hätte,	she **would have stopped** him. hätte sie ihn angehalten.
If Jerry **hadn't wanted** to be an actor,	he **wouldn't have come** to New York City.
If it **hadn't been** so cold,	we'**d have gone** to the beach.
past perfect	would + have + past participle (3. Verbform)

Beim Typ III weiß der Sprecher, dass die im if-Satz genannte Bedingung nicht mehr erfüllt werden kann: Man stellt sich bloß vor, was gewesen wäre, wenn …

Beispiel: If the police officer had seen Jerry earlier. =
Well, she **didn't** see him earlier.

Zu spät!
Das ist die Wirklichkeit!

Daran erkennst du Bedingungssätze vom Typ III:

Im *if*-Satz steht das *past perfect*.

Im Hauptsatz steht das *conditional perfect:* Es wird gebildet aus **would + have + past participle** (= die 3. Verbform).

If he **hurries,**
he**'ll catch** the bus.

If he **hurried**,
he **would catch** the bus.

If he **had hurried**,
he **would have caught** the bus.

What are his excuses?

They lost, because their best player was …
because …
because … (go on)

§ 8 Verben mit zwei Objekten   Verbs with two objects

Verben wie *give, send, lend, promise, show, sell, tell* und *offer* können zwei Objekte haben: ein **direktes Objekt** (meist eine **Sach**bezeichnung) und ein **indirektes Objekt** (meist eine **Personen**bezeichnung).
Du kannst diese Objekte auf zweierlei Weise an das Verb anschließen. Schau dir einfach das Beispiel mit *give* an:

SUBJEKT	VERB		DIREKTES OBJEKT (Sachobjekt)	
I	gave	the kids	some money.	
I	gave		some money	**to** the kids.

INDIREKTES OBJEKT (Personenobjekt): *the kids* / *to the kids*

Wie du siehst, steht das indirekte Objekt **ohne** Präposition vor dem direkten Objekt.

Wenn du das indirekte Objekt hinter dem direkten Objekt gebrauchst, musst du die Präposition **to** verwenden.

- Das indirekte Objekt wird meist dann **hinter** dem direkten Objekt verwendet, wenn es länger ist:

  I gave the book **to my friends from England. Nicht:** I gave my friends from England the book.

- Are you going to send your mother | this postcard of Manhattan?
  No, I'm going to send | **it** | to my girlfriend.

  Ist das direkte Objekt ein Pronomen, das sich auf eine Sache bezieht *(it* oder *them)* dann steht das indirekte Objekt (hier: *to my girlfriend*) mit **to** dahinter.

Unit 5

§ 9 Der unbestimmte Artikel ‚a/an' The indefinite article *a/an*

Manchmal unterscheidet sich der Gebrauch des unbestimmten Artikels im Englischen vom Deutschen:

Zeitangaben	
The speed limit in Texas is 55 miles **an** hour.	… pro Stunde.
This store is open 24 hours **a** day.	… am Tag geöffnet.
Alex called Daniel three times **a** week.	… pro Woche.
Mengenangaben	
Cream is 90 cents **a** pint.	… pro halben Liter.
Those apples are $ 1 **a** pound.	… das/pro Pfund.
Nach *quite* und *such*	
I think this is **quite a** good story.	… eine ganz gute Geschichte.
We had **such a** cold winter.	… solch einen kalten Winter.
It takes **quite a** long time to write everything down.	Es dauert ziemlich lang …

Beachte die Stellung des unbestimmten Artikels nach Wörtern wie ***quite*** und ***such.***

§ 10 Der bestimmte Artikel ‚the' The definite article 'the'

Der bestimmte Artikel zeigt an, dass Dinge oder Personen näher bezeichnet werden:

OHNE ARTIKEL	MIT ARTIKEL
Life is too short.	I've just read a book about **the life** of Elvis Presley.
Hier geht es um **das Leben allgemein.**	Hier ist **life** näher bezeichnet: Es geht nicht um das Leben allgemein, sondern um **das Leben von Elvis Presley.**

Music is wonderful.	I can't stand **the music my sister listens to.**
Money is always such a problem.	I've already spent all **the money I got for Christmas.**
Horses are beautiful animals.	**The horses in this picture** were used to pull wagons.
Houses are expensive today.	**The houses in this street** have big gardens.
Water is a problem in some parts of the US.	**The water in our rivers** is not very clean.
Actors act in plays, movies or on TV.	**The actors in this movie** are excellent.

Du musst den bestimmten Artikel *the* immer dann verwenden, wenn abstrakte Begriffe oder Personengruppen – meist durch eine *of-phrase* oder einen **Relativsatz** – näher bestimmt werden.

OHNE ARTIKEL	MIT ARTIKEL
Namen im Singular **Cindy** and **Soo** are friends. **Uncle Fred** called last night. **Poor Daniel** misses Rachel. • Personennamen im Singular stehen auch dann ohne Artikel, wenn ein Adjektiv vor ihnen steht.	**Namen im Plural** **The Chicago Bulls** are great. **The Alburgs** invited **the Chungs** to a barbecue.
Ländernamen im Singular **Switzerland** is a small country. **Turkey** is wonderful.	**Ländernamen im Plural, Gebirge, Flüsse, Meere(steile)** **The Netherlands** is a flat country. **The US** is visited by a lot of tourists. Mount McKinley is part of **the Alaska Range.**
Namen von Parks und Seen **Hyde Park** is in London and **Central Park** is in New York. Issaquah lies on **Lake Sammamish.**	**Namen mit *of-phrase*** **The Statue of Liberty** is in New York. **The Tower (of London)** is one of the city's most famous sights.
Namen von Monaten, Wochentagen, Mahlzeiten **June** is usually a warm month. Let's start on **Monday.** We can go to the lake after **dinner.**	**Näher bestimmte Monate, Wochentage, Mahlzeiten** **The June of 1990** was unusally warm. I'll never forget **the Monday I started my first job.** **The dinner we had last Friday** was very good.
School = Unterricht **bus = allgemeine Verkehrsverbindung** Tori and Alex go to **school** in Issaquah. Many Americans go to school by **bus.** • Wenn du bei ***school*** an den Unterricht denkst und bei ***bus*** an die Verkehrsverbindung allgemein, dann brauchst du kein ***the.***	**School = Gebäude** **bus = bestimmtes Fahrzeug** **The school he goes to** is modern. **The bus to New York** leaves at 8:00. • Den bestimmten Artikel ***the*** musst du bei ***school*** und ***bus*** gebrauchen, wenn du an ein bestimmtes Schulgebäude oder ein bestimmtes Fahrzeug denkst.

§ 11 Übersicht: Die Zeiten The tenses

Auf einen Blick

Active Voice

	simple	progressive
present	I always **take** lots of pictures when I'm on vacation. Tori always **takes** Alex to town in her car. Does she **take** tea or coffee?	Don't move, I'm **taking** a picture of you. She's **taking** her dad to the airport next Saturday.
past	Yesterday Lynn **took** the dog out. **Did** you **take** fish or steak?	While Lynn **was taking** the dog out, she met Cindy.
present perfect	**Have** you **taken** Daniel to Seattle yet? Bruce **hasn't taken** his medicine yet.	
past perfect	The Alburgs liked the pictures Daniel **had taken** of Stuttgart.	
will-future	I **will take** pictures of all the sights, in New York. I **won't take** a ride on this ferry again!	
going-to-future	We **are going to take** the train tonight.	
conditional	If Rachel went to Germany, she **would take** a present for Daniel with her.	
conditional perfect	If Daniel hadn't been to Seattle, he **wouldn't have taken** so many pictures.	

Passive Voice

present	Lots of pictures **are taken** of the Empire State Building.	
past	Daniel, Tori and Alex **were taken** on a tour of Colorado.	

Grammar list

Deutsch/Latein	Englisch	Englisches Beispiel	§
Adjektiv	adjective	nice, terrible	
Steigerung mit -er/-est	comparison with -er/-est	big, bigger, biggest	
Steigerung mit ‚more'/‚most'	comparison with 'more'/'most'	important, more important, most important	
Adjektiv nach bestimmten Verben	adjectives after certain verbs	This soup tastes nice.	
Adverbien	adverbs	sometimes, often	
Adverbien der Art und Weise	adverbs of manner	How does he drive? – He drives carefully.	
Steigerung des Adverbs	comparison of adverbs	slowly, more slowly, …	
Vergleiche mit Adverbien	comparisons with adverbs	as slowly as … more slowly than …	
Aktiv und Passiv	active and passive voice		6
einfache Gegenwart	simple present passive	... damage is done ...	
einfache Vergangenheit	simple past passive	… mountains of garbage were left …	
Apostroph (Auslassungszeichen)	apostrophe	Where's Mini?	
Artikel	article		
bestimmter Artikel	definite article	… the life of …	10
Namen im Plural		The Chicago Bulls are great.	
mit *of-phrase*		The Statue of Liberty is in New York.	
unbestimmter Artikel	indefinite article	a house, an apple	
Zeit-/Mengenangaben		55 miles an hour, $1 a pound …	9
nach ‚quite' und ‚such'		quite a good story, such a cold winter	
Bedingungssätze	conditional sentences		
Typ I (erfüllbar)		If it rains tomorrow, I won't play football.	
Typ II (theoretisch)		If someone offered her a role in a movie, she would feel lucky.	3
Typ III (nicht mehr erfüllbar)		If he had hurried, he would have caught the bus.	7
‚Each other'	each other	Soo and Daryl love each other.	
Einzahl (Singular)	singular	one house	

Deutsch/Latein	Englisch	Englisches Beispiel	§
Futur	future		
Going-to-Futur	going-to-future	I'm going to watch a movie.	
Will-Futur	will-future	Daniel will be 15 next year.	
Gegenwart (Präsens)	present tense		
einfache Form	simple present	I like tennis.	
Verlaufsform	present progressive	He's watching TV.	
Present progressive zur Wiedergabe der Zukunft	present progressive with a future meaning	I'm meeting Cindy in the evening.	
Gerund	gerund	reading, cooking	
als Objekt	as object	I love swimming.	
als Subjekt	as subject	Reading is fun.	
nach ‚what about'/ ‚it's no good'/ ‚I can't stand'	after 'what about'/ 'it's no good'/'I can't stand'	What about going to the shops?	
nach Präpositionen	after prepositions	I'm thinking of visiting my cousins. Are you good at working with …?	4
Grundform (Infinitiv)	infinitive	to see, to do etc.	
Infinitiv nach bestimmten Verben	the infinitive after certain verbs	Don't forget to write.	
Grundzahlen	cardinal numbers	1,045,986	
Hilfsverb (modales)	modal auxiliary		
‚Be allowed to'	be allowed to	I'm allowed to go home now!	
‚Have to'	have to	I have to do my homework.	
‚Mustn't'	mustn't	You mustn't play here!	
‚Needn't'	needn't	You needn't stay in bed.	
‚Must' und ‚needn't' und die Ersatzform ‚have to'	'must' and needn't' and the substitute form 'have to'	We must leave now. You don't have to go yet.	
‚Mustn't' und die Ersatzform ‚not be allowed to'	'mustn't' and the substitute form 'not be allowed to'	You aren't allowed to play football here.	
‚Can/could' und die Ersatzform ‚be able to'	'can/could' and the substitute form 'be able to'	Can I ask you a question? I wasn't able to call you.	
Bitte, Wunsch	will you?, would you?	Will you shut the door, please?	5
Vorschlag, Angebot	shall I?, should we?	Shall I open the window?	
Rat, Ermahnung	should, ought to	You should ask Rachel …	

Deutsch/Latein	Englisch	Englisches Beispiel	§
Mehrzahl (Plural)	plural	two women, five dogs	
Mitlaut (Konsonant)	consonant	b, p, k, l	
Nebensätze mit ‚when'	clauses with 'when'	When Alex is sixteen, he'll get his driver's license.	
Objekt	object	Tori has got a car.	
Partizip der Vergangenheit	past participle	asked, found, thrown	
Past perfect	past perfect	They had always wanted a farm.	
Präposition (Verhältniswort)	preposition	in, on, under	
Present Perfect	present perfect	I have known her	
mit ‚for' und ‚since'	with 'for' and 'since'	for two months/since July.	1
regelmäßige Formen	regular forms	He has cooked lunch.	
unregelmäßige Formen	irregular forms	We've eaten it.	
Fragen, Verneinung und Kurzformen	questions, negative sentences and short forms	Have you ever seen a monster? No, I haven't.	
Reflexivpronomen (-self, -selves)	reflexive pronouns (-self,-selves)	myself, themselves	
Relativsätze	relative clauses	This is the boy who won the race.	
Relativpronomen	relative pronouns	who, which, that, whose	
Relativsätze ohne Relativpronomen	relative clauses without relative pronouns	This is the story I like best.	
Selbstlaut (Vokal)	vowel	a, e, i, o, u	
‚Some' und ‚any'	'some' and 'any'	Have we got any bread?	
Zusammensetzungen	compounds	something, anything	
‚Some' in Fragen	'some' in questions	Would you like some cake?	
Subjekt	subject	The man was old.	
Substantiv (Nomen)	noun	dog, teacher, bike	
Verb	verb	to go, to see	
Verb+Objekt+Infinitiv (mit und ohne ‚to')	verb+object+infinitive (with or without 'to')	I want you to read the text at home. He made us write the text.	

Deutsch/Latein	Englisch	Englisches Beispiel	§
Verben mit Präposition oder Adverb	phrasal verbs	look after, turn up, take out	2
Verben mit zwei Objekten	verbs with two objects	I gave the kids some money.	
Vergangenheit	past		
einfache Vergangenheit von ‚to be' und ‚to have'	simple past of 'to be' and 'to have'	It was cold yesterday but I had fun in the snow.	
regelmäßige Formen	regular forms	Alex called Daniel.	
unregelmäßige Formen	irregular forms	Cindy went skating.	
Fragen mit ‚was' und ‚were'	questions with 'was' and 'were'	Were you on vacation last week?	
Fragen mit ‚did'	questions with 'did'	Did you like the movie?	
Verlaufsform der Vergangenheit	past progressive	Tori was watching TV.	
‚whose'	'whose'	We found a poor cat whose leg was broken.	
Zeiten	the tenses		11

Vocabulary

a) Aufbau des Vokabulars

Das Vokabular ist genau wie in deinem Buch vom letzten Schuljahr aufgebaut:
In der linken Spalte findest du die englischen Wörter in der Reihenfolge, in der sie in der Unit vorkommen. Dahinter steht die Lautschrift in eckigen Klammern. Wie du die Lautschrift lesen musst, steht unten auf dieser Seite.

In der mittleren Spalte stehen Beispielsätze oder kleine Zeichnungen sowie wichtige Hinweise, die dir beim Lernen helfen.

In der rechten Spalte findest du eine deutsche Übersetzung des englischen Wortes. Vergiss aber nicht, dass sich Wörter aus einer Sprache nicht einfach in die andere übersetzen lassen. Deshalb werden manchmal mehrere deutsche Übersetzungsmöglichkeiten angeboten.
Wie im Buch vom Vorjahr findest du Tipps zum Vokabellernen. Außerdem findest du *vocabulary boxes*, die Wörter und Wendungen wiederholen und zusammenfassen. Du lernst sie am besten in Gruppen.

b) Abkürzungen und Zeichen

(pl)	Plural, Mehrzahl
(sg)	Singular, Einzahl
s.th.	something
s.o.	someone
s.b.	somebody
umg.	umgangssprachlich
(AE)	American English
(BE)	British English

=	ist gleich
→	ist verwandt mit
←→	ist das Gegenteil von
°	Bei Wörtern mit diesem Zeichen frag bitte deine Lehrerin oder deinen Lehrer, ob du sie lernen musst. (Erläuterungen hierzu finden sich auf Seite 142.)

c) Lautschrift

Wie die englischen Wörter ausgesprochen werden, lernst du im Unterricht. Die Lautschrift im Vokabular hilft dir, die Aussprache und Betonung eines Wortes nachzusehen. Sie benutzt einige normale Buchstaben und einige besondere Zeichen. Die Aussprache der einzelnen Zeichen kannst du dir anhand eines einfachen Wortes merken. Die Betonung eines Wortes wird durch einen Betonungsstrich **vor** der betonten Silbe gezeigt: [ˈ] zeigt den Hauptakzent des Wortes, [ˌ] den Nebenakzent. Der Bindebogen [‿] zeigt, dass zwei Wörter in der Aussprache miteinander verbunden werden.

Konsonanten		**Vokale**		**Doppellaute**	
[ŋ]	morni**ng**	[ɑː]	f**a**ther	[aɪ]	**I**, m**y**
[r]	**r**ed	[ʌ]	b**u**t, **u**nder	[aʊ]	n**ow**, h**ou**se
[s]	cla**ss**	[e]	p**e**n	[eə]	th**ere**, p**air**
[z]	i**s**	[ə]	**a** sist**er**	[eɪ]	n**a**me, th**ey**
[ʒ]	televi**sio**n	[ɜː]	g**ir**l	[ɪə]	h**ere**, id**ea**
[dʒ]	**G**ermany, pa**ge**	[æ]	**a**pple	[ɔɪ]	b**oy**
[ʃ]	**sh**e	[ɪ]	**i**t	[əʊ]	**o**ld, hell**o**
[tʃ]	**ch**air, lun**ch**	[iː]	**ea**sy, sh**e**	[ʊə]	**you're**
[ð]	**th**e	[ɒ]	g**o**t, **o**n		
[θ]	**th**anks	[ɔː]	b**a**ll		
[v]	**v**ideo, ha**v**e	[ʊ]	b**oo**k		
[w]	**w**ord, **o**ne	[uː]	t**oo**, t**wo**		

Alle anderen Zeichen werden genau so ausgesprochen, wie sie im Deutschen geschrieben werden [j, k, …].

Lerntipps sind Tipps für den Grips!

Stress beim Vokabellernen muss nicht sein – zumindest kann man ihn in engen Grenzen halten.

- Unsere Mittelspalte will hier mit Erklärungen, Hinweisen, Beispielsätzen, Bildern usw. helfen, jedes einzelne Wort für den Hirnkasten „merk-würdig" zu machen.
- Dennoch lernt jeder von uns ein bisschen anders. Deshalb solltest du dir schon beim ersten Anschauen der Wörter überlegen, ob es für einzelne Vokabeln nicht schon einen Anknüpfungspunkt bei bereits gelernten Wörtern gibt.
  Das kann die gleiche Wortfamilie sein (z. B. *a look* → *to look*) oder das gleiche Wortfeld (z. B. *basketball* → *ball games* wie *volleyball* und *football*). Oder du kennst schon ein Wort mit gleicher oder sehr ähnlicher Bedeutung (*cool* = *great, fantastic*) oder das neue Wort ist das Gegenteil von einem schon bekannten (*dry* ⟷ *wet*).
- Ein neues Symbol in diesem Buch ist **FF** für *false friends*, das heißt „falsche Freunde". Bei diesen Wörtern muss man besonders aufpassen, weil sie auf den ersten Blick so wie oder so ähnlich wie deutsche Wörter aussehen. Aber nur auf den ersten Blick! Du kennst ja schon ein paar davon: *to become* heißt eben nicht „bekommen", sondern „werden". Und ein *gymnasium* ist in Großbritannien etwas ganz anderes als ein deutsches Gymnasium.
- Weil die Amerikaner sich manchmal in ihrer Wortwahl, Aussprache und Schreibung von den Briten unterscheiden, sind die Unterschiede mit den Abkürzungen BE (*British English)* und AE (*American English)* gekennzeichnet.

Und nicht vergessen:

- Die richtige Lernportion ist wichtig: nimm dir immer nur 10 bis 15 Wörter vor, dafür aber mehrmals täglich.
- Abwechslung fürs Gehirn ist wichtig, erst Englisch (was sonst?), dann Mathe, dann die andere Fremdsprache, dann Bio, dann wieder 10 Minuten Englischwörter, …
- Lege Lernpausen ein.
- Und … Eselsbrücken können über Merk-Hindernisse helfen.

Unit 1 Hello America!

coach [kəʊtʃ]	Our tennis ~ is really good.	Trainer/in

Step A **You'll like Issaquah, Daniel**

Issaquah [ˈɪzəˌkwɑː]		*Stadt in den USA*
WA (= Washington) [ˈdʌbljuː eɪ = ˈwɒʃɪŋtən]		*US-Bundesstaat*
USA (= United States of America, US) [ˌjuːesˈeɪ = juːˈnaɪtɪd steɪts‿əv‿əˈmerɪkə, ˌjuːˈes]	The ~ is one of the biggest countries in the world.	USA, die Vereinigten Staaten von Amerika
cool [kuːl]	*cool* = great, fantastic	toll, klasse, cool, super
hard [hɑːd]	It's ~ to remember that the US has five different time zones.	*hier:* schwer
to **meet** [miːt]		*hier:* sich kennen lernen

	Lake Sammamish [ˌleɪk səˈmæmɪʃ]		*See in den USA*
	to **go hiking** [ˌɡəʊ ˈhaɪkɪŋ]	We love *going hiking* in the mountains.	wandern gehen
	barbecue [ˈbɑːbɪkjuː]	We have a ~ every weekend in summer.	Grill, Grillfest, Barbecue
	backyard (*AE*) [ˌbækˈjɑːd]	BE = back garden	Garten (*hinter dem Haus*)
	relative [ˈrelətɪv]	*relatives*: parents, brother, aunt, ...	Verwandte/r
	mom (*AE*) [mɑːm]	BE = m**u**m, mother	Mutter, Mutti, Mama
	tape [teɪp]	Can you copy that CD onto a ~ for me?	Band, Kassette
	Seattle [sɪˈætl]		*Stadt in den USA*
	PS (= postscript) [piː ˈes]		PS, Postskriptum

Step A **The Alburgs' hometown**

	hometown [ˌhəʊmˈtaʊn]		Heimatstadt
2a)	**driver's license** (*AE*) [ˈdraɪvəz ˌlaɪsəns]		Führerschein
	part-time job [ˌpɑːt taɪm ˈdʒɒb]	Students often have ~s.	Teilzeitstelle
	gym [dʒɪm]		*hier:* Fitnessstudio
	favorite (*AE*) [ˈfeɪvərɪt]	BE = favo**u**rite	Lieblings-
3a)	**bye-bye** [baɪ ˈbaɪ]	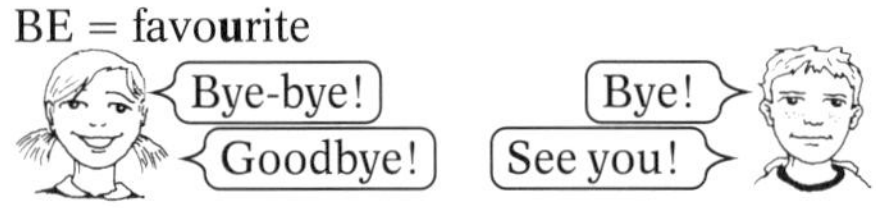	auf Wiedersehen
	What's up?		Was gibt's Neues?, Was ist los?
	How are you doing?		Wie geht es dir/euch/Ihnen?
	See you!		*umg.*: Tschüs!, Bis bald!, Bis dann!
4a)	**bowling alley** [ˈbəʊlɪŋ ˌælɪ]		Kegelbahn, Bowlingbahn
	drive-in restaurant [draɪv‿ɪn ˈrestərɒnt]		Autorestaurant

Step B **An American barbecue**

	since [sɪns]	I **have lived** here **since 1997**.	seit
	for ages [fɔː ˈeɪdʒɪz]	My grandma **has lived** here **for ages**.	seit langem, schon ewig
	coke float [ˌkəʊk ˈfləʊt]	For a ~, you need ice cream and ~.	*amer. Getränk*
	coke [kəʊk]		Cola
1	to **burn, burnt, burnt** [bɜːn, bɜːnt, bɜːnt]		(an)brennen, verbrennen
2	**on the phone** [ɒn ðə ˈfəʊn]	She's been ~ for half an hour.	am Telefon
	Mt. Rainier [ˌmaʊnt reɪˈnɪər]		*Berg im US-Bundesstaat Washington*
	Mt. (= Mount) [ˌmaʊnt]		Berg (*bei Namen*)

Step B **Can you pick up some flour, Tori?**

to **pick up** (*AE*) [pɪk‿ˈʌp]	BE = to go and buy	*hier:* kaufen, holen
flour [ˈflaʊə]	For a cake, you need eggs, butter, sugar and ~.	Mehl

basketball ['bɑːskɪtbɔːl]	~ is a very popular game in America.	Basketball
to **turn up** [tɜːn 'ʌp]	He always *turns* the radio *up* when he likes the song.	lauter drehen, hoch drehen
horrible ['hɒrəbl]	Turn that music down! It's ~!	grauenhaft, schrecklich
honey ['hʌnɪ]		Honig; *hier:* Liebling (*Kosename*)
store (*AE*) [stɔː]	BE = shop (*department store* = AE + BE)	Geschäft, Laden
apple pie [ˌæpl 'paɪ]		gedeckter Apfelkuchen
middle ['mɪdl]	left/~/right	Mitte
You only see the fun side. [jʊ 'əʊnlɪ siː ðə 'fʌn saɪd]	~ of the computer, I need it for my work.	Du siehst nur dein Vergnügen.
to **go places** [ˌgəʊ 'pleɪsɪz]		herumfahren, herumreisen
from time to time [frəm 'taɪm tə 'taɪm]	OK, you can listen to my new CD ~.	von Zeit zu Zeit
to **take out** [teɪk 'aʊt]	*Take* the glasses and the meat *out* to the barbecue, please.	hinaustragen
to **clean up** [kliːn‿'ʌp]		putzen, aufwischen, aufräumen
garbage (*AE*) ['gɑːbɪdʒ]	BE = rubbish	Abfall
5 **steak** [steɪk]	~s taste best when you cook them on the barbecue.	Steak
to **put down** [pʊt 'daʊn]	Don't *put* your glass *down* on the barbecue, it's too hot!	hinlegen, hinstellen; auflegen (*Telefon*)
6 **vanilla** [və'nɪlə]	~ tastes great in cakes or ice cream.	Vanille
straw [strɔː]	You only use a ~ for cold drinks.	Strohhalm, Trinkhalm

Eating and drinking

apple pie	*gedeckter Apfelkuchen*	**pepper**	*Pfeffer*	**to feed**	*füttern*
bean	*Bohne*	**pizza**	*Pizza*	**to peel**	*schälen*
beef	*Rindfleisch*	**porridge**	*Haferbrei*	**to wash up**	*abwaschen, spülen*
biscuit (*BE*)	*Keks*	**potato**	*Kartoffel*		
cabbage	*Kohl*	**salad**	*gemischter Salat*		
cake	*Kuchen, Torte*	**sandwich**	*belegtes Brot*	**barbecue**	*Grill, Grillfest, Barbecue*
carrot	*Karotte, Möhre*	**sausage**	*Wurst, Würstchen*	**breakfast**	*Frühstück*
cheese	*Käse*	**steak**	*Steak*	**dinner**	*Mittagessen, Abendessen*
chicken	*Huhn*	**tomato**	*Tomate*		
chips (*BE*)	*Pommes frites*	**vegetable**	*Gemüse*	**lunch**	*Mittagessen*
chocolate	*Schokolade*			**picnic**	*Picknick*
coconut	*Kokosnuss*	**coffee**	*Kaffee*	**tea**	*Mahlzeit am frühen Abend*
cookie (*AE*)	*Keks*	**lemonade**	*Limonade*		
cream	*Sahne*	**milk**	*Milch*		
crisps (*BE*)	*Kartoffelchips*	**milkshake**	*Milchmix-getränk*	**cafeteria**	*Cafeteria*
curry	*Currygericht*			**restaurant**	*Restaurant*
egg	*Ei*	**tea**	*Tee*	**snack bar**	*Imbissstube*
fish fingers	*Fischstäbchen*				
flour	*Mehl*	**to be hungry**	*Hunger haben*	**bottle**	*Flasche*
fruit	*Frucht, Obst*	**to be thirsty**	*Durst haben*	**cup**	*Tasse*
ham	*gekochter Schinken*	**to burn**	*(an)brennen, verbrennen*	**fork**	*Gabel*
				glass	*Glas*
honey	*Honig*	**to cook**	*kochen, backen, braten*	**kettle**	*Kessel*
ice cream	*Eiskrem*			**knife**	*Messer*
mince (*BE*)	*Hackfleisch*	**to drink**	*trinken*	**plate**	*Teller*
orange	*Orange*	**to eat**	*essen*	**spoon**	*Löffel*

Step C **Big night in a small town**

to **suggest** [sə'dʒest]	What can we do? Can't you ~ anything?	vorschlagen; andeuten, hindeuten auf
to **protest** [prəʊ'test]	I think he likes her, but he ~s that he doesn't!	protestieren
Snoqualmie Falls [snəʊˌkwɑːlmɪ 'fɔːlz]		*Wasserfall bei Issaquah*
smile [smaɪl]	a *smile* → to smile 	Lächeln
look [lʊk]	a *look* → to look	Blick
dark [dɑːk]	It gets ~ early in the winter.	dunkel
waterfall ['wɔːtəfɔːl]	water + fall 	Wasserfall
foot, feet (= ft.) (*pl*) [fʊt, fiːt]	A meter is a bit more than three *feet*.	Fuß (*Maßeinheit*)
Here we come!		Jetzt kommen wir!
to **walk down** [wɔːk 'daʊn]	We walked down the hill, then we walked up it again.	hinuntergehen
trail (*AE*) [treɪl]	BE = path	Spur; Weg, Pfad
phone booth (*AE*) ['fəʊn ˌbuːð]	BE = telephone box	Telefonzelle
teenager ['tiːnˌeɪdʒə]	= a boy or girl betwen thir**teen** and nine**teen**	Jugendliche/r; Teenager
bush [bʊʃ]	bush [bʊʃ]; bushes [bʊʃɪz]	Busch
Yeah! [jeə]		*umg.:* Ja!
to **reach** [riːtʃ]	It was after 12 o'clock when we ~ed the hotel, and there were no lights on.	erreichen, greifen (nach)
to **agree** [ə'griː]	Oh, yes, you're right, I ~ with you.	übereinstimmen
to **get in line** (*AE*) [ˌget ɪn 'laɪn]	BE = to stand in a queue	sich anstellen
counter ['kaʊntə]	You can pay at the ~ in the middle of the store.	Theke, Ladentisch
to **rent** (*AE*) [rent]	We could ~ a car or go by train.	mieten
to **bowl** [bəʊl]		kegeln, bowlen
to **mean, meant, meant** [miːn, ment, ment]	I didn't ~ to hurt you.	*hier:* wollen
to **bump into s.o./s.th.** [bʌmp]	 He *bumped into* a tree and hurt his head.	gegen jdn./etw. stoßen, mit jdm. zusammenstoßen
rude [ruːd]	*rude* ⟷ polite	unhöflich, grob
dollar (= $) ['dɒlə]	Wie beim britischen £ steht das Währungszeichen vor der Zahl: $20, £20.	Dollar (*amer. Geldeinheit*)
to **reach for s.th.** ['riːtʃ fɔː]	She *reached for* a book on the shelf above her head.	nach etw. greifen
zipper (*AE*) ['zɪpə]		Reißverschluss
wallet (*AE*) ['wɒlɪt]	BE = purse	Geldbeutel, Portmonee
to **be shocked** [ʃɒkt]	He *was shocked* when he saw how ill she was.	schockiert sein
3 **Thank goodness!** [θæŋk 'gʊdnɪs]	- Here are your keys. - ~, I thought I'd lost them.	Gott sei Dank!

⟨5⟩ on my mind [ɒn maɪ 'maɪnd]	im Kopf	out of sight [aʊt‿əv 'saɪt]	außer Sichtweite, nicht zu sehen
to nag [næg]	herumnörgeln		
Gonna (= I'm going to) [gɒnə]	Ich werde …	to bug [bʌg]	nerven
bread [bred]	*hier:* Geld	rich [rɪtʃ]	reich
fine [faɪn]	schön	mad [mæd]	verrückt

Step D **Let's check**

a) **Mexico** [ˈmeksɪkəʊ]	A lot of people from ~ now live in the US.	Mexiko
Pacific Northwest [pəˌsɪfɪk nɔ:θˈwest]		*Region in den USA*
to **belong (to)** [bɪˈlɒŋ tʊ]		dazu gehören, gehören (zu)
canoe [kəˈnu:]	Die Betonung ist anders als im Deutschen.	Kanu
neighbor (*AE*) [ˈneɪbə]	BE = neighb**ou**r	Nachbar/in

American English/British English

Dieses Buch hat die USA zum Thema, deshalb ist es durchgängig in amerikanischem Englisch gehalten. Hier sind einige Unterschiede zwischen britischem und amerikanischem Englisch:

Unterschiedliche Wörter
Einige Wörter im amerikanischen Englisch sind unterschiedlich zum britischen Englisch.

Einige Beispiele aus *Unit* 1 sind:	**backyard (AE)**	**back garden (BE)**
	garbage (AE)	**rubbish (BE)**
	to get in line (AE)	**to queue (BE)**

Unterschiedliche Schreibung
Die meisten amerikanischen Wörter werden gleich geschrieben wie im britischen Englisch, bei einigen unterscheidet sich jedoch die Schreibung:

BE **-our** ist normalerweise **-or** im AE	**color**	**colour**
BE **-gramme** ist normalerweise **-gram** im AE	**program**	**programme**
BE **-re** ist normalerweise **-er** im AE	**center**	**centre**

Unterschiedliche Aussprache
Auf den Tonaufnahmen für dieses Buch wirst du amerikanische Sprecherinnen und Sprecher hören. Sie sprechen einige Laute anders aus als du es bisher von Band 1–3 gewohnt bist.

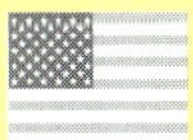 

Wörter wie *possible, hot, problem* werden	[ɑ:] im AE,	[ɒ] im BE	gesprochen.
Wörter wie *half* und *after* werden	[æ] im AE,	[ɑ:] im BE	gesprochen.
In Wörtern wie *student, Tuesday* hörst du oft	[(s)tu:] im AE,	[(s)tju:] im BE.	

In Wörtern wie *understand, other, word* wird das ‚r' im amerikanischen Englisch gesprochen. Und in Wörtern wie *water, better, notice* klingt das ‚t' wie ein ‚d'.

Die Lautschrift in diesem Buch ist immer in britischem Englisch. Wenn die Amerikanerinnen und Amerikaner das Wort ganz anders aussprechen, weist dich der *coach* darauf hin.

Workshop A Working with words

Part 1: **Understanding new words**

	fridge (= refrigerator) [frɪdʒ]	You put food and drink in a ~ to keep it cool. 	Kühlschrank
	microwave (oven) ['maɪkrəweɪv]	A ~ cooks food very quickly.	Mikrowelle(nherd)
	neighborhood watch (*AE*) [ˌneɪbəhʊd 'wɒtʃ]	Neighbors who try to keep their	*Nachbarschaftshilfe zum Schutz vor Kriminalität*
	neighborhood (*AE*) ['neɪbəhʊd]	~ safe from burglars.	Nachbarschaft, Wohnviertel
	till (= until) [tɪl]		bis
	definitely ['defɪnɪtlɪ]	Will you be at Jane's party? – Yes, ~.	hundertprozentig, ganz sicher; endgültig, definitiv
	Colorado [ˌkɒlə'rɑːdəʊ]		*US-Bundesstaat*
	°**red-eye flight** (*AE*) ['red‿aɪ‿flaɪt]	On a night flight you don't get much sleep, so it's called a ~.	*umg.:* Nachtflug
	Denver ['denvə]	~ is the capital of Colorado.	*Stadt in Colorado*
	midnight ['mɪdnaɪt]	12.00 pm = ~	Mitternacht
	to **tour around** [tʊə ə'raʊnd]	You can ~ the US by car, bus, …	eine Tour/(Rund-)Reise machen, herumreisen
	motorhome ['məʊtəhəʊm]	motorbike, motorway, *motorhome*	Wohnmobil
	river-rafting ['rɪvə‿ˌrɑːftɪŋ]		Schlauchboot fahren (*auf einem Fluss*)
	river [rɪvə]	You can go river-rafting on many ~s in America and Europe.	Fluss
	to **be over at** … [biː‿'əʊvər‿æt]	Sorry, Tori isn't in, she's ~ Soo's.	bei … sein
	to **install** [ɪn'stɔːl]	I can't ~ that on my computer.	installieren
	software ['sɒftweə]	– Hm. Are you sure you've got the right ~?	Software
	to **give s.o. a hand** [gɪv‿ə 'hænd]	This cupboard's heavy. Can you *give me a hand* with it?	*hier:* jdm. helfen
	movie (*AE*) ['muːvɪ]	BE = film	Film
	at the movies (*AE*) [ˌæt‿ðə 'muːvɪz]	BE = at the cinema	im Kino
1a)	**micro** ['maɪkrəʊ]		Mikro-

Part 2: **Working with your dictionary**

1	to **warm up** [wɑːm‿'ʌp]	It's important to ~ before you start training.	aufwärmen
2	°**headword** ['hedwɜːd]		Stichwort
	to **pronounce** [prə'naʊns]	How do you ~ 'Issaquah'?	aussprechen
	°**abbreviation** [əˌbriːvɪ'eɪʃn]	short form of a word	Abkürzung
	if [ɪf]	I don't know yet ~ I'll go river-rafting tomorrow.	*hier:* ob
	related [rɪ'leɪtɪd]	Your relatives are ~ to you.	verwandt; zusammenhängend
	°**compound word** [kəm'paʊnd wɜːd]		zusammengesetztes Wort

	°**separate entry** ['seprət‿ˌentrɪ]	eigener Eintrag
	entry ['entrɪ]	Eingang, Einfahrt
	guided tour [ˌgaɪdɪd 'tʊə]	Führung
	guide [gaɪd]	*hier:* Reiseführer (*Buch*)
	at the moment [æt ðə‿'məʊmənt]	zur Zeit
3	to **sail** [seɪl]	segeln

Part 3: **Using your skills**

skill [skɪl]	You want to go sailing? Do you have the right ~s?	Fertigkeit, Fähigkeit
°**whitewater rafting** [ˌwaɪt'wɔːtə 'rɑːftɪŋ]	You will find all the new words from this leaflet in the Alphabetical word list; here are the most important ones.	Wildwasser-Rafting
Arkansas River ['ɑːkənsɔː ˌrɪvə]	Achte auf die Aussprache.	*Fluss in den USA*
suitable ['suːtəbl]	Please wear ~ shoes for the hiking trip.	geeignet, passend
enjoyable [ɪn'dʒɔɪəbl]	The trip will not be ~ if your feet hurt all the time.	nett; unterhaltsam, amüsant
company ['kʌmpənɪ]		Firma, Unternehmen
involvement [ɪn'vɒlvmənt]		Engagement, Mitarbeit
equipment [ɪ'kwɪpmənt]	You need special ~ for rock climbing.	Ausstattung, Ausrüstung
guide [gaɪd]	A ~ can show you the best places in town.	*hier:* Führer/in
excellent ['eksələnt]	good → very good → ~	ausgezeichnet, hervorragend
management ['mænɪdʒmənt]		Führung, Leitung, Management
reasonable ['riːznəbl]		vernünftig, angemessen
reservation [ˌrezə'veɪʃn]	to make a *reservation* = to book	Reservierung
to **require** [rɪ'kwaɪə]	*to require* = to need	benötigen, brauchen; erfordern
rest [rest]		Rest
to **dry** [draɪ]		trocknen
shorts (*sg + pl*) [ʃɔːts]	My ~ **are** green, my jeans **are** blue.	Shorts, kurze Hose, kurze Hosen
pants (*AE*) (*sg + pl*) [pænts]	BE = trousers	Hose, Hosen
sunglasses (*sg + pl*) ['sʌnglɑːsɪz]	Do you like my ~? I bought **them** in America.	Sonnenbrille, Sonnenbrillen
sweater ['swetə]		Pullover
dry [draɪ]	*dry* ⟷ wet	trocken
available [ə'veɪləbl]	There are cheaper prices ~ for teenagers in some museums.	vorrätig, verfügbar, erhältlich
sleeping bag ['sliːpɪŋ bæg]		Schlafsack
type [taɪp]	What ~ of holiday do you want?	Typ; Art, Sorte
Royal Gorge [ˌrɔɪəl 'gɔːdʒ]		*Name einer Schlucht am Arkansas River*
rapids (*sg + pl*) ['ræpɪds]		Stromschnellen
condition [kən'dɪʃn]		Bedingung, Umstand; Verhältnis
to **force s.o. to do s.th.** [fɔːs]	The bad weather *forced* us to go back down the mountain.	jdn. zwingen, etw. zu tun
outdoor ['aʊtdɔː]	*outdoor* activities: cycling, riding, hiking, …	draußen, im Freien, Freiluft-

2	**washable** ['wɒʃəbl]		waschbar
	to **wash** [wɒʃ]		waschen
	reason ['ri:zn]	**why** you do something	Grund, Ursache
3	to **involve** [ɪn'vɒlv]		beteiligen
	to **inform** [ɪn'fɔ:m]	*to inform* → information	benachrichtigen, informieren
4	to **exist** [ɪg'zɪst]		existieren
	hyphen ['haɪfn]	Is there a ~ in river-rafting?	Bindestrich
	weight [weɪt]		Gewicht

Vokabellernen mit Verstand

- Warte nicht mit dem Lernen bis zum letzten Augenblick, verteile die zu lernenden Vokabeln möglichst gleichmäßig auf die Zeit, die zur Verfügung steht.
- Vokabeln, die du dir nur schwer merken kannst, musst du dir möglichst oft vors Auge halten. Das kann ein Zettel an der Tür oder am Spiegel oder ein Lernplakat an der Wand sein.
- Auch kannst du diese „Problemfälle" in deinem Vokabelheft mit einem Markierstift hervorheben. Denn erst Markierungen lenken die Aufmerksamkeit und leiten das Auge.
- Und wenn du einzelne Wörter immer wieder falsch schreibst, hilft es, wenn du dir diese paar Wörter immer wieder hintereinander aufschreibst und die Buchstabenfolge laut vor dir hersagst.
- Wiederholen auf immer die gleiche Art ist langweilig und nicht besonders erfolgreich. Versuch's beim zweiten und dritten Mal lieber auf unterschiedliche Art und Weise.
- Dass eine Vokabelkartei oder etwas Ähnliches auf dem Computer hilfreich ist, weißt du schon.
- Lege dir möglichst viele verschiedene Wortfelder in deinem Heft, auf dem Computer oder in der Vokabelkartei an. Versuche jedes neue Wort diesen Wortfeldern zuzuordnen. Oder du stellst als Wiederholung alle *opposites* aus dieser Lektion zusammen. Oder alle Wörter mit gleicher oder - ähnlicher Bedeutung. Oder alle Wörter, die zur gleichen Wortfamilie gehören, z. B. *sun, sunglasses*, … Und dies müssen nicht immer Listen sein, sondern können auch Wörternetze oder Bilder sein.

- **Einige spielerische Möglichkeiten Wortschatz zu üben:** Du nimmst einfach ein Quadrat mit 15 × 15 Kästchen und versteckst möglichst viele Wörter der Lektion oder eines Wortfelds darin, senkrecht, waagrecht, vorwärts und rückwärts geschrieben. Oder du nimmst 10 Wörter eines Wortfelds wie "*river-rafting*", zerlegst sie in Silben, ordnest diese alphabetisch und lässt deine Freunde diese Wörter suchen und zusammensetzen. Oder du stellst ihnen die Aufgabe, fünf Wörter aus der neuen Lektion zu benennen, wenn du ihnen alte Wörter nennst, auf die sich die neuen reimen. Also *better – (sweater), sports – (shorts), green – (sunscreen), that's all – (to install)*, usw.

What you can say about people

angry	*böse, verärgert*	**important**	*wichtig*
annoyed	*verärgert*	**interesting**	*interessant*
awful	*schrecklich*	**nervous**	*aufgeregt, nervös*
boring	*langweilig*	**nice**	*nett, sympathisch*
brave	*mutig, tapfer*	**nosy**	*neugierig*
careful	*vorsichtig, sorgfältig*	**pleased**	*erfreut*
careless	*nachlässig, unvorsichtig*	**pretty**	*hübsch*
clever	*intelligent, klug*	**proud**	*stolz*
cool	*cool, toll*	**quiet**	*still, ruhig*
crazy	*verrückt*	**small**	*klein*
disappointed	*enttäuscht*	**strong**	*stark*
excited	*aufgeregt*	**stupid**	*dumm*
friendly	*freundlich*	**tidy**	*ordentlich*
funny	*lustig, komisch*	**tired**	*müde*
glad	*froh*	**unhappy**	*unglücklich*
great	*toll, großartig*	**unfriendly**	*unfreundlich*
happy	*fröhlich, glücklich*	**untidy**	*unordentlich*
horrible	*grauenhaft, schrecklich*	**worried**	*besorgt, beunruhigt*

Umgang mit dem Wörterbuch

Du hast jetzt viele Tipps für die Benutzung eines Wörterbuches gefunden.
Hier sind noch weitere:

- **Das Alphabet** musst du wirklich gut beherrschen, um nicht unnötig viel Zeit mit Blättern zu verlieren. Mit Freunden kannst du Wettbewerbe gegen die Uhr veranstalten. Ihr könnt Wörterlisten – auch auf Deutsch – wie auf Seite 16 zusammenstellen und sehen, wer sie zuerst richtig sortieren kann, oder ihr sucht abwechselnd ein kniffeliges Wort aus und versucht, das jeweilige Wort binnen sechs Sekunden im Wörterbuch zu finden.
  Vergiss nicht: die zwei Wörter, die oben **fett** gedruckt sind, sind eine große Hilfe. Sie zeigen dir das **erste** und das **letzte** Wort auf der Seite.
- Du hast schon gesehen, dass Wörter, die zu einer bestimmten Wortfamilie gehören, unter einem gemeinsamen **Stichwort** im Wörterbuch zusammengestellt werden. Du musst also gut überlegen, welches Stichwort du brauchst, wenn du ein Wort nachschlagen möchtest. Versuche, das passende Stichwort zu diesen Wörtern zu finden:
  a) gemütlich; ohnehin; blau machen; Lautstärke; lückenhaft
  b) *quietly; worried; to go wrong; from time to time*
- Es lohnt sich oft, **die ganze Eintragung** unter einem Stichwort durchzulesen, denn vielleicht findest du die vollständige Redewendung, die du suchst. Wenn das z. B. „die Sache hat einen Haken" ist, findest du unter „Haken" den entsprechenden englischen Ausdruck "*there's a snag or a catch*". Das funktioniert natürlich auch umgekehrt. "*To be black and blue*" z. B. findest du unter "*black*" mit der Überstzung „überall blaue Flecken haben".
  In den Beispielsätzen findest du dann auch eher die Präpositionen, die du nach einem Wort brauchst: *be crazy **about** ..., different **from** ..., to land **at** ...*
- Wenn du **dein eigenes Wörterbuch** hast, solltest du dir die Mühe machen, es richtig kennen zu lernen. Mache dich vertraut mit der Einleitung, wo die Anordnung erklärt wird, und mit den verwendeten Abkürzungen. Finde heraus, welche hilfreichen Listen z. B. mit unregelmäßigen Verben, Maßeinheiten, geographischen Namen usw. es gibt. Meist stehen sie hinten im Buch.

Aber denk dran, so hilfreich ein Wörterbuch auch sein mag, es kann die Englischkenntnisse in deinem Kopf nur ergänzen, nicht ersetzen!

Unit 2 A patchwork quilt

patchwork quilt [ˌpætʃˌwɜːk ˈkwɪlt]	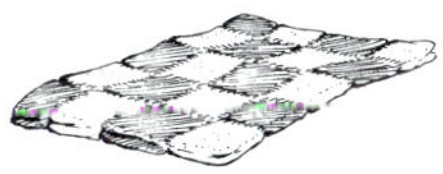	aus bunten Flicken zusammengesetzte Decke

Step A **A land of immigrants**

immigrant [ˈɪmɪgrənt]	A person who leaves his/her country to live in another one.	Einwanderer/ Einwanderin
high school (*AE*) [ˈhaɪ ˌskuːl]	FF *high school* ≠ Hochschule BE = comprehensive school	Gesamtschule
student (*AE*) [ˈstjuːdnt]	BE = pupil Americans say: [ˈstuːdnt] 	Schüler/in; Student/in
foreigner [ˈfɒrənə]	Someone from another country.	Ausländer/in
origin [ˈɒrɪdʒɪn]		Ursprung, Herkunft
citizen [ˈsɪtɪzn]		Bürger/in
2 **journey** [ˈdʒɜːnɪ]	The ~ to America was long for the immigrants.	(lange) Reise

	to **settle** ['setl]		(be)siedeln, sich niederlassen
a)	**slave** [sleɪv]	~s had to work hard and live like prisoners.	Sklave/Sklavin
	rich [rɪtʃ]	*rich* ⟷ poor	reich
	Virginia [və'dʒɪnjə]		*US-Bundesstaat*
	to **smoke** [sməʊk]	You mustn't ~ in a no-smoking zone.	rauchen
	So what? [səʊ 'wɒt]		Na und?
	settler ['setlə]	to settle → *settler*	Siedler/in
	°**Native American** ['neɪtɪv ə'merɪkən]	The first people who lived in America.	indianisch, *amer. Ureinwohner/in*
	Siberia [saɪ'bɪərɪə]		Sibirien
	Alaska [ə'læskə]		Alaska
	colony ['kɒlənɪ]	The English took *colonies* on the east coast of the US.	Kolonie
	on business [ɒn 'bɪznɪs]	He is going to the US ~, not on holiday.	geschäftlich
	business ['bɪznɪs]		Geschäft
	paved [peɪvd]	paved 	gepflastert
	New York [ˌnjuː 'jɔːk]		*Stadt in den USA; US-Bundesstaat*
	Latin America [ˌlætɪn ə'merɪkə]		Lateinamerika
	illegal [ɪ'liːgəl]	Some people try to get into the US ~ly.	illegal, ungesetzlich
3	**on foot** [ɒn 'fʊt]	by train, by bus, by car – but **on** foot	zu Fuß
	truck (*AE*) [trʌk]	BE = lorry 	Lkw, Lastwagen
	to **take, took, taken** [teɪk, tʊk, 'teɪkn]	How long did your journey ~?	erfordern; *hier:* dauern
	traveled (*AE*) ['trævld]		reiste, reistest, reisten
	less [les]	You can fly to America in ~ than a day.	weniger

Step A **A look at Seattle**

5	**during** ['djʊərɪŋ]	What did you do ~ the summer?	während
	view [vjuː]		Blick, Aussicht
	earthquake ['ɜːθkweɪk]	An ~ can destroy towns.	Erdbeben
	The Sonics (= The Seattle Supersonics) [ˌdə 'sɒnɪks]		*Name einer Basketballmannschaft*
	Chicago Bulls [ʃɪ'kɑːgəʊ 'bʊlz]	The Supersonics play the ~ next week.	*Name einer Basketballmannschaft*
⟨6⟩	nationality [ˌnæʃə'nælətɪ]	German, English, American, French, …	Nationalität
	chart [tʃɑːt]		Tabelle, Diagramm

In and around Seattle

the International District [ˌɪntə'næʃənl 'dɪstrɪkt]
Lake Sammamish [ˌleɪk sə'mæmɪʃ]
Mt. Rainier [ˌmaʊnt reɪ'nɪər]
the Pike Place Market [paɪk pleɪs 'mɑːkɪt]
Pioneer Square [paɪəˌnɪə 'skweə]
Snoqualmie Falls [snəʊˌkwɑːlmɪ 'fɔːlz]
the Space Needle [ðə 'speɪs ˌniːdl]

Step B **Tricky Situations**

Tricky Situations ['trɪkɪ ˌsɪtjʊ'eɪʃnz]		*Name einer Fernsehsendung*
tricky ['trɪkɪ]	Driving cars in big towns can be ~.	schwierig
to **barbecue** ['bɑːbɪkjuː]	Daniel: Some people ~ snakes!	grillen
Yuck! [jʌk]	Tori: ~! That's nasty.	Igitt!, Pfui!, Bäh! (*Ausruf des Ekels*)
to **be sick** [bɪ 'sɪk]		sich übergeben
to **offer** ['ɒfə]	If you ~ him money, he will do it.	(an)bieten
gang [gæŋ]	He will join the ~.	Bande, Gang
change [tʃeɪnʒ]		Wechselgeld, Kleingeld
manager ['mænɪdʒə]	The ~ of the shop was angry when	Geschäftsführer/in, Manager/in
cashier [kæ'ʃɪə]	the ~ gave me the wrong change.	Kassierer/in
as if … [ˌæz‿'ɪf]		als ob …
to **press** [pres]		drücken
alarm [ə'lɑːm]	You can press the ~ if the lift stops.	Alarm
elevator (*AE*) ['elɪveɪtə]	BE = lift	Aufzug, Fahrstuhl
to **get bored** [bɔːd]		Langeweile haben/ bekommen
4 to **go (out) with s.o.** [gəʊ 'aʊt wɪð]		mit jdm. (aus)gehen
°**Korean** [kə'rɪən]		koreanisch, Koreanisch, Koreaner/in
not … **any more** [nɒt 'enɪˌmɔː]		nicht mehr
Worldfest [wɜːld'fest]		*Name eines internat. Festes in Seattle*

5⟩ melting pot ['meltɪŋ pɒt]	Schmelztiegel	to be tossed out [biː tɒst 'aʊt]	hinausgeworfen werden
to mix [mɪks]	mischen	to pass [pɑːs]	*hier:* überqueren
nation ['neɪʃn]	Nation	brim [brɪm]	Kante, Rand
magic ['mædʒɪk]	magisch, Zauber-	private ['praɪvɪt]	Privat-
to step in [step 'ɪn]	hineingehen, hineinsteigen	stain [steɪn]	Klecks, Fleck
Czech [tʃek]	tschechisch, Tschechisch, Tscheche/ Tschechin	I don't give a damn. [ˌaɪ dəʊnt gɪv‿ə 'dæm]	Das ist mir piepegal.
		Shove your old pot. [ʃʌv]	*etwa:* Steckt euch euren bloden Topf an den Hut.
Scot [skɒt]	Schotte/Schottin		
to step out [step 'aʊt]	hinausgehen, hinaussteigen	Dudley Randall ['dʌdlɪ 'rændl]	*Personenname*
freshly christened [freʃlɪ 'krɪsnd]	gerade getauft		

Step B **At the Worldfest**

Korea [kə'rɪə]	~ is in Asia.	Korea
to **be interested in s.th.** [bɪ 'ɪntrəstɪd ɪn]		interessiert sein an
to **be used to s.th.** [bɪ 'juːst tʊ]		gewöhnt sein an
°**chopstick** ['tʃɒpstɪk]	Let's eat with ~s. 	(Ess-)Stäbchen

Vocabulary

	to **be tired of s.th.** [bɪ 'taɪəd‿əv]		von etw. genug haben
	all the time [ɔ:l θə‿'taɪm]		die ganze Zeit
	to **look forward to s.th.** [lʊk 'fɔ:wəd]	Soo isn't *looking forward* to telling her parents about Daryl.	sich auf etw. freuen
6	°**African-American** [ˌæfrɪkən‿ə'merɪkən]		afroamerikanisch, Afroamerikaner/in
7a)	**-ing-form** ['ɪŋ fɔ:m]		-ing-Form, Gerundium
b)	**neither** ['naɪðə]	I'm not interested in history. Me ~.	*hier:* auch nicht

Step C **The fortune cookie**

	°**fortune cookie** ['fɔ:tʃu:n ˌkʊkɪ]		*Keks, der eine Art Lebensweisheit enthält*
	fortune ['fɔ:tʃu:n]		Schicksal
	cookie (*AE*) ['kʊkɪ]	BE = biscuit	Keks
	color (*AE*) ['kʌlə]	BE = colour	Farbe
	The Jackals [ðə 'dʒækɔ:lz]		*Name einer Gang*
	heart [hɑ:t]		Herz
	S.th. is wrong. [rɒŋ]		*hier:* Es stimmt etw. nicht.
	truth [tru:θ]		Wahrheit
	apartment (*AE*) [ə'pɑ:tmənt]	BE = flat	Wohnung
	worry ['wʌrɪ]		Sorge
	Pugwacket ['pʌgwækɪt]		*Name eines Hundes*
	true [tru:]		wahr
	blind [blaɪnd]	People who cannot see are ~.	blind
	°**prejudice** ['predʒʊdɪs]	Many people have ~s against others.	Vorurteil
	to **deliver** [dɪ'lɪvə]		liefern
	°**Asian** ['eɪʃn]	Asia → *Asian*	asiatisch, Asiate/Asiatin
	flame [fleɪm]		Flamme
	building [bɪldɪŋ]		Gebäude
	damn [dæm]		verdammt
	fire ['faɪə]		Feuer
	kiss [kɪs]		Kuss
	after all [a:ftər‿'ɔ:l]		doch, doch noch
3	to **interview** ['ɪntəvju:]		interviewen
	firefighter ['faɪəˌfaɪtə]	The ~s put the fire out in 10 minutes.	Feuerwehrmann/-frau

Step C **Not only hot dogs**

4	**Suquamish** [sʊ'kwɑ:mɪʃ]		*Name eines Indianerstamms*
	festival ['festəvl]	Most young people like pop ~s.	Fest, Festival
5	°**Hispanic** [hɪ'spænɪk]	People from Mexico are ~.	hispanisch, *Amerikaner/in lateinamer. Herkunft*
	Japan [dʒə'pæn]		Japan
	Switzerland ['swɪtsələnd]		Schweiz

6⟩ Americano [əˌmerɪˈkɑːnəʊ]	spanisch für „Amerikaner/in“
cent (=c) (*AE*) [sent]	Cent (*amer. Geldeinheit*)
to grow up [ˌgrəʊ ˈʌp]	aufwachsen
president [ˈprezɪdənt]	Präsident
Magic Kingdom [ˌmædʒɪk ˈkɪŋdəm]	*Zauberreich*
Barbie doll [ˈbɑːbɪ dɒl]	Barbie-Puppe
chinos (*sg + pl*) [tʃiːnəʊz]	leichte Baumwollhose
Pepsi [ˈpepsɪ]	*Markenname*
Oreo (*AE*) [ˈɒriːəʊ]	*amer. Keksmarke*
to advertise [ˈædvətaɪz]	werben
to take no bull (*AE*) [bʊl]	*etwa:* sich nicht für dumm verkaufen lassen
soul (= soul music) [səʊl]	Soul (*Musikrichtung*)
to create [kriːˈeɪt]	(er)schaffen, kreieren, erfinden
rock ’n’ roll [ˌrɒkn'rəʊl]	Rock ’n’ Roll (*Musikrichtung*)
low-riding Chicano [ˌləʊ raɪdɪŋ tʃɪˈkɑːnəʊ]	*Fahrer mexikanischer Herkunft mit tiefergelegtem Auto*
satellite station [ˈsætəlaɪt ˌsteɪʃn]	Satellitensender
cable TV [ˌkeɪbl tiːˈviː]	Kabelfernsehen
pot [pɒt]	Topf
pan [pæn]	Pfanne
crime [kraɪm]	Kriminalität; Verbrechen
leisure time [ˈleʒə ˌtaɪm]	Freizeit
shark [ʃɑːk]	*hier:* Schlitzohr
fool [fuːl]	Dummkopf

Step D **Let’s check**

1 °**Mexican** [ˈmeksɪkn]	A ~ comes from Mexico.	mexikanisch, Mexikaner/in
°**Swiss** [swɪs]	~ chocolate is very famous.	schweizerisch
2 **star** [stɑː]		Star; Stern
3 **Asterix** [ˈæstərɪks]		*Comicfigur*
Lois Lane [ˌləʊɪs ˈleɪn]		*Figur aus Superman-Comics*
Superman [ˈsuːpəmæn]		*Comicfigur*
Spiderman [ˈspaɪdəmæn]		*Comicfigur*
wall [wɔːl]	There is a big ~ in our backyard.	Wand, Mauer
Bugs Bunny [ˌbʌgz ˈbʌnɪ]		*Zeichentrickfigur*
Charlie Brown [tʃɑːlɪ ˈbraʊn]		*Comicfigur*
baseball [ˈbeɪsbɔːl]		Baseball
Kermit [ˈkɜːmɪt]		*Figur aus der Muppets-Show*
Miss Piggy [mɪs ˈpɪgɪ]		*Figur aus der Muppets-Show*
Batman [ˈbætmæn]		*Comicfigur*
the Joker [ðə ˈdʒəʊkə]		*Figur aus Batman-Comics*
James Bond [ˌdʒeɪmz ˈbɒnd]		*Filmfigur*

⟨Revision 1⟩

5⟩ Where there’s a will, there’s a way. [weə ðeəz‿ə ˈwɪl ðeəz‿ə ˈweɪ]	Wo eine Wille ist, ist auch ein Weg.

⟨5⟩	vacation (*AE*) [və'keɪʃn]	Ferien, Urlaub
	robot ['rəʊbɒt]	Roboter/in
	private ['praɪvɪt]	privat
	interactive [ˌɪntər'æktɪv]	interaktiv
	forever [fə'revə]	ewig, für immer
	Super-Youth pill [sʌpə‿'ju:θ pɪl]	*Name einer Pille*
b)	transportation [ˌtrænspɔ:'teɪʃn]	Verkehrsmittel, Transport

True friends and false friends

A: True friends
Du kennst schon eine Menge englischer Wörter, die in ihren deutschen Entsprechungen dem englischen Wort sehr ähnlich oder gar gleich sind. Denke z. B. an *hotel*, *camera* oder *tourist*. Solche Wörter machen beim Lernen ja überhaupt keine Schwierigkeiten. Ein Teil davon unterscheidet sich dann doch noch ein bisschen, z. B. in der Aussprache wie *finger* oder in der Betonung wie *pullover* oder in der Schreibung wie *address*.

B: False friends FF
Allerdings gibt es auch *false friends*, also falsche Freunde. Diese Wörter sehen wie ein deutsches Wort aus oder wenigstens so ähnlich. Aber sie haben im Englischen eine ganz andere Bedeutung.

Im Vokabelverzeichnis sind diese Wörter mit dem Symbol FF gekennzeichnet.

Versuche doch mal dir ein System auszudenken mit dem du diese Wortpaare besser behalten kannst. Es gibt da verschiedene Möglichkeiten:

So: become = werden ≠ bekommen = get

oder so:	E:	D:
	become	*werden*
	get	*bekommen, werden*

Du kannst dir ja jedes Doppel-Wortpaar auf eine kleine Karteikarte schreiben und bekommst so im Laufe der Zeit eine gute Lern- und Wiederholungskartei mit *false friends*.

art – *Kunst*	**note** – *Zettel, Notiz*	**map** – *Landkarte*
kind – *Art (u. Weise)*	**mark** – *Note*	NICHT MAPPE

Wenn du das zweite englische Wort noch nicht kennst, kannst du dir das auch so wie im letzten Beispiel notieren.

Workshop B Listening and speaking

Part 1: **Understanding and explaining**

1	**gist** [dʒɪst]	I didn't understand, but I got the ~.	Wesentliches
	material [mə'tɪərɪəl]	Texts, books and pictures are learning ~.	Material, Stoff
	conversation [ˌkɒnvə'seɪʃn]	B ⟨bla, bla, …⟩ ⟨bla, bla, …⟩ A A and B are having a ~.	Unterhaltung, Gespräch
	rough [rʌf]	A ~ idea does not give you many details.	grob

〈The Pledge of Allegiance of the United States of America〉	Das Treuegelöbnis der Vereinigten Staaten von Amerika
“I pledge allegiance to the flag of the United States of America, and to the republic for which it stands, one nation under God, indivisible, with liberty and justice for all.”	„Ich gelobe Treue auf die Flagge der Vereinigten Staaten von Amerika und auf die Republik, für die sie steht – eine Nation unter Gott, unteilbar, in welcher Freiheit und Gerechtigkeit für alle herrschen.“

schedule (*AE*) [ˈʃedjuːl]	BE = timetable Americans say [ˈskedʒwəl] 	Stundenplan; Fahrplan
period (*AE*) [ˈpɪərɪəd]	BE = lesson	*hier:* Unterrichtsstunde
Math (*AE*) [mæθ]	BE = Maths	Mathe, Mathematikunterricht
Computer Science [kəmˈpjuːtə ˈsaɪəns]		Informatik
IHS (= Issaquah High School) [ˌaɪ‿eɪtʃ‿ˈes = ˈɪzəˌkwɑː ˈhaɪ skuːl]		*Name einer Schule*
yearbook (*AE*) [ˈjɪəbʊk]	There are pictures, postcards and stories in the IHS ~.	Jahrbuch *(einer Schule)*
chess [tʃes]	 ← Let’s have a game of ~.	Schach
choir [ˈkwaɪə]	 Achtung Aussprache! [ˈkwaɪə]	Chor
football [ˈfʊtbɔːl]		*hier:* American Football
golf [gɒlf]		Golf
soccer [ˈsɒkə]	ball games: ~, golf, tennis, table tennis, basketball	Fußball
wrestling [ˈreslɪŋ]		Ringen
paper (= newspaper) [ˈpeɪpə]	 news – newsagent’s – *newspaper*	Zeitung
nature [ˈneɪtʃə]	*nature* = wild animals, trees, flowers	Natur
Student Council (*AE*) [ˌstjuːdnt ˈkaʊnsl]		Schülermitverwaltung
cheerleader [ˈtʃɪəliːdə]	Many teams in the US have ~s. 	Cheerleader/in
locker [ˈlɒkə]		Schließfach
2 **exact** [ɪgˈzækt]	What is the ~ price of this book?	genau, exakt
3 **advice** [ədˈvaɪs]	*advice* = help, tip	Rat(schlag)
named [neɪmd]		namens, mit dem Namen
1) **ought to** [ˈɔːt‿tʊ]	– I don’t feel well. – You ~ go to the doctor.	sollte, solltest, solltet, sollten
to **ask s.o. for a date** [deɪt]		jdn. nach einer Verabredung fragen
9) **grade** (*AE*) [greɪd]	When Tori was in the first ~, her ~s were very good.	Note (*in der Schule*); Klasse

Part 2: **Discussing and making suggestions**

to **discuss** [dɪˈskʌs]		besprechen, diskutieren
suggestion [səˈdʒestʃn]	I don’t agree with your ~. Do you want to discuss it?	Vorschlag

Vocabulary

	staff [stɑ:f]		Mitarbeiterteam, Personal
	°**wake boarding** (*A*E) ['weɪk ˌbɔ:dɪŋ]		*Wassersportart*
	°to **fly high** ['flaɪ ˌhaɪ]		gute Laune haben
	°to **let the dirt fly** [let ðə 'dɜ:t flaɪ]		Spaß haben
	°**mud ball** ['mʌd bɔ:l]		Schlammball
	to **figure out** ['fɪgər‿aʊt]		(heraus)finden
1	**announcement** [ə'naʊnsmənt]	A: There was an ~ for	Durchsage, Ansage, Ankündigung, Bekanntmachung
	P.A. system (= public address system) [pi: eɪ 'sɪstəm = 'pʌblɪk ə'dres sɪstəm]	Mr. Steven Long on the ~.	Lautsprecheranlage
	mind map ['maɪnd ˌmæp]		Wörternetz
2a)	**campus** ['kæmpəs]	I like walking on the ~ best.	Campus, Schul-, Universitätsgelände
b)	to **disagree** [ˌdɪsə'gri:]	I *disagree*.	nicht übereinstimmen; anderer Meinung sein
c)	**would rather** ['rɑ:ðə]	I ~ go walking on the beach.	lieber

Part 3: **Listening to a story**

°**babysitter** ['beɪbɪˌsɪtə]		Kinderbetreuer/in, Babysitter/in
to **accuse s.o. of s.th.** [ə'kju:z]	The German teacher *accused me of* cheating.	jdn. beschuldigen/anklagen, etw. getan zu haben
°**mystery** ['mɪstrɪ]		Geheimnis, Rätsel
extract ['ekstrækt]		Auszug
test paper (*AE*) [test 'peɪpə]	BE = test, exam	Klassenarbeit
to **plan** [plæn]		planen
to **show s.th. off** [ʃəʊ‿'ɒf]		mit etw. protzen, mit etw. angeben
notebook (*AE*) ['nəʊtbʊk]	BE = exercise book	(Übungs-)Heft
gotten (*AE*) ['gɒtn]	A: I've ~ 8 out of 10 right.	bekommen
percent [pə'sent]	B: That's 80 ~.	Prozent
problem ['prɒbləm]		*hier:* Aufgabe
to **get at s.th.** ['get æt]	I don't understand. What are you *getting at*?	auf etw. hinauswollen
though [ðəʊ]		jedoch; *hier:* aber
private lesson [ˌpraɪvɪt 'lesn]	I'm not so good at Math, I have to have ~s.	Nachhilfeunterricht
°**probability** [ˌprɒbə'bɪlətɪ]		Wahrscheinlichkeit
zero ['zɪərəʊ]	Look at the sun, the probability of rain is ~.	Null
in turn [ɪn 'tɜ:n]		der Reihe nach, abwechselnd
this suggests … [ðɪs sə'dʒests]		das legt den Schluss nahe
fear [fɪə]		Angst, Furcht
confused [kənˌfju:zd]	Is it Mark or Mike? I'm ~.	durcheinander, verwirrt
bright [braɪt]	The light is so ~, I can't see.	hell, leuchtend; klug
to **speak up** [spi:k 'ʌp]		sich äußern, die Meinung sagen; lauter sprechen

that well [ðæt 'wel]		*hier:* besonders gut
to **nod** [nɒd]		nicken
°**principal** (*AE*) ['prɪnsəpl]	BE = headteacher	Schuldirektor/in
to **take care of s.th.** [teɪk 'keər‿ɒv ˌsʌmθɪŋ]		etw. erledigen; nach etw. schauen; sich um etw. kümmern
to **lead, led, led** [li:d, led, led]	I was *leading* the race, when I fell over.	führen

Unit 3 America's national parks

national park ['næʃənl 'pɑ:k]		Nationalpark

Step A **All kinds of places**

Some American national parks

Denali [de'nɑ:lɪ]	**Mesa Verde** [ˌmesə 'vədɪ]
Everglades ['evəgleɪdz]	**Sequoia** [sɪ'kwɔɪə]
Grand Canyon [ˌgrænd 'kænjən]	**Shenandoah** [ˌʃenən'dəʊə]
Kings Canyon [ˌkɪŋz 'kænjən]	**Yosemite** [jəʊ'semɪtɪ]

canyon ['kænjən]		Schlucht, Cañon
swampland ['swɒmplænd]		Sumpf(-gebiet)
landscape ['lænskeɪp]		Landschaft
to **protect** [prə'tekt]	People ought to ~ America's beautiful landscape.	schützen, beschützen
1 **description** [dɪ'skrɪpʃn]	to describe → *description*	Beschreibung
giant ['dʒaɪənt]		Riese; riesig, Riesen-
redwood ['redwʊd]	Yosemite is famous for its giant ~s.	*Baumart*
Alaska Range [ə'læskə reɪndʒ]		*Name einer Berggruppe*
Skyline Drive [ˌskaɪlaɪn 'draɪv]		*Straßenname*
alligator ['ælɪgeɪtə]	In the Everglades there are lots of ~s.	Alligator
:a) **grid** [grɪd]	Today's homework is easy. We only have to fill in a ~.	*hier*: Tabelle
3⟩ travel agent's ['trævl ˌeɪdʒənts]		Reisebüro
CD-ROM [si: di: 'rɒm]		CD-ROM
Internet ['ɪntənet]		Internet
state [steɪt]		(Bundes-)Staat
4 **present progressive** [ˌpreznt prəʊ'gresɪv]		*Verlaufsform*
vacation (*AE*) [və'keɪʃn]	BE = holiday	Ferien, Urlaub
to **smell, smelt, smelt** [smel, smelt, smelt]	Redwoods ~ wonderful.	riechen
luck [lʌk]	*luck*, lucky, to be lucky 	Glück
ranger ['reɪndʒə]	~s work in national parks.	Aufseher/in, Ranger/in
5 **Mt. McKinley** [ˌmaʊnt mə'kɪnlɪ]		*Berg in Alaska*
hurricane ['hʌrɪkən]		Wirbelsturm

6	**tall story** [tɔːl ˈstɔːrɪ]	I don't think that's true. Someone has told you a ~.	Lügengeschichte
	tall [tɔːl]		groß; hoch
a)	**California** [ˌkælɪˈfɔːnjə]		*US-Bundesstaat*
	cloud [klaʊd]		Wolke
	to **dive** [daɪv]		ins Wasser springen; tauchen
	dolphin [ˈdɒlfɪn]	 The ~ dived deep into the sea.	Delphin

Step B **Parks and people**

	to **do damage** [ˈdæmɪdʒ]	Hurricanes *do* a lot of *damage* to towns.	Schaden anrichten
	to **damage** [ˈdæmɪdʒ]		beschädigen
	garbage can (*AE*) [ˈgɑːbɪdʒ kæn]	In the US you put your garbage in a ~. 	Abfalleimer
	can [kæn]		Dose
	recycling bin [ˌriːˈsaɪklɪŋ bɪn]		Recyclingtonne
	bin [bɪn]		Mülleimer
	rare [reə]		selten, rar
	plant [plɑːnt]		Pflanze
	to **get frightened** [ˈfraɪtnd]		Angst bekommen
2b)	°**chief** [tʃiːf]		(Indianer-)Häuptling
⟨4⟩	wood [wʊd]		Holz; Wald
	leather [ˈleðə]	Shoes, bags, pencil cases are made of ~.	Leder

Step B **A newspaper report**

	remote [rɪˈməʊt]	~ places are often beautiful and quiet.	entfernt, abgelegen
	huge [hjuːdʒ]	*huge* = giant, enormous	riesig
	meter (*AE*) [ˈmiːtə]	BE = metr**e**	Meter
	by [baɪ]		von, vom (*in Passivsätzen*); bis
	everywhere [ˈevrɪweə]	*everywhere*, everybody, everyone, everything	überall
2	**talk-radio program** (*AE*) [tɔːk ˈreɪdɪəʊ prəʊgræm]	There are many ~s in the US.	*Radiosendung, bei der die Hörer und Hörerinnen anrufen können*
	program (*AE*) [ˈprəʊgræm]	BE = program**me**	Sendung (*im Radio oder TV*); Programm
	host [həʊst]		Gastgeber; *hier:* Moderator/in
	Florida [ˈflɒrɪdə]		*US-Bundesstaat*
	farmland [ˈfɑːmlænd]	You will not find ~ in big cities.	Ackerland
[3a)]	to bring down (trees) [brɪŋ daʊn]		abknicken, ausreißen
	passive [ˈpæsɪv]		Passiv-
	auxiliary [ɔːgˈzɪljərɪ]		Hilfs-; Hilfsverb
[b)]	headline [ˈhedlaɪn]	Look at the ~! **Hurricane brings down Redwoods in Yosemite.**	Titel, Schlagzeile
4	**center** *(AE)* [ˈsentə]		Mitte, Zentrum

Step C **A bear problem**

	General Grant Tree [ˌdʒenrl ˌgrɑːnt 'triː]		*Name eines Baumes*
	Pittsburgh ['pɪtsbɜːg]		*Stadt in Pennsylvania*
	Malibu ['mælɪbʊ]		*Vorort von Los Angeles*
	arrival [ə'raɪvl]	to arrive → *arrival*	Ankunft
	campground (*AE*) ['kæmpgraʊnd]	 ← *campground*	Campingplatz
	wherever [weər'evə]	We take our dog ~ we go.	wo auch immer, egal wo
	to **attack** [ə'tæk]	Last week a bear ~ed a child.	angreifen
	hiker ['haɪkə]	Wild animals rarely attack ~s.	Wanderer/Wanderin
	ugly ['ʌglɪ]	beautiful, pretty ←→ *ugly*	hässlich
	to **kill** [kɪl]		töten
	guy (*AE*) [gaɪ]		Mann, Kerl
	to **hit the trail** [hɪt ðə 'treɪl]	Debbie wanted to ~ early.	*umg.:* sich auf den Weg machen
	deer (*sg + pl*) [dɪə]	1 deer, 2 deer; 1 sheep, 2 sheep	Reh, Hirsch; Rotwild
	scream [skriːm]		Schrei
	to **grab** [græb]	*to grab* = to take s.th. quickly	greifen, schnappen
	backpack ['bækpæk]	*backpack* → backpacking	Rucksack
	several ['sevrl]		mehrere, einige
	to **shake, shook, shaken** ['ʃeɪk, ʃʊk, 'ʃeɪkn]	It was so cold we were all *shaking*.	zittern, schütteln
b)	to **react** [rɪ'ækt]		reagieren
a)	**result** [rɪ'zʌlt]	You will find all the new words from this text in the Alphabetical word list; here are the most important ones.	Ergebnis, Resultat; *hier:* Folge
	human ['hjuːmən]		menschlich
	powerful ['paʊəfʊl]		stark, kraftvoll, kräftig
	to **continue** [kən'tɪnjuː]		weitermachen, fortfahren
b)〉	wall display ['wɔːl dɪ'spleɪ]		Wandzeitung

5〉	bare necessity [beə nɪ'sesətɪ]	das Notwendigste	to rest at ease ['rest‿ət 'iːz]	sich zurücklehnen, sich wohl fühlen
	simple ['sɪmpl]	einfach		
	strife [straɪf]	Unfriede, Streit	to pick [pɪk]	pflücken
	Mother Nature ['mʌðə 'neɪtʃə]	Mutter Natur	paw-paw ['pɔː pɔː]	*Obstsorte*
			prickly pear ['prɪklɪ peə]	Kaktusfeige
	to wander ['wɒndə]	umherwandern	to prick [prɪk]	stechen
	to roam [rəʊm]	streifen durch	raw [rɔː]	*hier:* nackt
	to be fond of s.o./s.th. [fɒnd]	jdn./etw. (sehr) gern haben	paw [pɔː]	Pfote
			to beware [bɪ'weə]	aufpassen
	bee [biː]	Biene	claw [klɔː]	Kralle, Klaue
	to buzz [bʌz]	brummen	to relax [rɪ'læks]	(sich) entspannen
	to take a glance at [glɑːns]	einen Blick werfen auf	to fall apart [ˌfɔːl ə'pɑːt]	*hier:* sich entspannen
	fancy ['fænsɪ]	fein, toll, schick	Cool it … ['kuːl‿ɪt]	Reg dich ab …
	ant [ænt]	Ameise	little britches [ˌlɪtl 'brɪtʃɪz]	Dreikäsehoch

Step D **Let's check**

2	**countdown** ['kaʊntdaʊn]	*countdown:* 10, 9, 8, 7, 6, 5, 4, 3, 2, 1	Countdown
	within [wɪ'ðɪn]		innerhalb
	watch [wɒtʃ]	Look at your ~ and tell me what time it is, please. 	Armbanduhr

Back to Nature

alligator	*Alligator*	**farmland**	*Ackerland*	**ranger**	*Aufseher/in, Ranger/in*
backpack	*Rucksack*	**field**	*Feld, Wiese*		
bear	*Bär*	**forest**	*Wald*	**rapids**	*Stromschnellen*
bush	*Busch*	**ground**	*Boden*	**river**	*Fluss*
campground *(AE)*	*Campingplatz*	**hill**	*Hügel*	**rock**	*Fels*
		hurricane	*Wirbelsturm*	**stone**	*Stein*
canyon	*Schlucht, Cañon*	**island**	*Insel*	**storm**	*Sturm*
cliff	*Klippe, Fels*	**lake**	*See, Teich*	**swampland**	*Sumpf(-gebiet)*
climate	*Klima*	**landscape**	*Landschaft*	**trail** (*AE*)	*Spur; Weg, Pfad*
cloud	*Wolke*	**map**	*Landkarte*	**tree**	*Baum*
country(side)	*Land(schaft)*	**mountain**	*Berg*	**valley**	*Tal*
deer	*Reh, Hirsch; Rotwild*	**national park**	*Nationalpark*	**waterfall**	*Wasserfall*
		path	*Pfad, Weg*	**weather**	*Wetter*
earthquake	*Erdbeben*	**plant**	*Pflanze*	**youth hostel**	*Jugendherberge*

⟨Revision 2⟩

2	drive-in movie theater (*AE*) [draɪv‿ɪn ˌmu:vɪ 'θɪetə]	Autokino
	Richard Milton Hollingshead [ˌrɪtʃəd ˌmɪltn 'hɒlɪŋzhed]	*Personenname*
	to project [prə'dʒekt]	projizieren
	New Jersey [nju: 'dʒɜ:zɪ]	*US-Bundesstaat*
	simple ['sɪmpl]	einfach
	teenage ['ti:nˌeɪdʒ]	Jugend-, Teenager-
	open-air concert [ˌəʊpn‿eə 'kɒnsət]	Freiluftkonzert
	typical ['tɪpɪkl]	typisch
	to run [rʌn]	*hier:* betreiben
3	Smokey ['sməʊkɪ]	*Tiername*
5b)	unbreakable [ʌn'breɪkəbl]	unzerbrechlich

Workshop C Reading and understanding

Part 1: **Starting off**

The Great Spirit [ðə greɪt ˈspɪrɪt]		„Großer Geist" (*Indianergottheit*)
°to **interfere (with)** [ˌɪntəˈfɪə wɪð]	It's not your problem, so please don't ~.	sich einmischen (in)
civilized [ˈsɪvɪlaɪzd]	Please be ~ and stand quietly in line.	zivilisiert
reservation [ˌrezəˈveɪʃn]	Land kept for a special group of people or animals is a ~.	Reservat
Indian [ˈɪndjən]	~s live in India, American ~s live in America.	indianisch, Indianer/in
tribe [traɪb]	There are lots of different Indian ~s.	Stamm
to **group** [gruːp]	We can ~ trees into two main kinds – those that lose their leaves and those that don't.	gruppieren, in Gruppen einteilen
°**geographical** [dʒɪəˈgræfɪkəl]		geografisch
region [ˈriːdʒən]	Die Betonung ist anders im Deutschen.	Region
settlement [ˈsetlmənt]		Siedlung
gradually [ˈgrædʒʊəlɪ]	The white settlers ~ built more roads.	nach und nach, allmählich
to **force** [fɔːs]	The Europeans ~ed the Native Americans to leave their land.	zwingen
Pike [paɪk]		*Stadt in den USA*
wide [waɪd]		weit, breit
prairie [ˈpreərɪ]	All you can see is grass for miles and miles on the ~.	Prärie
°**teepee** [tiːˈpiː]		Tipi (*kegelförmiges Zelt der Prärie-Indianer*)
open-air museum [ˌəʊpn‿ˈeə mjuːˈzɪəm]	In an ~ you can see how people lived and worked in earlier times.	Freilichtmuseum
°**longhouse** [ˈlɒŋhaʊs]		*langes Holzhaus der Indianer des amer. Nordwestens*
cabin [ˈkæbɪn]	Early settlers built themselves ~s that were made of wood.	Blockhaus
shotgun [ˈʃɒtgʌn]		Schrotflinte
beside [bɪˈsaɪd]	~ the door, ~ his chair, ~ the river, ...	neben

Es ist oft besser, sich Wörter nicht nur einzeln zu merken, sondern zusammen mit anderen Wörtern, in typischen Ausdrücken (Sätzen/Phrasen). In der Mittelspalte findest du immer wieder Beispiele, wie hier für *beside*. Sammle selber Beispiele, und merke dir, wenn ein bekanntes Wort in einem neuen Zusammenhang auftaucht. So fällt dir das Wort zur passenden Gelegenheit – im Kontext – eher wieder ein.

Winchester [ˈwɪnʃɪstə]		*Name eines Gewehrs*
Walker Colt [ˌwɔːkə ˈkəʊlt]		*Name eines Revolvers*
to **beat, beat, beaten** [biːt, biːt, ˈbiːtn]	His heart ~ fast as he ran up the stairs.	schlagen
Apache [əˈpætʃɪ]		*Indianerstamm*
to **lift** [lɪft]	Can you help me ~ this heavy box?	(hoch-)heben
buffalo [ˈbʌfələʊ]	buffalo → buffal**oes**	Büffel, Bison

1	**heading** [ˈhedɪŋ]	The ~ usually shows what a text is about.	Überschrift
	Wild West [waɪld ˈwest]	Movies about the ~ are very popular.	Wilder Westen
2	°**covered wagon** [ˈkʌvəd ˌwæɡən]		Planwagen
	wagon [ˈwæɡən]		Planwagen
4	**speech** [spiːtʃ]		Rede
	to **expect** [ɪkˈspekt]	You don't ~ to see snow in June.	erwarten

Part 2: **Finding out more**

1	°**wagon train** [ˈwæɡən ˌtreɪn]	We saw a ~ with so many wagons, it was a mile long!	Planwagentreck
	according to [əˈkɔːdɪŋ tʊ]		nach, laut, gemäß
	crowded [ˈkraʊdɪd]	You will find all the new words from this leaflet in the Alphabetical word list; here are the most important ones.	voll mit Leuten, überfüllt
	naturally [ˈnætʃrəlɪ]	He won the competition, so ~ he was happy.	natürlich; selbstverständlich
	hunter [ˈhʌntə]	A ~ shoots animals for their meat or skin.	Jäger/in
	°**trapper** [ˈtræpə]		Fallensteller/in, Trapper/in
	route [ruːt]	Columbus only expected to find a new ~ to India.	Weg, Route
	°**cattle rancher** [ˈkætl rɑːntʃə]		Rancher/in, Viehzüchter/in
	cattle (*pl*) [ˈkætl]	Farmers keep ~ for milk or meat.	Rind(-vieh)
	railroad (*AE*) [ˈreɪlrəʊd]	BE = railway 	Eisenbahn
	Mississippi [ˌmɪsɪˈsɪpɪ]		*Fluss in den USA*
	further [ˈfɜːðə]	Boston is ~ north than New York.	weiter
	wilderness [ˈwɪldənes]	Try the ~ of the North for hiking.	Wildnis
	to **camp** [kæmp]	If you ~ you don't have to worry about booking hotel rooms.	zelten, kampieren
	to **form** [fɔːm]	*to form* = to make	bilden, formen
	circle [ˈsɜːkl]	circle: ○ square: □	Kreis
	peaceful [ˈpiːsfʊl]	At first the Native Americans were ~ and friendly.	friedlich
	to **swear, swore, sworn** [sweə, swɔː, swɔːn]		schwören; fluchen
	to **manage to do s.th.** [ˈmænɪdʒ]	Did you *manage to do* all those jobs?	schaffen etw. zu tun
	to **survive** [səˈvaɪv]		überleben
	because of [bɪˈkɒz‿əv]	We didn't go hiking ~ the bad weather.	wegen
	the Pilgrims [ðə ˈpɪlɡrɪmz]		*die ersten engl. Kolonisten im heutigen Massachusetts*
	tradition [trəˈdɪʃn]		Tradition, Brauch
	way of life [ˌweɪ‿əv ˈlaɪf]	The Indians' ~ was better for the environment.	Lebensstil
	°**savage** [ˈsævɪdʒ]		Wilde/r
	government [ˈɡʌvnment]		Regierung
	army [ˈɑːmɪ]		Armee
	disease [dɪˈziːz]		Krankheit
2	**paragraph** [ˈpærəɡrɑːf]	letter → word → sentence → ~	Absatz, Abschnitt
3	**religion** [rɪˈlɪdʒən]	The Indians had a different ~ from the white settlers.	Religion

°**tribal land** [ˌtraɪbl ˈlænd]		Stammesland
Sioux [suː]		*Prärie-Indianerstamm*
lifestyle [laɪfˌstaɪl]	The ~ of Indians today is very different from 100 years ago.	Lebensstil
pipe [paɪp]	The Indians smoked ~s to show they were friendly.	Pfeife
warrior [ˈwɒrɪə]		Krieger/in
use of s.th. [juːs‿ɒv]		Gebrauch von etw.

Part 3: **Reacting to a text**

You will find all the new words from this text in the Alphabetical word list; here are the most important ones.

to **pass** [pɑːs]	The new motorway ~es too close to the village.	vorbeigehen; bestehen
as though [æz ˈðəʊ]		als ob
she didn't blame him [ʃiː dɪdnt ˈbleɪm hɪm]		*hier:* sie konnte ihn gut verstehen
to **look up** [lʊk‿ʌp]	She *looked up* from her book when he came in.	hochschauen, aufsehen
silent [ˈsaɪlənt]	The first movies were ~.	still, stumm, geräuschlos; schweigsam
collar [ˈkɒlə]	Dogs should wear a ~ with their name on it.	*hier:* Halsband
to **reply** [rɪˈplaɪ]		antworten
to **drag** [dræg]		schleppen, ziehen
to **tie** [taɪ]	Please help me ~ my shoes.	(fest-)binden, anbinden
°**tin** [tɪn]		Zinn, Blech
°**tobacco** [təˈbækəʊ]		Tabak
to **fill** [fɪl]		stopfen
to **light** [laɪt]	~ a pipe, ~ a fire, …	anzünden; beleuchten
to **rise up, rose up, risen up** [ˈraɪz‿ʌp, ˈrəʊz‿ʌp, ˈrɪzn‿ʌp]		*hier:* aufstehen
gun [gʌn]	A ~ is a very dangerous weapon.	Schusswaffe, Pistole, Gewehr
perfect [ˈpɜːfɪkt]		vollkommen
camp [kæmp]		Lager
to **treat** [triːt]		behandeln
stable [ˈsteɪbl]	Horses are kept in a ~.	Stall
eagle [ˈiːgl]	~s are big birds.	Adler
feather [ˈfeðə]		Feder
to **wave** [weɪv]		wehen; winken
to **point s.th. at s.o.** [pɔɪnt]		etw. auf jdn. richten
to **step between** [step bɪˈtwiːn]	He *stepped between* the two boys.	dazwischen treten
farther [ˈfɑːðə]	~ means the same as further.	weiter
mad [mæd]		verrückt; *hier:* böse, verärgert
firm [fɜːm]		fest
Wilder [ˈwaɪldə]		*Familienname*
b) **impression** [ɪmˈpreʃn]	She made a good ~ at the job interview and got the job.	Eindruck
2 **author** [ˈɔːθə]		Autor/in

American History

army	*Armee*	**hunter**	*Jäger/in*	**slave**	*Sklave/Sklavin*
buffalo	*Büffel, Bison*	**immigrant**	*Einwanderer/ Einwanderin*	**teepee**	*Tipi*
cabin	*Blockhaus*			**tradition**	*Tradition, Brauch*
cattle rancher	*Rancher/in, Viehzüchter/in*	**prairie**	*Prärie*	**tribe**	*Stamm*
		reservation	*Reservat*	**wagon**	*Planwagen*
civilized	*zivilisiert*	**region**	*Region*	**wagon train**	*Planwagentreck*
colony	*Kolonie*	**to settle**	*besiedeln*	**warrior**	*Krieger/in*
freedom	*Freiheit*	**settlement**	*Siedlung*	**way of life**	*Lebensstil*
government	*Regierung*	**settler**	*Siedler/in*	**wilderness**	*Wildnis*

Ähnliches Wort – ähnliche Bedeutung

Denke daran, dass englische Wörter, die deutschen Wörtern ähnlich sehen, in den meisten Fällen eine ähnliche Bedeutung haben. Einige Beispiele aus diesem Workshop:

region = *Region*
reservation = *Reservat*
route = *Route*
civilized = *zivilisiert*

} *aber Vorsicht! Die Aussprache ist oft anders!*

Finde weitere Wörter in dieser Lektion, die *true friends* sind, weil sie dir gleich ihre Bedeutung verraten. Viele Wörter haben aber mehr als eine Bedeutung, manchmal stimmt nur eine Bedeutung mit den verschiedenen deutschen Bedeutungen überein, z. B.

cabin – heißt in dieser Lektion ‚Blockhütte'. Auf einem Schiff kann es auch ‚Kabine' heißen, während die Fußballer sich in einem *changing room* umziehen.

to manage – heißt hier ‚etwas schaffen', kann aber ‚managen' bedeuten, wenn man von einer Firma oder einem Geschäft spricht.

False friends sind sehr lästig! Das sind Wörter, die wie gute Bekannte aussehen, sie entpuppen sich aber als etwas völlig anderes! Sei also auf der Hut! Im Zweifelsfall aber, wenn du meinst, ein Wort zu erkennen, ist es wahrscheinlich ein Freund – ein Wort, das in sehr vielen europäischen Sprachen die gleiche oder eine sehr ähnliche Bedeutung hat. Es gibt also viel mehr gute Freunde als falsche Freunde!

Unit 4 New York, New York

Step A **The Big Apple**

Places in New York

Chinatown [ˈtʃaɪnəˌtaʊn]
Greenwich Village [ˌgrenɪdʒ ˈvɪlɪdʒ]
Harlem [ˈhɑːləm]
Little Italy [ˌlɪtl ˈɪtəlɪ]
Little Ukraine [ˌlɪtl juːˈkreɪn]
Manhattan [mænˈhætn]
Queens [kwiːnz]
Staten Island [ˌstætn‿ˈaɪlənd]
the Bronx [ðə ˈbrɒŋks]

Broadway [ˈbrɔːdweɪ]
Central Park [ˌsentrl ˈpɑːk]
the Empire State Building [ˌempaɪə ˈsteɪt ˌbɪldɪŋ]
the Hard Rock Café [ˌhɑːd rɒk‿ˈkæfeɪ]
Lincoln Square [ˌlɪŋkən ˈskweə]
Madison Avenue [ˌmædɪsən ˈævənjuː]
Plaza Hotel [ˌplɑːzə həʊˈtel]
the Statue of Liberty [ðə ˌstætʃuː əv ˈlɪbətɪ]
Times Square [ˌtaɪmz ˈskweə]
the World Trade Center [wɜːld ˈtreɪd ˌsentə]

The Big Apple [ðə ˌbɪg ˈæpl]		*Spitzname von New York*
New York City [ˌnjuː ˈjɔːk sɪtɪ]		*Stadt in den USA*
courier [ˈkʊrɪə]	A ~ takes things from one place to another.	Bote/Botin; Kurier
package [ˈpækɪðʒ]		Paket
agency [ˈeɪdʒənsɪ]		Agentur
mail [meɪl]		Post
subway (*AE*) [ˈsʌbweɪ]	BE = underground 	U-Bahn
cab [kæb]	BE = taxi	Taxi
whatever [wɒtˈevə]	~ you do, don't cycle without a helmet.	was (auch immer), egal was
Nebraska [nɪˈbræskə]		*US-Bundesstaat*
actor [ˈæktə]	to act → *actor*	Schauspieler
to **try out for** [ˌtraɪ ˈɒʊt fɔː]		*hier:* vorsingen, vorspielen
musical [ˈmjuːzɪkəl]		Musical
tip [tɪp]		Trinkgeld
café [ˈkæfeɪ]		Café
°**billboard** [ˈbɪlbɔːd]	New York is famous for its huge ~s.	Reklametafel
°**neon sign** [ˌnɪɒn ˈsaɪn]	There are a lot of bright ~s in Times Square.	Leuchtreklame
to **skate** [skeɪt]	She is ~ing. 	Rollschuh/Schlittschuh laufen
to **jog** [dʒɒg]	to walk, ~, to run	joggen
grass [grɑːs]		Gras
skyscraper [ˈskaɪˌskreɪpə]	 There are ~s in most big cities of the world.	Wolkenkratzer
°**borough** [ˈbʌrə]	any of the five parts of New York City	Bezirk
atmosphere [ˈætməˌsfɪə]		Atmosphäre, Stimmung
multi-cultural [ˌmʌltɪ‿ˈkʌltʃərəl]		multikulturell
multi- [ˈmʌltɪ]		multi-
multi-ethnic [ˌmʌltɪ‿ˈeθnɪk]		multiethnisch, Vielvölker-
artist [ˈɑːtɪst]	An ~ draws or paints pictures.	Künstler/in
last but not least [ˌlɑːst bʌt nɒt ˈliːst]		nicht zuletzt
gallery [ˈgælərɪ]		Kunstgalerie
the **Hard Rock Café** [ˌhɑːd rɒk‿ˈkæfeɪ]		berühmtes Café
theater (*AE*) [θɪˈetə]	BE = theatre	Theater
a) **Puerto Rico** [ˈpwɜːtəʊ ˈriːkəʊ]		*Insel in der Karibik (US-Territorium)*
passenger [ˈpæsɪndʒə]		Passagier/in; Beifahrer/in
to **study** [stʌdɪ]		studieren; beobachten; *hier:* lesen
3 **reception** [rɪˈsepʃn]	In a hotel you check in at ~.	Rezeption
avenue [ˈævənjuː]	A long, wide street is often called an ~.	Straße, Allee

Vocabulary

Step B **Jerry – in a hurry**

2	**Kansas** ['kænzəs]		*US-Bundesstaat*
	°**bagel** ['beɪgl]	A ~ is a small, hard ring of bread.	*jüdisches Gebäck*
	°**sushi** ['suːʃɪ]	Small cakes of rice with fish on top are called ~.	*japanisches Fischgericht*
	raw [rɔː]	*raw* ⟷ cooked	roh
	°**burrito** [bə'riːtəʊ]	~s are filled with chicken, cheese, beef, …	*mexikanisches Gericht (gefüllte Pfannkuchen)*
	°**nacho** ['nʌtʃəʊ]		*mexikanische Vorspeise*
	°**chopsuey** [ˌtʃɒp'suːɪ]	Chinese dish with small pieces of meat and vegetables.	*chinesisches Gericht*
	°**pastrami** [pə'strɑːmɪ]		*Wurstsorte*
	°**sundae** ['sʌndeɪ]	ice cream + fruit + cream + chocolate = ~	Eisbecher
	°**dessert** [dɪ'zɜːt]	Something sweet at the end of a meal is a ~.	Nachtisch

Step B **Graffiti Girl: a true success story**

	graffiti [grə'fiːtɪ]		Wandmalereien, Graffiti
	to **spray** [spreɪ]		sprühen
	creative [kriː'eɪtɪv]	Achte auf die Aussprache!	kreativ, schöpferisch
	rather than ['rɑːðə]		*hier:* eher
	criminal ['krɪmɪnl]		kriminell; Straftäter/in
	work of art [wɜːk‿əv 'ɑːt]		Kunstwerk
	a deal for s.th. [diːl]		ein Angebot für etw.
	stuff [stʌf]	This is a fantastic music store, they have some great ~.	Zeug; Stoff
	to **look s.o. up** [lʊk‿'ʌp]	*Look me up* if you come to the US.	bei jdm. vorbeischauen
5	**painting** ['peɪntɪŋ]	to paint, paint, ~s	Bild, Gemälde
6a)	**financial** [faɪ'nænʃəl]	The ~ heart of a city is where the big banks are.	finanziell

⟨7⟩	to spread the news [spred]	weitersagen	top of the heap [hiːp]	der/die Beste
	vagabond ['vægəbɒnd]	Vagabund/in	these little town blues [ðiːz lɪtl taʊn 'bluːz]	*etwa:* diese Kleinstadtdepressionen
	are longing to stray [ɑː 'lɒŋɪŋ tʊ streɪ]	sich danach sehnen herumzustreunen	to melt away [melt‿ə'weɪ]	wegschmelzen
	right through the very heart of it [raɪt θruː ðə 'verɪ hɑːt‿əv‿ɪt]	mitten durch sein Herz	brand new ['brænd njuː]	brandneu
			to make it ['meɪk‿ɪt]	Erfolg haben; es rechtzeitig schaffen

City life

airport	*Flughafen*	**hotel**	*Hotel*	**service station**	*Tankstelle, Raststätte*
bowling alley	*Kegelbahn, Bowlingbahn*	**ice rink**	*Eisbahn*	**skyscraper**	*Wolkenkratzer*
building	*Gebäude*	**job**	*Beruf, Arbeit*	**snack bar**	*Imbissstube*
bus stop	*Bushaltestelle*	**movies**	*Kino*	**square**	*Platz*
cab (*AE*)	*Taxi*	**theater** (*AE*)		**street**	*Straße*
café	*Café*	**museum**	*Museum*	**station**	*Bahnhof*
cathedral	*Dom*	**musical**	*Musical*	**statue**	*Statue, Denkmal*
church	*Kirche*	**neighbor-hood**	*Wohnviertel*	**subway** (*AE*)	*U-Bahn*
cinema	*Kino*	**neon sign**	*Leuchtreklame*	**swimming pool**	*Schwimmbad*
company	*Firma*	**office**	*Büro, Amt*	**taxi**	*Taxi*
department store	*Warenhaus*	**park**	*Park*	**theater** (*AE*)	*Theater*
factory	*Fabrik*	**playground**	*Spielplatz, Schulhof*	**traffic**	*Verkehr*
gallery	*Kunstgalerie*	**phone booth** (*AE*)	*Telefonzelle*	**traffic jam**	*Stau*
garage	*Garage*	**post office**	*Postamt*	**traffic lights**	*Verkehrsampel*
garden	*Garten*	**school**	*Schule*	**underground**	*U-Bahn*
hospital	*Krankenhaus*			**youth centre**	*Jugendzentrum*

Step C **All in a day's work**

All in a day's work. ['ɔːl ɪn‿ə 'deɪz wɜːk]		*etwa:* Das gehört zu meiner täglichen Arbeit.
passport ['pɑːspɔːt]	You need a ~ to travel to most countries.	Reisepass
helicopter ['helɪkɒptə]	balloon, kite, plane, ~ 	Hubschrauber
receptionist [rɪ'sepʃənɪst]	reception → *receptionist*	Empfangschef/-dame
customer ['kʌstəmə]		Kunde/Kundin
limo ['lɪməʊ]	FF limo ≠ Limo (Limonade)	Stretchlimousine
speed [spiːd]		Geschwindigkeit, Schnelligkeit, Tempo
death [deθ]	life ⟷ *death*	Tod
to **crash into s.th.** [kræʃ]		in etw. hineinkrachen
to **race** [reɪs]	a race → *to race*	rennen, rasen
°**Damn idiot!** [dæm‿'ɪdɪət]		Verdammter Idiot!
crime [kraɪm]	*crime* → criminal	Kriminalität; Verbrechen
to **brake** [breɪk]	When you see a red light you must ~ and stop.	bremsen
°**mugger** ['mʌgə]		Straßenräuber/in
to **thank s.o.** [θæŋk]		jdm. danken
crash [kræʃ]		Unfall, Zusammenstoß; Absturz
to **bend, bent, bent** [bend, bent, bent]	You've sat on my new folder and *bent* it.	biegen, verbiegen
button [bʌtn]		Knopf
to **make it** ['meɪk‿ɪt]		Erfolg haben; es rechtzeitig schaffen
°**Damn you!** ['dæm‿juː]		Zur Hölle mit dir/Ihnen!
°**producer** [prə'djuːsə]		Produzent/in
2 to **report** [rɪ'pɔːt]		berichten
°**incident** ['ɪnsɪdənt]		Vorfall, Ereignis
bicycle ['baɪsɪkl]		Fahrrad

⟨3⟩	hell [hel]		Hölle
	no U turns [nəʊ 'juː‿tɜːnz]		nicht wenden
	back [bæk]		Rücken
	to touch [tʌtʃ]		anfassen, berühren

Step D **Let's check**

⟨4⟩	cartoon [kɑː'tuːn]		Cartoon
	but no one [bʌt 'nəʊ‿wʌn]		*hier:* aber auch gar niemand

In diesem Zusammenhang

Du seufzt innerlich, wenn du nach einer bestimmten Wortbedeutung fragst und dein Lehrer schon wieder antwortet: „Na ja, es kommt auf den Zusammenhang an."
Es kommt aber wirklich darauf an, in welcher Situation man ein Wort benutzt – worüber man gerade spricht, mit wem, wo oder sogar zu welcher Tages- oder Jahreszeit, nicht zuletzt auch darauf, ob man sich mündlich oder schriftlich mitteilt. Es kommt auf den Zusammenhang, den Kontext an.
Du hast, zum Beispiel, eine dritte Bedeutung von *to look up* kennengelernt.

to look s.th. up = nachschlagen	*She had to look up some words in her dictionary.*
to look up = aufblicken	*The cat looked up when he came into the room.*
to look s.o. up = aufsuchen/besuchen	*He likes to look up old friends when he's travelling.*

Diese verschiedenen Bedeutungen werden oft mit verschiedenen Wörtern übersetzt; es lohnt sich, im Wörterbuch nach einem passenden Satzbeispiel zu suchen, wenn dir die erste Übersetzungsmöglichkeit spanisch vorkommt!

Workshop D Writing letters

Part 1: **Looking at model letters**

1a)	**Lake View Drive** [ˌleɪk vjuː 'draɪv]		*Straße in Issaquah*
	°**Valentine's card** ['væləntaɪnz kɑːd]		Valentinskarte
	Valentine ['væləntaɪn]		*Freund/in, dem/der man am Valentinstag einen Gruß schickt*
	to **go to camp** [gəʊ tə 'kæmp]	Many US children ~ in the summer.	ins Ferienlager fahren
b)	**Superbowl** ['suːpəbəʊl]		*Endspiel um die Meisterschaft im American Football*
	°**Valentine's Day** ['væləntaɪnz deɪ]		Valentinstag
	°**Halloween** [ˌhæləʊ'iːn]		*Halloween*
	costume ['kɒstjuːm]	 Achtung Aussprache! <u>costume</u> – ['kɒstjuːm]	Kostüm
	trick-or-treat [trɪk‿ɔː‿'triːt]	Kids play *tricks* on Halloween if they don't get candy.	*etwa:* „Streich-oder-Leckerei"

	°**Thanksgiving** ['θæŋks,gɪvɪŋ]		Erntedankfest
	turkey ['tɜːkɪ]	On Thanksgiving Americans eat ~ for dinner.	Pute/r, Truthahn/ Truthenne
	harvest ['hɑːvɪst]		Ernte
	°**Independence Day** [,ɪndɪ'pendəns deɪ]		*Unabhängigkeitstag*
	parade [pə'reɪd]	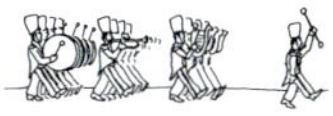	Umzug, Parade
	fireworks (*pl*) ['faɪəwɜːks]		Feuerwerk
	to **celebrate** ['selɪbreɪt]	You ~ birthdays, Christmas, Thanksgiving, …	feiern
2	**formal** ['fɔːml]		formell, förmlich
	Spokane [spɒ'kæn]		*Stadt in Washington*
	Madam ['mædəm]	You use ~ in a formal letter.	*Anrede für eine Dame*
	as soon as possible [əz_suːn_əz 'pɒsəbl]	*as soon as possible* = very fast, at once	so bald wie möglich
	so (that) ['səʊ ðæt]	She decided to give the kids more candy ~ they would not play tricks.	damit
	Sincerely, [sɪn'sɪəlɪ]	Vergiss das Komma nicht.	Mit freundlichen Grüßen (*Schlussformel in Briefen*)
	Golden ['gəʊldən]		*Stadt in den USA*
	basics ['beɪsɪks]	Always begin with the ~ when you start learning something.	Grundlagen
	to **enclose** [ɪn'kləʊz]		beilegen, beifügen
	application form [,æplɪ'keɪʃn 'fɔːm]		Anmeldeformular; Bewerbungsformular
	aged [eɪdʒd]		im Alter von, … Jahre alt
	to **improve** [ɪm'pruːv]	*to improve* = to make better	verbessern
	to **let s.o. know** [let 'nəʊ]	Sorry the hotel is full. I'll ~ if we have any cancellations.	jdm. Bescheid geben/ sagen; wissen lassen
	Sincerely yours, (*AE*) [sɪn'sɪəlɪ jɔːz]	BE = Yours sincerely Vergiss das Komma nicht.	Mit freundlichen Grüßen (*Schlussformel in Briefen*)
3	**sad** [sæd]		traurig

Special days

birthday	*Geburtstag*	**Happy Birthday!**	*Herzlichen Glückwunsch zum Geburtstag!*
calendar	*Kalender*		
candle	*Kerze*	**Independence Day**	*Unabhängigkeitstag*
carnival	*Karneval, Volksfest*	**Merry Christmas!**	*Fröhliche Weihnachten!*
to celebrate	*feiern*	**parade**	*Umzug, Parade*
Christmas	*Weihnachten*	**party**	*Party, Feier*
costume	*Kostüm*	**present**	*Geschenk*
Easter	*Ostern*	**Thanksgiving**	*Erntedankfest*
festival	*Fest*	**vacation** (*AE*)	*Urlaub, Ferien*
fete	*Schulfest, Stadtfest*	**Valentine's card**	*Valentinskarte*
fireworks	*Feuerwerk*	**Valentine's Day**	*Valentinstag*
Halloween	*Halloween*		

Part 2: **Using your skills**

	pie [paɪ]	apple ~, vegetable ~, meat ~, …	Kuchen; Pastete
	not … **either** ['aɪðə]		auch nicht
	as [æz]		da, während
	candy (*AE*) (*sg* + *pl*) ['kændɪ]	BE = sweets	Süßigkeit, Süßigkeiten
1	**fortunately** ['fɔːtʃnətlɪ]		glücklicherweise, zum Glück
	stack [stæk]	Who's eaten that ~ of pies?	Stapel
	to **flow** [fləʊ]	This text is difficult to read, it just doesn't ~.	fließen
3	**handwriting** ['hænd,raɪtɪŋ]		Handschrift
	to **recommend** [,rekə'mend]		empfehlen
	organization [,ɔːgənaɪ'zeɪʃn]		Organisation
⟨6⟩	werewolf ['wɪəwʊlf]		Werwolf
	witch [wɪtʃ]		Hexe
	corpse [kɔːps]		Leiche
	scary ['skærɪ]		unheimlich, gruselig, gespenstisch
⟨7⟩	bee [biː]		Biene
	rose [rəʊz]		Rose
	to be a laugh [lɑːf]		ein Witz sein
	to be a scream [skriːm]		zum Schreien sein

Unit 5 Communication and Technology

communication [kə,mjuːnɪ'keɪʃn]	Radio, computers and TV are different forms of ~.	Kommunikation, Informationsaustausch, Verständigung

Step A **Ways to communicate**

	to **communicate** [kə'mjuːnɪkeɪt]		kommunizieren, Informationen austauschen, sich verständigen
1a)	**fax** [fæks]	~, phone and e-mail are the fastest ways to communicate.	Telefax
b)	**teletext** ['telɪtekst]	You can read the ~ on TV.	Videotext
2	**instructions** (*pl*) [ɪn'strʌkʃnz]	You will find all the new words from this text in the Alphabetical word list; here are the most important ones.	Betriebsanleitung, Anweisungen
	index ['ɪndeks]		Inhaltsverzeichnis
a)	**operation** [,ɒpə'reɪʃn]		Arbeitsgang; *hier:* Bedienung
	to **select** [sɪ'lekt]		auswählen
	to **view** [vjuː]		anschauen, betrachten
	to **display** [dɪ'spleɪ]		ausstellen; *hier:* zeigen
	to **input** ['ɪnpʊt]		eingeben
	digit ['dɪdʒɪt]	*digit* = number	Zahl, Ziffer

	to **type** [taɪp]	When I was *typing*,	tippen
	error ['erə]	I made three ~s.	Fehler
b)	to **match s.th. with s.th.** [mætʃ]		das Passende zu etw. finden
3	**advantage** [əd'vɑːntɪdʒ]	It's an ~ if you can speak English, if you want to work in the US.	Vorteil
	disadvantage [ˌdɪsəd'vɑːntɪdʒ]	It's a ~ if you don't.	Nachteil

Step B **Telephone talk**

	shock [ʃɒk]	It was a big ~ when Uncle Tom died.	Schock(-zustand)
	such a [sʌtʃ‿ə]		solch ein/e, ein/e solche/r
	telephone bill ['telɪfəʊn ˌbɪl]	We never had such a huge ~.	Telefonrechnung
	bill [bɪl]		Rechnung
	hotline ['hɒtˌlaɪn]	If you have a problem, you can call the ~.	Hotline, „heißer Draht"
	to **scowl** [skaʊl]		ein böses Gesicht machen
	engineer [ˌendʒɪ'nɪə]		Ingenieur/in
	millionaire [ˌmɪljə'neə]	She won a lot of money and is now a ~.	Millionär/in
	quite a [kwaɪt‿ə]		ziemlich, ein/e ziemliche/r/s
2	**indefinite article** [ɪn'defɪnət ˌɑːtɪkl]	'A' and 'An' are ~s.	unbestimmter Artikel
5	**definite article** ['defɪnət ˌɑːtɪkl]	The ~ is '**the**'. The indefinite article is '**a**' or '**an**'.	bestimmter Artikel
6	to **limit** ['lɪmɪt]		begrenzen, limitieren

Technology words

assembly line	*Fließband*	**hotline**	*Hotline, „heißer Draht"*
camera	*Fotoapparat, Kamera*	**instructions**	*Betriebsanleitung, Anweisungen*
camcorder	*Videokamera*	**to input**	*eingeben*
cassette	*Kassette*	**to install**	*installieren*
CD	*CD*	**modern**	*modern*
CD player	*CD-Spieler*	**operation**	*Bedienung*
communication	*Kommunikation, Verständigung, Informationsaustausch*	**P.A. System**	*Lautsprecheranlage*
to communicate	*kommunizieren, sich verständigen, Informationen austauschen*	**program**	*Sendung, Programm*
computer	*Computer*	**to record**	*aufnehmen*
engineer	*Ingenieur/in*	**recording**	*Aufnahme*
error	*Fehler*	**software**	*Software*
fax	*Telefax*	**technology**	*Technologie*
fridge	*Kühlschrank*	**teletext**	*Videotext*
headphones	*Kopfhörer*	**TV**	*Fernsehen*
		to type	*tippen*
		video	*Video*

Step C **A future world**

Vocabulary

Autogram ['ɔːtəgræm]		*Bezeichnung für eine lebensgroße Spielzeugfigur*
life-sized [ˌlaɪf'saɪzd]	The artist did a ~ painting of me.	lebensgroß
image ['ɪmɪdʒ]		Bild, Figur
to **respond** [rɪ'spɒnd]	*to respond* = to answer	antworten, reagieren auf
°**housing unit** ['haʊzɪŋ‿juːnɪt]	*housing unit*: apartment, house, …	Wohneinheit
Factcenter ['fæktˌsentə]		*Name eines Kommunikationsgeräts*
walkway ['wɔːkweɪ]		Fußweg
Captain Courage [ˌkæptɪn 'kʌrɪdʒ]		*Personenname*
captain ['kæptɪn]		Hauptmann; Kapitän
Beowulf ['beɪəʊwʊlf]		*Personenname*
Lance [lɑːns]		*Personenname*
Arty ['ɑːtɪ]		*Personenname*
Hydro [ˌhaɪdrə]		*Abk.*: Hydrophonic facilities
°**control module** [kən'trəʊl ˌmɒdjuːl]	You will find all the new words from this text in the Alphabetical word list; here are the most important ones.	Fernsteuerung
soldier ['səʊldʒə]		Soldat/in
°**Commando** [kə'mɑːndəʊ]		Mitglied einer Kommandotruppe
What's it meant to do? [ment tʊ]		Was soll er/sie/es eigentlich tun/machen?
personalized ['pɜːsnəlaɪzd]	My pen is ~. It has got my name on it.	auf eine bestimmte Person bezogen
silence ['saɪləns]		Ruhe, Stille
°to **blow s.o. away** [bləʊ ə'weɪ]		*hier:* jdn. abknallen
°**Who's a pretty boy, then?**	You can say this to a pet bird.	*etwa:* Ach, bist du niedlich!
to **program** ['prəʊgræm]	The engineer *programmed* the computer.	programmieren
to **be stuck** [bɪ 'stʌk]		*hier:* klemmen
to **be stuck with** [bɪ 'stʌk wɪð]		etw. am Hals haben
to **come along** [kʌm ə'lɒŋ]		*hier:* gedeihen
shout [ʃaʊt]	to shout → *shout*	Schrei
out of action [aʊt‿əv 'ækʃn]	The computer doesn't work. It's ~.	außer Betrieb
to **lose s.o.** [luːz]		*hier:* jdn. abhängen
wool [wʊl]		Wolle
to **knit** [nɪt]		stricken
harmless ['hɑːmles]	The dog won't hurt you, she's ~.	harmlos
to **go ahead** [ə'hed]		vorangehen
height [haɪt]		Höhe

⟨6⟩ space oddity [speɪs 'ɒdɪtɪ]	*etwa:* seltsamer Zwischenfall im Weltall	ignition [ɪg'nɪʃn]	Zündung
ground control ['graʊnd kən'trəʊl]	Bodenstation	You've really made the grade. [juːv 'rɪəlɪ meɪd ðə 'greɪd]	Du hast es wirklich geschafft.
Major Tom [meɪdʒə 'tɒm]	*Personenname*	capsule ['kæpsjuːl]	Kapsel
protein ['prəʊtiːn]	Eiweiß	to dare [deə]	wagen
pill [pɪl]	Pille, Tablette	to float [fləʊt]	treiben, schweben
to commence [kə'mens]	anfangen	peculiar [pɪ'kjuːljə]	eigenartig, komisch

tin can [tɪn 'kæn]	Blechdose	spaceship ['speɪsʃɪp]	Raumschiff
planet ['plænɪt]	Planet	circuit ['sɜːkɪt]	Stromkreis, Leitung

Step D **Let's check**

2 **motel** [məʊ'tel] — Motel
low rate [ləʊ 'reɪt] — *hier:* günstig
Gala apples ['gɑːlə] — *Äpfelname*

American English – British English

Different spelling

AE	BE
color	colour
favorite	favourite
meter	metre
mom	mum
Mr./Mrs./Ms.	Mr/Mrs/Ms
neighbor	neighbour
to practice	to practise
program	programme
traveled	travelled

Different words

AE	BE	AE	BE
apartment	*flat*	**pants**	*trousers*
at the movies	*at the cinema*	**period**	*lesson*
backyard	*back garden*	**phone booth**	*telephone box*
candy	*sweets*	**principal**	*headteacher*
cookie	*biscuit*	**schedule**	*timetable*
elevator	*lift*	**store**	*shop*
garbage	*rubbish*	**student**	*pupil*
to get in line	*to queue*	**subway**	*underground*
grade	*mark, form, class*	**trail**	*path*
		truck	*lorry*
Math	*Maths*	**vacation**	*holiday*
movie	*film*	**wallet**	*purse*

Alphabetical word list

In dieser alphabetischen Liste ist das gesamte Vokabular von *Red Line New 1* bis *4* enthalten. Namen werden in einer gesonderten Liste nach dem Vokabular aufgeführt.

Der Wortschatz aus Übungen und Texten, die in Spitzklammern ⟨ ⟩ stehen, ist wahlfrei.
Der Wortschatz in rechteckigen Klammern [ ] kommt in Texten bzw. Übungen vor, die nicht für alle Bundesländer verbindlich sind.
Die mit einem ° gekennzeichneten Wörter zeichnen den rezeptiven Wortschatz aus. In Bundesländern, in denen nicht ausdrücklich rezeptiver Wortschatz verlangt wird, werden diese Wörter genauso behandelt wie der übrige Wortschatz. Die rezeptiv gekennzeichneten Wörter können innerhalb der *Unit*, in der sie erstmalig vorkommen, eigenständig von den Schülerinnen und Schülern angewandt werden. Falls sie in späteren *Units* auftauchen, werden sie nur mit Hilfe von Vorgaben verlangt.
Das Zeichen * nach einem Verb bedeutet: unregelmäßiges Verb.

Die Zahlen verweisen auf das erstmalige Vorkommen der Wörter, z. B.
about [ə'baʊt] über **I** = Red Line New Band 1
actor ['æktə] Schauspieler **IV 4**, 54 = Red Line New Band 4, Unit 4, Seite 54

A

'A' level ['eɪ ˌlevl] Abschlussprüfung (*entspricht in etwa dem Abitur*) **III**
a [ə] ein/eine **I**
a deal for s.th. [di:l] ein Angebot für etw. **IV 4**, 58
a hundred years ago [ə 'hʌndrəd jɪəz ə'gəʊ] vor hundert Jahren **II**
° **abbreviation** [əˌbri:vɪ'eɪʃn] Abkürzung **IV WSA**, 17
to be **able to** [bɪ 'eɪbl tə] können **III**
about [ə'baʊt] über **I**; ungefähr **III**
to talk about ['tɔ:k‿ə'baʊt] reden über, sprechen über **I**
What about ...? [wɒt‿ə'baʊt] Was ist mit ...? **I**
above [ə'bʌv] über **II**
accent ['æksent] Akzent **III**
accident ['æksɪdənt] Unfall **I**
according to [ə'kɔ:dɪŋ tʊ] nach, laut, gemäß **IV WSC**, 50
to **accuse s.o. of s.th.** [ə'kju:z] jdn. beschuldigen/anklagen, etw. getan zu haben **IV WSB**, 35
across [ə'krɒs] über **III**
to **act** [ækt] spielen, nachspielen **I**
to act normal [ˌækt 'nɔ:ml] sich normal benehmen **III**
action ['ækʃn] Handlung, Geschehen **II**
out of action [aʊt‿əv 'ækʃn] außer Betrieb **IV 5**, 75
activity [æk'tɪvɪtɪ] Tätigkeit **I**
actor ['æktə] Schauspieler **IV 4**, 54
to **adapt** [ə'dæpt] adaptieren, anpassen **III**
to **add** [æd] addieren, hinzufügen **II**
address [ə'dres] Adresse, Anschrift **III**
adjective ['ædʒɪktɪv] Adjektiv **II**
⟨Adscan⟩ ['ædskæn] *eine Art Katalog für Teleshopping* **IV 5**, 74
adult ['ædʌlt] Erwachsene/r **II**
advantage [əd'vɑ:ntɪdʒ] Vorteil **IV 5**, 71
adventure [əd'ventʃə] Abenteuer **II**
⟨adventurer⟩ [əd'ventʃərə] Abenteurer/in **IV WSC**, 50
adverb ['ædvɜ:b] Adverb **III**
⟨to advertise⟩ ['ædvətaɪz] werben **IV 2**, 28
advertisement (= **ad**) [əd'vɜtɪsment] Anzeige, Werbung **II**
advice [əd'vaɪs] Rat(schlag) **IV WSB**, 33
African ['æfrɪkən] afrikanisch, Afrikaner/in **III**
° African-American [ˌæfrɪkən‿ə'merɪkən] afroamerikanisch, Afroamerikaner/in **IV 2**, 25
after ['ɑ:ftə] nach **I**
after all [ɑ:ftər‿'ɔ:l] doch, doch noch **IV 2**, 27
afternoon [ɑ:ftə'nu:n] Nachmittag **I**
Good afternoon. [gʊd ɑ:ftə'nu:n] Guten Tag. (*Anrede am Nachmittag*) **I**
in the afternoon [ɪn ðiː‿ɑ:ftə'nu:n] nachmittags, am Nachmittag **I**
this afternoon [ðɪs‿ɑ:ftə'nu:n] heute Nachmittag **I**
again [ə'gen] wieder, noch einmal **I**
again and again [əˌgen‿ənd‿ə'gen] immer wieder **III**
against [ə'genst] gegen **III**
aged [eɪdʒd] im Alter von, ... Jahre alt **IV WSD**, 65
agency ['eɪdʒənsɪ] Agentur **IV 4**, 54
for **ages** [fɔ: 'eɪdʒɪz] seit langem, schon ewig **IV 1**, 10
⟨aggressive⟩ [ə'gresɪv] aggressiv **IV 3**, 43
ago [ə'gəʊ] vor (*nachgestellt*) **II**
to **agree** [ə'gri:] übereinstimmen **IV 1**, 12
to go **ahead** [ə'hed] vorangehen **IV 5**, 75
air [eə] Luft **III**
air stream travel ['eə stri:m ˌtrævl] „Luftstromtransport" **III**
airhead ['eəhed] „Spinner", dumme Person **III**
airport ['eəpɔ:t] Flughafen **I**
alarm [ə'lɑ:m] Alarm **IV 2**, 23
all [ɔ:l] alle/alles **I**; ganz **I**
All in a day's work. ['ɔ:l ɪn‿ə 'deɪz wɜ:k] *etwa:* Das gehört zu meiner täglichen Arbeit. **IV 4**, 60
all over ['ɔ:l‿ˌəʊvə] überall auf **I**
all right (= alright) ['ɒl 'raɪt] in Ordnung **II**
all the time [ɔ:l θə‿'taɪm] die ganze Zeit **IV 2**, 25
alligator ['ælɪgeɪtə] Alligator **IV 3**, 36
to be **allowed to** [bɪ ə'laʊd tə] dürfen **III**
almost ['ɔ:lməʊst] fast, beinahe **II**
alone [ə'ləʊn] allein **II**
to leave s.o. alone [li:v ə pɜ:sn ə'ləʊn] jdn. in Ruhe lassen **II**
along [ə'lɒŋ] entlang **III**
alphabet ['ælfəbɪt] Alphabet **I**
alphabetical order [ˌælfə'betɪkl 'ɔ:də] alphabetische Reihenfolge **II**
already [ɔ:l'redɪ] schon **II**
also ['ɔ:lsəʊ] außerdem **II**
although [ɔ:l'ðəʊ] obwohl **III**
always ['ɔ:lweɪz] immer **I**
am [ˌeɪ 'em] 0.00–12.00 Uhr **III**
ambulance ['æmbjʊləns] Krankenwagen **I**
American [ə'merɪkən] amerikanisch, Amerikaner/in **II**
° Native American ['neɪtɪv ə'merɪkən] indianisch, *amer. Ureinwohner/in* **IV 2**, 20
an [ən] ein/eine **I**
and [ænd] und **I**
angel ['eɪnʒəl] Engel **III**

angry ['æŋgrɪ] böse, verärgert **I**
animal ['ænɪml] Tier **I**
announcement [ə'naʊnsmənt] Durchsage, Ansage, Ankündigung, Bekanntmachung **IV WSB**, 34
annoyed [ə'nɔɪd] verärgert **III**
anorak ['ænəræk] Anorak **I**
another [ə'nʌðə] noch einen/eine/eins **I**
answer ['ɑ:nsə] Antwort **I**
to **answer** ['ɑ:nsə] (be)antworten **I**
answering machine ['ɑ:nsərɪŋ mə'ʃi:n] Anrufbeantworter **III**
⟨ant⟩ [ænt] Ameise **IV 3**, 44
any ['enɪ] (irgend)welche **II**
anybody ['enɪbədɪ] (irgend)jemand **II**
not ... **any more** [nɒt 'enɪˌmɔ:] nicht mehr **IV 2**, 24
anyone ['enɪwʌn] (irgend)jemand **II**
anything ['enɪθɪŋ] (irgend)etwas **II**
Anything else? ['enɪθɪŋ 'els] Sonst noch etwas? **I**
anyway ['enɪweɪ] sowieso; jedenfalls **III**
anywhere ['enɪweə] irgendwo **II**
Apache [ə'pætʃɪ] *Indianerstamm* **IV WSC**, 49
apartment (*AE*) [ə'pɑ:tmənt] Wohnung **IV 2**, 26
to **appear** [ə'pɪə] erscheinen **III**
appendix [ə'pendɪks] Blinddarm **II**
apple ['æpl] Apfel **I**
apple pie [ˌæpl 'paɪ] gedeckter Apfelkuchen **IV 1**, 11
application form [ˌæplɪ'keɪʃn 'fɔ:m] Anmeldeformular; Bewerbungsformular **IV WSD**, 65
April ['eɪprəl] April **I**
⟨are longing to stray⟩ [ɑ: 'lɒŋɪŋ tʊ streɪ] sich danach sehnen herumzustreunen **IV 4**, 59
area ['eərɪə] Gebiet, Region, Fläche **III**
to have an **argument** [ˌhæv‿ən 'ɑ:gjʊmənt] einen Streit, eine Auseinandersetzung haben **II**
arm [ɑ:m] Arm **I**
armour ['ɑ:mə] Rüstung **III**
army ['ɑ:mɪ] Armee **IV WSC**, 51
around [ə'raʊnd] um, herum **II**
arrival [ə'raɪvl] Ankunft **IV 3**, 42
to **arrive** [ə'raɪv] ankommen **I**
arrow ['ærəʊ] Pfeil **II**
Art [ɑ:t] Kunst **II**
work of art [wɜ:k‿əv 'ɑ:t] Kunstwerk **IV 4**, 58
article ['ɑ:tɪkl] Artikel, Bericht **III**
definite article ['defɪnət ˌɑ:tɪkl] bestimmter Artikel **IV 5**, 73
indefinite article [ɪn'defɪnət ˌɑ:tɪkl] unbestimmter Artikel **IV 5**, 72
artist ['ɑ:tɪst] Künstler/in **IV 4**, 54
as [æz] als **II**; wie **II**; da, während **IV WSD**, 66
(not) as ... as [æz ... æz] (nicht) so ... wie **II**
as if ... [ˌæz‿'ɪf] als ob ... **IV 2**, 23
as soon as possible [əz‿su:n‿əz 'pɒsəbl] so bald wie möglich **IV WSD**, 65
as though [æz 'ðəʊ] als ob **IV WSC**, 52
°**Asian** ['eɪʃn] asiatisch, Asiate/Asiatin **IV 2**, 26
to **ask** [ɑ:sk] fragen **I**
to ask for ['ɑ:sk fɔ:] bitten um **I**
to ask s.o. for a date [deɪt] jdn. nach einer Verabredung fragen **IV WSB**, 33
assembly [ə'semblɪ] Versammlung **I**
Assembly Hall [ə'semblɪ hɔ:l] Aula **II**
assembly line [ə'semblɪ ˌlaɪn] Fließband **III**
assistant [ə'sɪstənt] Helfer/in, Assistent/in **I**
at [æt, ət] an **I**
at all [ət‿'ɔ:l] überhaupt **III**
at home [ət 'həʊm] zu Hause **I**
at least [ət 'li:st] wenigstens, mindestens **II**
at once [ˌət 'wʌns] sofort **II**
at the bottom of [ət ðə 'bɒtəm‿əv] unten, am unteren Ende **I**
at the moment [æt ðə‿'məʊmənt] zur Zeit **IV WSA**, 17
at the movies (*AE*) [ˌæt‿ðə 'mu:vɪz] im Kino **IV WSA**, 16
at the same time [ət ðə ˌseɪm 'taɪm] gleichzeitig **III**
at the top of [ət ðə 'tɒp‿əv] ganz oben **I**
at this time [ət 'ðɪs taɪm] um diese Zeit **II**
at ... o'clock [ət ... ə'klɒk] um ... Uhr **I**
athletics [æθ'letɪks] Leichtathletik **III**
Atishoo! [ə'tɪʃu:] Hatschi! **III**
atmosphere ['ætməˌsfɪə] Atmosphäre, Stimmung **IV 4**, 54
to **attack** [ə'tæk] angreifen **IV 3**, 42
attraction [ətrækʃn] Attraktion **III**
August ['ɔ:gəst] August **I**
aunt [ɑ:nt] Tante **I**
Aunty ['ɑ:ntɪ] *Anrede für eine Tante* **I**
Australian [ɒ'streɪljən] australisch, Australier/in **III**
author ['ɔ:θə] Autor/in **IV WSC**, 53
Autogram ['ɔ:'təgræm] *Bezeichnung für eine lebensgroße Spielzeugfigur* **IV 5**, 74
autumn ['ɔ:təm] Herbst **I**
[auxiliary] [ɔ:g'zɪljərɪ] Hilfs-; Hilfsverb **IV 3**, 41
available [ə'veɪləbl] vorrätig, verfügbar, erhältlich **IV WSA**, 19
avenue ['ævənju:] Straße, Allee **IV 4**, 56
to **avoid** [ə'vɔɪd] vermeiden **III**
away [ə'weɪ] weg **II**
awful ['ɔ:fʊl] schrecklich **III**

B

baby ['beɪbɪ] Baby **III**
°**babysitter** ['beɪbɪˌsɪtə] Kinderbetreuer/in, Babysitter/in **IV WSB**, 35
babysitting ['beɪbɪˌsɪtɪŋ] Babysitten **II**
⟨back⟩ [bæk] Rücken **IV 4**, 62
back [bæk] zurück **I**
back door ['bæk 'dɔ:] Hintertür **I**
backpack ['bækpæk] Rucksack **IV 3**, 42
backpacking ['bækˌpækɪŋ] Bergtouren machen, Bergwandern; mit dem Rucksack reisen **IV WSA**, 19
backstage ['bæksteɪdʒ] hinter der Bühne **II**
backyard (*AE*) [ˌbæk'jɑ:d] Garten (*hinter dem Haus*) **IV 1**, 7
bad [bæd] schlimm, schlecht **I**
badminton ['bædmɪntən] Federballspiel **I**
bag [bæg] Tasche **I**
°**bagel** ['beɪgl] *jüdisches Gebäck* **IV 4**, 57
bagpipes (*pl*) ['bægpaɪps] Dudelsack **II**
ball [bɔ:l] Ball **I**
balloon [bə'lu:n] Luftballon **I**
banana [bə'nɑ:nə] Banane **I**
band [bænd] Gruppe, (Musik-)Kapelle **III**; [Kapelle, Musikgruppe] **II**
bank [bæŋk] Bank **I**
bank clerk ['bæŋk‿klɑ:k] Bankangestellte/r **I**
bar [bɑ:] Tafel **I**
barbecue ['bɑ:bɪkju:] Grill, Grillfest, Barbecue **IV 1**, 7
to **barbecue** ['bɑ:bɪkju:] grillen **IV 2**, 23
⟨Barbie doll⟩ ['bɑ:bɪ dɒl] Barbie-Puppe **IV 2**, 28
⟨bare necessity⟩ [beə nɪ'sesətɪ] das Notwendigste **IV 3**, 44
to **bark** [bɑ:k] bellen **I**
baseball ['beɪsbɔ:l] Baseball **IV 2**, 29

basic ['beɪsɪk] Grund- **IV 5**, 71
basics ['beɪsɪks] Grundlagen **IV WSD**, 65
basketball ['bɑ:skɪtbɔ:l] Basketball **IV 1**, 11
bat [bæt] Schläger **III**
bath [bɑ:θ] Bad, Badewanne **I**
to have a bath [hæv‿ə 'bɑ:θ] baden **I**
bathroom ['bɑ:θrʊm] Badezimmer **I**
battle ['bætl] Schlacht, Kampf **III**
to **be*** [bɪ] sein **I**
Be careful! [bɪ 'keəfʊl] Pass auf!, Vorsicht! **I**
to be able to [bɪ 'eɪbl tə] können **III**
to be allowed to [bɪ ə'laʊd tə] dürfen **III**
to be called [bɪ 'kɔ:ld] genannt werden **II**
to be good at [bɪ 'gʊd‿ət] gut sein in ... **I**
to be in a hurry [bɪ ɪn‿ə'hʌrɪ] in Eile sein **III**
to be lucky [bɪ 'lʌkɪ] Glück haben **I**
to be on [bɪ‿'ɒn] eingeschaltet sein **I**
to be over at ... [bi:‿'əʊvər‿æt] bei ... sein **IV WSA**, 16
to be proud of [bɪ 'praʊd‿əv] stolz sein auf **II**
to be shocked [ʃɒkt] schockiert sein **IV 1**, 13
to be sick [bɪ 'sɪk] sich übergeben **IV 2**, 23
to be sorry about s.th. [bɪ 'sɒrɪ əbaʊt] Leid tun, dass ..., Leid tun wegen **II**
to be sorry for s.o. [bɪ 'sɒrɪ fə] Mitleid haben mit jdm. **II**
to be stuck [bɪ 'stʌk] klemmen **IV 5**, 75
to be stuck with [bɪ 'stʌk wɪð] etw. am Hals haben **IV 5**, 75
to be tired of s.th. [bɪ 'taɪəd‿əv] von etw. genug haben **IV 2**, 25
to be trapped [bɪ 'træpt] in der Falle sein, abgeschnitten sein **III**
to be unlucky [bɪ ʌn'lʌkɪ] Pech haben **III**
beach [bi:tʃ] Strand **I**
bean [bi:n] Bohne **II**
bear [beə] Bär **II**
beard [bɪəd] Bart **II**
beat [bi:t] Rhythmus **III**
to **beat*** [bi:t] schlagen **IV WSC**, 49
beautiful ['bju:təfʊl] schön **II**
because [bɪ'kɒz] weil **I**
because of [bɪ'kɒz‿əv] wegen **IV WSC**, 50
to **become*** [bɪ'kʌm] werden **III**
bed [bed] Bett **I**
bed and breakfast [bed‿ən 'brekfəst] Übernachtung mit Frühstück **II**
⟨bedpost⟩ ['bedpəʊst] Bettpfosten **IV WSC**, 52
bedroom ['bedrʊm] Schlafzimmer **I**
⟨bee⟩ [bi:] Biene **IV 3**, 44
beef [bi:f] Rindfleisch **II**
beetle ['bi:tl] Käfer **I**
before [bɪ'fɔ:] vorher, vor **II**
to **begin*** [bɪ'gɪn] anfangen, beginnen **II**
behind [bɪ'haɪnd] hinter **I**
from behind [frɒm bɪ'haɪnd] von hinten **II**
Belgian ['beldʒən] belgisch, Belgier/in **III**
to **believe** [bɪ'li:v] glauben **III**
bell [bel] Glocke, Klingel **III**
to **belong** (to) [bɪ'lɒŋ tʊ] dazu gehören, gehören (zu) **IV 1**, 15
below [bɪ'ləʊ] unten **III**
bench [bentʃ] (Park-)Bank **III**
to **bend*** [bend] biegen, beugen **II**; verbiegen **IV 4**, 60
beside [bɪ'saɪd] neben **IV WSC**, 49
best [best] beste/bester/bestes **I**
better ['betə] besser **I**
I hope you're better soon. [aɪ 'həʊp jʊə ˌbetə 'su:n] Ich hoffe, es geht dir bald besser. **I**
to do better [ˌdu: 'betə] besser sein **III**

between [bɪ'twi:n] zwischen **II**
⟨to beware⟩ [bɪ'weə] aufpassen **IV 3**, 44
bicycle ['baɪsɪkl] Fahrrad **IV 4**, 62
big [bɪg] groß **I**
bigger ['bɪgə] größer **II**
bike [baɪk] Fahrrad **I**
bill [bɪl] Rechnung **IV 5**, 72
telephone bill ['telɪfəʊn ˌbɪl] Telefonrechnung **IV 5**, 72
°**billboard** ['bɪlbɔ:d] Reklametafel **IV 4**, 54
bin [bɪn] Mülleimer **IV 3**, 39
Biology [baɪ'ɒlədʒɪ] Biologie **II**
bird [bɜ:d] Vogel **II**
bird watcher ['bɜ:dˌwɒtʃə] Vogelbeobachter/in **II**
biro ['baɪrəʊ] Kugelschreiber **I**
birthday ['bɜ:θdeɪ] Geburtstag **I**
biscuit ['bɪskɪt] Keks **I**
bit [bɪt] Teil, Stück **III**
a bit [a'bɪt] etwas, ein bisschen **I**
black [blæk] schwarz **I**
⟨to blame s.o.⟩ [bleɪm] jdm. die Schuld geben, jdn. beschuldigen **IV 3**, 43
she didn't blame him [ʃi: dɪdnt 'bleɪm hɪm] sie konnte ihn gut verstehen **IV WSC**, 52
Bless you! ['bles‿ju:] Gesundheit! **III**
blind [blaɪnd] blind **IV 2**, 26
blood [blʌd] Blut **III**
°to **blow s.o. away** [bləʊ ə'weɪ] jdn. abknallen **IV 5**, 75
blue [blu:] blau **I**
boarding school ['bɔ:dɪŋsku:l] Internat **III**
boat [bəʊt] Boot **I**
boating lake ['bəʊtɪŋ leɪk] Bootsteich **I**
body ['bɒdɪ] Körper **I**
book [bʊk] Buch **I**
to **book** [bʊk] buchen, reservieren **III**
bookshelf ['bʊkʃelf] Bücherregal **III**
bookshop ['bʊkʃɒp] Buchhandlung **I**
to get **bored** [bɔ:d] Langeweile haben/bekommen **IV 2**, 23
boring ['bɔ:rɪŋ] langweilig **I**
she was **born** [ˌʃi: wɒz 'bɔ:n] sie ist geboren **III**
°**borough** ['bʌrə] Bezirk **IV 4**, 54
to **borrow** ['bɒrəʊ] borgen, leihen **III**
both [bəʊθ] beide **II**
bottle ['bɒtl] Flasche **I**
at the **bottom of** [ət ðə 'bɒtəm‿əv] unten, am unteren Ende **II**
bow [bəʊ] Bogen **II**
to **bowl** [bəʊl] kegeln, bowlen **IV 1**, 13
bowling alley ['bəʊlɪŋ ˌælɪ] Kegelbahn, Bowlingbahn **IV 1**, 9
box [bɒks] Schachtel, Kiste, Dose **I**
lunch box ['lʌntʃ bɒks] *Dose für belegte Brote zum Mittagessen* **I**
boy [bɔɪ] Junge **I**
boyfriend ['bɔɪfrend] Freund **III**
brainstorming ['breɪnstɔ:mɪŋ] Ideensammeln **III**
to **brake** [breɪk] bremsen **IV 4**, 60
⟨brand new⟩ ['brænd nju:] brandneu **IV 4**, 59
brave [breɪv] mutig, tapfer **III**
bread [bred] Brot **I**; ⟨Geld⟩ **IV 1**, 14
break [breɪk] Pause **II**
to **break over** [breɪk 'əʊvə] hereinbrechen **III**
breakfast ['brekfəst] Frühstück **I**
bridge [brɪdʒ] Brücke **III**
bright [braɪt] hell, leuchtend; klug **IV WSB**, 35
⟨brim⟩ [brɪm] Kante, Rand **IV 2**, 24
[bring-and-buy sale] [brɪŋ‿ənd 'baɪ seɪl] Wohltätigkeitsbazar **II**

to **bring*** [brɪŋ] bringen **I**; mitbringen **I**
[to bring down (trees)] [brɪŋ daʊn] abknicken, ausreißen **IV 3**, 41
British ['brɪtɪʃ] britisch **I**
Britons ['brɪtnz] Briten, *(Ur-)Einwohner von Großbritannien* **III**
⟨to broadcast⟩ ['brɔːdkɑːst] senden **IV 5**, 71
brochure ['brəʊʃə] Broschüre, Prospekt **III**
broken ['brəʊkən] kaputt, zerbrochen **I**
brother ['brʌðə] Bruder **I**
brown [braʊn] braun **I**
bubble bath ['bʌbl ˌbɑːθ] Schaumbad **I**
bucket ['bʌkɪt] Eimer **I**
budgie ['bʌdʒɪ] Wellensittich **II**
buffalo ['bʌfələʊ] Büffel, Bison **IV WSC**, 49
⟨to bug⟩ [bʌg] nerven **IV 1**, 14
to **build*** [bɪld] bauen **III**
building [bɪldɪŋ] Gebäude **IV 2**, 26
⟨to take no bull (AE)⟩ [bʊl] *etwa:* sich nicht für dumm verkaufen lassen **IV 2**, 28
bully ['bʊlɪ] Rabauke, Rüpel, Tyrann **II**
to **bump into s.o./s.th.** [bʌmp] gegen jdn./etw. stoßen, mit jdm. zusammenstoßen **IV 1**, 13
bungee-jumping ['bʌndʒɪ ˌdʒʌmpɪŋ] „Bungee"-Springen *(an einem Gummiseil aus großer Höhe springen)* **III**
burglar ['bɜːglə] Einbrecher/in **I**
to **burn*** [bɜːn] (an)brennen, verbrennen **IV 1**, 10
°**burrito** [bə'riːtəʊ] *mexikanisches Gericht (gefüllte Pfannkuchen)* **IV 4**, 57
bus [bʌs] Bus **I**
bus shelter ['bʌs ˌʃeltə] überdachte Bushaltestelle **III**
bus stop ['bʌs stɒp] Bushaltestelle **I**
bush [bʊʃ] Busch **IV 1**, 12
business ['bɪznɪs] Geschäft **IV 2**, 21
busy ['bɪzɪ] beschäftigt **I**
but [bʌt] aber **I**
⟨but no one⟩ [bʌt 'nəʊ‿wʌn] aber auch gar niemand **IV 4**, 63
butter ['bʌtə] Butter **I**
button [bʌtn] Knopf **IV 4**, 60
to **buy*** [baɪ] kaufen **I**
⟨to buzz⟩ [bʌz] brummen **IV 3**, 44
by [baɪ] mit **I**; von, vom *(in Passivsätzen)*; bis **IV 3**, 40
⟨by the 1830s⟩ [baɪ ðə 'eɪtiːn 'θɜːtɪz] um die 1830er-Jahre **IV WSC**, 50
⟨by the fire⟩ [baɪ ðə 'faɪə] am Feuer **IV WSC**, 52
Bye! [baɪ] Tschüs! *(kurze gesprochene Form von* Goodbye) **I**
bye-bye [baɪ 'baɪ] auf Wiedersehen **IV 1**, 8

C

cab [kæb] Taxi **IV 4**, 54
cabbage ['kæbɪdʒ] Kohl **II**
cabin ['kæbɪn] Blockhaus **IV WSC**, 49
⟨cable TV⟩ [ˌkeɪbl tiː'viː] Kabelfernsehen **IV 2**, 28
café ['kæfeɪ] Café **IV 4**, 54
cafeteria [ˌkæfɪ'tɪərɪə] Cafeteria **III**
cage [keɪdʒ] Käfig **II**
cake [keɪk] Kuchen, Torte **I**
calendar ['kælɪndə] Kalender **I**
call [kɔːl] Anruf **III**
to **call** [kɔːl] rufen, anrufen **I**; nennen **III**
to be called [bɪ 'kɔːld] genannt werden **II**
calm [kɑːm] ruhig **III**
camcorder ['kæmkɒːdə] Videokamera **II**
camera ['kæmərə] Fotoapparat, Kamera **I**
camp [kæmp] Lager **IV WSC**, 52
to go to camp [gəʊ tə 'kæmp] ins Ferienlager fahren **IV WSD**, 64
to **camp** [kæmp] zelten, kampieren **IV WSC**, 50
campground *(AE)* ['kæmpgraʊnd] Campingplatz **IV 3**, 42
campus ['kæmpəs] Campus, Schul-, Universitätsgelände **IV WSB**, 34
can [kæn] Dose **IV 3**, 39
can [kæn] können **I**
cancellation [ˌkænsə'leɪʃn] Stornierung, Absage **III**
candle ['kændl] Kerze **I**
candy *(AE)* *(sg + pl)* ['kændɪ] Süßigkeit, Süßigkeiten **IV WSD**, 66
canoe [kə'nuː] Kanu **IV 1**, 15
canyon ['kænjən] Schlucht, Cañon **IV 3**, 36
capital ['kæpɪtl] Hauptstadt **III**
⟨capsule⟩ ['kæpsjuːl] Kapsel **IV 5**, 76
captain ['kæptɪn] Hauptmann; Kapitän **IV 5**, 74
car [kɑː] Auto **I**
car park ['kɑː ˌpɑːk] Parkplatz, -haus **II**
caravan ['kærəvæn] Wohnwagen **II**
card [kɑːd] Karte **I**
to take **care of s.th.** [teɪk 'keər‿ɒv ˌsʌmθɪŋ] etw. erledigen; nach etw. schauen; sich um etw. kümmern **IV WSB**, 35
careful ['keəfʊl] vorsichtig, sorgfältig **III**
Be careful! [bɪ 'keəfʊl] Pass auf!, Vorsicht! **I**
careless ['kɜəlɪs] nachlässig **III**; unvorsichtig **III**
carnival ['kɑːnɪvl] Karneval, Volksfest **III**
carrot ['kærət] Karotte, Möhre **II**
to **carry** ['kærɪ] tragen **III**
⟨cartoon⟩ [kɑː'tuːn] Cartoon **IV 4**, 63
case [keɪs] Etui, Hülle **I**
pencil case ['pensl keɪs] Federmäppchen **I**
cashier [kæ'ʃɪə] Kassierer/in **IV 2**, 23
cassette [kæ'set] Kassette **II**
castle ['kɑːsl] Burg **I**
cat [kæt] Katze **I**
to **catch*** [kætʃ] fangen **II**
to catch up with s.o. [ˌkætʃ‿'ʌp wɪð] jdn. einholen **III**
catchy ['kætʃɪ] eingängig **III**
cathedral [kə'θiːdrɪəl] Kathedrale **III**
cattle *(pl)* ['kætl] Rind(-vieh) **IV WSC**, 50
°cattle rancher ['kætl rɑːntʃə] Rancher/in, Viehzüchter/in **IV WSC**, 50
cave [keɪv] Höhle **II**
CD [siː 'diː] CD **I**
CD player [siː 'diː pleɪə] CD-Spieler **I**
⟨CD-ROM⟩ [siː diː 'rɒm] CD-ROM **IV 3**, 37
to **celebrate** ['selɪbreɪt] feiern **IV WSD**, 64
⟨cent (=c) (AE)⟩ [sent] Cent *(amer. Geldeinheit)* **IV 2**, 28
center *(AE)* ['sentə] Mitte, Zentrum **IV 3**, 41
central ['sentrl] in der Mitte, zentral, Zentral-, Mittel- **IV 4**, 54
centre ['sentə] Mitte, Zentrum **I**
century ['sentʃʊrɪ] Jahrhundert **III**
certainly ['sɜːtnlɪ] gewiss, bestimmt **III**
chair [tʃeə] Stuhl **I**
chance [tʃɑːns] Chance, Möglichkeit **III**
change [tʃeɪnʒ] Wechselgeld, Kleingeld **IV 2**, 23
to **change** [tʃeɪndʒ] (sich) (ver)ändern, wechseln **II**
to change onto [tʃeɪndʒ] umsteigen auf **III**
channel ['tʃænl] (Fernseh-)Kanal, Programm **III**

character ['kærəktə] Figur, Person **III**
[charity] ['tʃærətɪ] Wohltätigkeitsverein **II**
⟨chart⟩ [tʃɑ:t] Tabelle, Diagramm **IV 2**, 22
cheap [tʃi:p] billig **II**
to **cheat** [tʃi:t] schummeln **III**
to **check** [tʃek] überprüfen, kontrollieren **I**
to check in [ˌtʃek‿'ɪn] einchecken, anmelden **III**
checklist ['tʃeklɪst] Checkliste **III**
Cheer up! ['tʃɪər‿ʌp] Kopf hoch! **III**
cheerleader ['tʃɪəli:də] Cheerleader/in **IV WSB**, 32
cheese [tʃi:z] Käse **I**
chemist's ['kemɪsts] Apotheke **II**
chess [tʃes] Schach **IV WSB**, 32
chicken [tʃɪkɪn] Huhn **II**
°**chief** [tʃi:f] (Indianer-)Häuptling **IV 3**, 39
child [tʃaɪld] Kind **I**
children (*pl*) ['tʃɪldrən] Kinder **I**
Chinese [ˌtʃaɪ'ni:z] chinesisch, Chinesisch, Chinese/ Chinesin **II**
⟨chinos (sg + pl)⟩ [tʃi:nəʊz] leichte Baumwollhose **IV 2**, 28
chips (*pl*) [tʃɪps] Pommes frites **I**
chocolate ['tʃɒkələt] Schokolade **I**
choir ['kwaɪə] Chor **IV WSB**, 32
to **choose*** [tʃu:z] wählen, aussuchen **II**
°**chopstick** ['tʃɒpstɪk] (Ess-)Stäbchen **IV 2**, 25
°**chopsuey** [ˌtʃɒp'su:ɪ] *chinesisches Gericht* **IV 4**, 57
chorus ['kɔ:rəs] Refrain **II**
Christmas ['krɪsməs] Weihnachten **II**
church [tʃɜ:tʃ] Kirche **I**
cinema ['sɪnɪmə] Kino **I**
circle ['sɜ:kl] Kreis **IV WSC**, 50
⟨circuit⟩ ['sɜ:kɪt] Stromkreis, Leitung **IV 5**, 76
circus ['sɜ:kəs] Zirkus, Ring **III**
citizen ['sɪtɪzn] Bürger/in **IV 2**, 20
city ['sɪtɪ] (Groß-)Stadt **I**
civilized ['sɪvɪlaɪzd] zivilisiert **IV WSC**, 48
⟨to claim⟩ [kleɪm] beanspruchen; behaupten **IV WSC**, 50
to **clap** [klæp] klatschen **II**
[Clap'n' Rap] [ˌklæp‿n 'ræp] Klatschen und „Rappen" **II**
class [klɑ:s] Klasse (*in einer deutschen Schule*) **I**
classroom ['klɑ:srʊm] Klassenzimmer **I**
⟨claw⟩ [klɔ:] Kralle, Klaue **IV 3**, 44
to **clean** [kli:n] putzen **II**
to clean up [kli:n‿'ʌp] putzen, aufwischen, aufräumen **IV 1**, 11
clean [kli:n] sauber **II**
clear [klɪə] klar, deutlich **III**
clerk [klɑ:k] Büroangestellte/r **I**
bank clerk ['bæŋk‿klɑ:k] Bankangestellte/r **I**
clever ['klevə] intelligent, klug **I**
to **click on** ['klɪk‿ˌɒn] „anklicken", mit der Maus auswählen **III**
cliff [klɪf] Klippe, Fels **III**
climate ['klaɪmɪt] Klima **III**
to **climb** [klaɪm] klettern **III**
to climb up [ˌklaɪm 'ʌp] hochklettern, erklettern **I**
climbing ['klaɪmɪŋ] Bergsteigen, Klettern **II**
clock [klɒk] Uhr **II**
close (to) [kləʊs] nah (bei) **III**
⟨close⟩ [kləʊs] knapp **IV WSC**, 53
to **close** [kləʊz] schließen, zumachen **I**
closed [kləʊzd] geschlossen **III**
clothes (*pl*) ['kləʊðz] Kleider **I**
cloud [klaʊd] Wolke **IV 3**, 38
clown ['klaʊn] Clown **III**
club [klʌb] Klub, Verein **II**
clue [klu:] Hinweis **III**
coach [kəʊtʃ] Trainer/in **IV**, 3
coal [kəʊl] Kohle **III**
coast [kəʊst] Küste **III**
on the coast [ˌɒn ðə 'kəʊst] an der Küste **III**
coastguard ['kəʊstgɑ:d] Küstenwache **III**
coat [kəʊt] Mantel **II**
coconut ['kəʊkənʌt] Kokosnuss **II**
coconut shy ['kəʊkənʌt 'ʃaɪ] Wurfbude mit Kokosnüssen **II**
coffee ['kɒfɪ] Kaffee **II**
coke [kəʊk] Cola **IV 1**, 10
coke float [ˌkəʊk 'fləʊt] *amer. Getränk* **IV 1**, 10
cold [kəʊld] Erkältung **II**
cold [kəʊld] kalt **I**
collar ['kɒlə] Halsband **IV WSC**, 52
to **collect** [kə'lekt] (ein)sammeln **I**; abholen **I**
colony ['kɒlənɪ] Kolonie **IV 2**, 21
color (*AE*) ['kʌlə] Farbe **IV 2**, 26
colour ['kʌlə] Farbe **I**
colourful ['kʌləfʊl] bunt **III**
to **come*** [kʌm] kommen **I**
Come on! [kəm‿'ɒn] Komm schon!, Kommt schon! **I**
to come along [kʌm ə'lɒŋ] gedeihen **IV 5**, 75
to come home [kʌm 'həʊm] nach Hause kommen **I**
to come off [kʌm‿'ɒf] abgehen **II**
to come over to s.o. [ˌkʌm‿'əʊvə] auf jdn. zukommen **III**
to come round [kʌm 'raʊnd] vorbeikommen **III**
comic ['kɒmɪk] Comic **I**
comma ['kɒmə] Komma **III**
⟨to commence⟩ [kə'mens] anfangen **IV 5**, 76
comment ['kɒment] Bemerkung, Kommentar **III**
to **communicate** [kə'mju:nɪkeɪt] kommunizieren, Informationen austauschen, sich verständigen **IV 5**, 70
communication [kəˌmju:nɪ'keɪʃn] Kommunikation, Informationsaustausch, Verständigung **IV 5**, 70
⟨compact⟩ ['kɒmpækt] kompakt **IV WSA**, 19
company ['kʌmpənɪ] Firma, Unternehmen **IV WSA**, 19
to **compare** [kəm'peə] vergleichen **II**
comparison [kəm'pærɪsn] Vergleich **III**
to **compete in** [kəm'pi:t‿ɪn] teilnehmen an (*Wettbewerb*) **III**
competition [kɒmpə'tɪʃn] Wettbewerb, Preisausschreiben **I**
to **complete** [kəm'pli:t] vervollständigen, ausfüllen, durchmachen **III**
complete [kəm'pli:t] vollständig **III**
complicated ['kɒmplɪkeɪtɪd] kompliziert **III**
°**compound word** [kəm'paʊnd wɜ:d] zusammengesetztes Wort **IV WSA**, 17
comprehensive (school) [ˌkɒmprɪ'hensɪv ˌsku:l] Gesamtschule **III**
computer [kəm'pju:tə] Computer **I**
Computer Science [kəm'pju:tə 'saɪəns] Informatik **IV WSB**, 32
to **concentrate** (on) ['kɒnsəntreɪt‿ˌɒn] sich konzentrieren (auf) **III**
concert ['kɒnsət] Konzert **III**
condition [kən'dɪʃn] Bedingung, Umstand; Verhältnis **IV WSA**, 19
conference ['kɒnfərəns] Konferenz, Tagung **III**
confused [kən'fju:zd] durcheinander, verwirrt **IV WSB**, 35
to **connect** [kə'nekt] verbinden **III**
connecting [kə'nektɪŋ] verbindend **III**
to **conquer** ['kɒŋkə] erobern **III**

〈to contact〉 ['kɒntækt] aufsuchen, Kontakt aufnehmen **IV WSA**, 19
context ['kɒntekst] Kontext, Zusammenhang **III**
to **continue** [kən'tɪnjuː] weitermachen, fortfahren **IV 3**, 43
° **control module** [kən'trəʊl ˌmɒdjuːl] Fernsteuerung **IV 5**, 74
conversation [ˌkɒnvə'seɪʃn] Unterhaltung, Gespräch **IV WSB**, 32
to **cook** [kʊk] kochen **II**
cookie (*AE*) ['kʊkɪ] Keks **IV 2**, 26
cool [kuːl] toll, klasse, cool, super **IV 1**, 7
〈Cool it …〉 ['kuːl‿ɪt] Reg dich ab … **IV 3**, 44
to **copy** ['kɒpɪ] abschreiben, kopieren **III**
〈corn〉 [kɔːn] Mais **IV WSC**, 50
corner ['kɔːnə] Ecke **II**
cornflakes (*pl*) ['kɔːnfleɪks] Cornflakes **I**
〈corpse〉 [kɔːps] Leiche **IV WSD**, 67
to **correct** [kə'rekt] korrigieren, verbessern **I**
to **cost*** [kɒst] kosten **I**
costume ['kɒstjuːm] Kostüm **IV WSD**, 64
〈cotton〉 ['kɒtn] Baumwolle, Baumwoll- **IV WSA**, 19
to **count** [kaʊnt] zählen **I**
countdown ['kaʊntdaʊn] Countdown **IV 3**, 45
counter ['kaʊntə] Theke, Ladentisch **IV 1**, 13
country ['kʌntrɪ] Land **III**
in the country [ɪn ðə 'kʌntrɪ] auf dem Lande **III**
countryside ['kʌntrɪsaɪd] Landschaft **III**
courier ['kʊrɪə] Bote/Botin; Kurier **IV 4**, 54
course [kɔːs] Kurs, Lehrgang **III**
of course [əv‿'kɔːs] natürlich, selbstverständlich **I**
court [kɔːt] Hof **II**
cousin ['kʌzn] Cousin/e **I**
° **covered wagon** ['kʌvəd ˌwægən] Planwagen **IV WSC**, 48
cow [kaʊ] Kuh **I**
crab [kræb] Krebs **I**
crash [kræʃ] Unfall, Zusammenstoß; Absturz **IV 4**, 60
to **crash** [kræʃ] schlagen, krachen **III**
to crash into s.th. [kræʃ] in etw. hineinkrachen **IV 4**, 60
Crash! [kræʃ] Rums! **I**
crayon ['kreɪən] Buntstift **I**
crazy ['kreɪzɪ] verrückt **I**
cream [kriːm] Sahne **II**
〈to create〉 [kriː'eɪt] (er)schaffen, kreieren, erfinden **IV 2**, 28
creative [kriː'eɪtɪv] kreativ, schöpferisch **IV 4**, 58
cricket ['krɪkɪt] *englischer Rasensport* **I**
crime [kraɪm] Kriminalität; Verbrechen **IV 4**, 60
criminal ['krɪmɪnl] kriminell; Straftäter/in **IV 4**, 58
crisps (*pl*) [krɪsps] Kartoffelchips **I**
〈to cross〉 [krɒs] überqueren **IV WSC**, 48
crowd [kraʊd] Menschenmenge **II**
crowded ['kraʊdɪd] voll mit Leuten, überfüllt **IV WSC**, 50
to **cry** [kraɪ] weinen **II**
cup [kʌp] Tasse **II**; Pokal, Kelch **III**
cupboard ['kʌbəd] Schrank **I**
curry ['kʌrɪ] Curry (*indisches Gericht*) **II**
customer ['kʌstəmə] Kunde/Kundin **IV 4**, 60
to **cut*** [kʌt] schneiden **II**
to cut out [ˌkʌt‿'aʊt] ausschneiden **III**
to **cycle** ['saɪkl] Rad fahren **III**
cycling ['saɪklɪŋ] Fahrradfahren **II**
cyclist ['saɪklɪst] Radfahrer/in **III**
〈Czech〉 [tʃek] tschechisch, Tschechisch, Tscheche/Tschechin **IV 2**, 24

D

Dad [dæd] Vati, Papa **I**
to do **damage** ['dæmɪdʒ] Schaden anrichten **IV 3**, 39
to **damage** ['dæmɪdʒ] beschädigen **IV 3**, 39
damn [dæm] verdammt **IV 2**, 27
° Damn idiot! [dæm‿'ɪdɪət] Verdammter Idiot! **IV 4**, 60
° Damn you! ['dæm‿juː] Zur Hölle mit dir/Ihnen! **IV 4**, 61
dance [dɑːns] Tanz **III**
to **dance** [dɑːns] tanzen **I**
dancer [dɑːnsə] Tänzer/in **III**
dangerous ['deɪndʒərəs] gefährlich **II**
Danish ['deɪnɪʃ] dänisch, Dänisch **III**
〈to dare〉 [deə] wagen **IV 5**, 76
dark [dɑːk] dunkel **IV 1**, 12
〈darned〉 [dɑːnd] verflixt **IV WSC**, 53
date [deɪt] Datum **I**
to ask s.o. for a date [deɪt] jdn. nach einer Verabredung fragen **IV WSB**, 33
daughter ['dɔːtə] Tochter **II**
day [deɪ] Tag **I**
day off [ˌdeɪ 'ɒf] freier Tag, Urlaubstag **III**
in … days [ɪn … deɪz] in … Tagen **I**
dead [ded] tot **I**
dear [dɪə] liebe/lieber/liebes **I**
Oh **dear!** [əʊ 'dɪə] Oh je! **I**
death [deθ] Tod **IV 4**, 60
December [dɪ'sembə] Dezember **I**
to **decide** [dɪ'saɪd] sich entscheiden, beschließen **III**
decimal number [ˌdesɪml 'nʌmbə] Dezimalzahl **III**
deep [diːp] tief **III**
deer (*sg + pl*) [dɪə] Reh, Hirsch; Rotwild **IV 3**, 42
to **defend** [dɪ'fend] verteidigen **III**
definite article ['defɪnət ˌɑːtɪkl] bestimmter Artikel **IV 5**, 73
definitely ['defɪnɪtlɪ] hundertprozentig, ganz sicher; endgültig, definitiv **IV WSA**, 16
to **deliver** [dɪ'lɪvə] liefern **IV 2**, 26
department store [dɪ'pɑːtment 'stɔː] Warenhaus **II**
〈deposit〉 [dɪ'pɒzɪt] Anzahlung **IV WSA**, 19
to **describe** [dɪ'skraɪb] beschreiben **III**
description [dɪ'skrɪpʃn] Beschreibung **IV 3**, 36
desk [desk] Schreibtisch, Pult **I**
° **dessert** [dɪ'zɜːt] Nachtisch **IV 4**, 57
to **destroy** [dɪ'strɔɪ] zerstören **III**
detail ['diːteɪl] Einzelheit, Detail **II**
to get **detention** [dɪ'tenʃn] nachsitzen müssen **III**
to **dial** ['daɪəl] wählen, eintippen (*Telefonnummer*) **III**
dialogue ['daɪəlɒg] Dialog, Gespräch **I**
diary ['daɪərɪ] Tagebuch, Terminkalender **II**
dice (*sg + pl*) [daɪs] Würfel **I**
dictionary ['dɪkʃənrɪ] Wörterbuch **II**
to **die** [daɪ] sterben **I**
difference ['dɪfrəns] Unterschied **III**
different ['dɪfrənt] unterschiedlich, anders **I**
difficult ['dɪfɪkəlt] schwierig **II**
digit ['dɪdʒɪt] Zahl, Ziffer **IV 5**, 71
dinner ['dɪnə] Mittagessen, Abendessen **III**
dinner lady ['dɪnə ˌleɪdɪ] *Dame an der Essensausgabe* **III**
〈direct〉 [dɪ'rekt] direkt **IV 3**, 43
dirty ['dɜːtɪ] schmutzig, dreckig **I**
disadvantage [ˌdɪsəd'vɑːntɪdʒ] Nachteil **IV 5**, 71
to **disagree** [ˌdɪsə'griː] nicht übereinstimmen; anderer Meinung sein **IV WSB**, 34
to **disappear** [ˌdɪsə'pɪə] verschwinden **III**
disappointed [ˌdɪsə'pɔɪntɪd] enttäuscht **III**

disappointing [ˌdɪsəˈpɔɪntɪŋ] enttäuschend **III**
disco [ˈdɪskəʊ] [Disko, Tanzveranstaltung mit Popmusik] **II**; Diskothek **III**
to **discuss** [dɪˈskʌs] besprechen, diskutieren **IV WSB**, 34
disease [dɪˈziːz] Krankheit **IV WSC**, 51
to **display** [dɪˈspleɪ] ausstellen; zeigen **IV 5**, 71
to **dive** [daɪv] ins Wasser springen; tauchen **IV 3**, 38
to **divide** [dɪˈvaɪd] teilen, aufteilen **III**
to **do*** [duː] tun, machen **I**
to do better [ˌduː ˈbetə] besser sein **III**
do it yourself [ˌduː ɪt jɔːˈself] heimwerken **III**
So do I. [ˌsəʊ duː ˈaɪ] Ich auch. **II**
to do the washing-up [ˈdʊ ðə ˌwɒʃɪŋˈʌp] spülen, abwaschen **I**
to do well [ˌduː ˈwel] gut sein, gut abschneiden **III**
Do you? [ˈduː juː] Oder?, Nicht wahr? **III**
doctor [ˈdɒktə] Arzt/Ärztin **I**
dodgem car [ˈdɒdʒəm kɑː] Autoscooter **II**
dog [dɒg] Hund **I**
dog biscuit [ˈdɒg ˌbɪskɪt] Hundekuchen **I**
dog-free zone [ˈdɒgfriː ˈzəʊn] hundefreie Zone **I**
How are you **doing?** Wie geht es dir/euch/Ihnen? **IV 1**, 8
dollar (= **$**) [ˈdɒlə] Dollar *(amer. Geldeinheit)* **IV 1**, 13
dolphin [ˈdɒlfɪn] Delphin **IV 3**, 38
door [dɔː] (Garagen-)Tor **I**; Tür **I**
back door [ˈbæk ˈdɔː] Hintertür **I**
front door [ˈfrʌnt ˈdɔː] Haustür **I**
⟨doorway⟩ [ˈdɔːweɪ] Eingang **IV WSC**, 52
double [ˈdʌbl] zweimal, Doppel- **I**
double decker [ˈdʌbl ˌdekə] Doppeldecker **I**
down [daʊn] herunter, hinunter **I**
to sit down [sɪt ˈdaʊn] sich hinsetzen **I**
downstairs [ˌdaʊnˈsteəz] unten *(im Gebäude)* **I**
⟨downstream⟩ [ˈdaʊnˈstriːm] flussabwärts **IV WSA**, 19
Dr [ˈdɒktə] Doktor *(Anrede)* **II**
to **drag** [dræg] schleppen, ziehen **IV WSC**, 52
dragon [ˈdrægən] Drache **III**
drama group [ˈdrɑːmə gruːp] Theatergruppe **I**
to **draw*** [drɔː] zeichnen **I**
⟨to be drawn to s.th.⟩ [drɔːn] von etw. angezogen werden **IV 3**, 43
dream [driːm] Traum **II**
dress [dres] Kleid **II**
drink [drɪŋk] Getränk **III**
to **drink*** [drɪŋk] trinken **I**
drive-in restaurant [draɪv‿ɪn ˈrestərɔnt] Autorestaurant **IV 1**, 9
⟨drive-in movie theater *(AE)*⟩ [draɪv‿ɪn ˌmuːvɪ ˈθɪetə] Autokino **IV RII**, 46
to **drive*** [draɪv] fahren **I**
⟨to drive s.o. off⟩ [ˌdraɪv ˈɒf] jdn. vertreiben **IV WSC**, 50
driver [ˈdraɪvə] Fahrer/in **I**
driver's license *(AE)* [ˈdraɪvəz ˌlaɪsəns] Führerschein **IV 1**, 8
[drop] [drɒp] Tropfen **II**
to **drop** [drɒp] fallen (lassen) **II**
to **drown** [draʊn] ertrinken, ertränken **II**
to **dry** [draɪ] trocknen **IV WSA**, 19
dry [draɪ] trocken **IV WSA**, 19
duck [dʌk] Ente **I**
during [ˈdjʊərɪŋ] während **IV 2**, 22
Dutch [dʌtʃ] niederländisch, Niederländisch **III**

E

e-mail [ˈiːmeɪl] E-Mail *(elektronischer Briefverkehr)* **III**
each [iːtʃ] jede/jeder/jedes **II**
each other [ˌiːtʃ‿ˈʌðə] einander, sich gegenseitig **III**
eagle [ˈiːgl] Adler **IV WSC**, 53
ear [ɪə] Ohr **II**
early [ˈɜːlɪ] früh **I**
earth [ɜːθ] Erde **III**
What on earth ...? [ˌwɒt ɒn ˈɜːð] Was um alles in der Welt ...? **II**
earthquake [ˈɜːθkweɪk] Erdbeben **IV 2**, 22
easily [iːzɪlɪ] leicht *(Adverbialform)* **III**
east [iːst] östlich, Ost-, Osten **II**
Easter [ˈiːstə] Ostern **II**
easy [ˈiːzɪ] einfach, leicht **I**
to **eat*** [iːt] essen **I**
egg [eg] Ei **I**
Egyptian [ɪˈdʒɪpʃn] ägyptisch, Ägypter/in **III**
elephant [ˈelɪfənt] Elefant **II**
elevator *(AE)* [ˈelɪveɪtə] Aufzug, Fahrstuhl **IV 2**, 23
else [els] sonst (noch) **I**
emergency [ɪˈmɜːdʒənsɪ] Notfall **III**
empty [ˈemptɪ] leer **II**
to **enclose** [ɪnˈkləʊz] beilegen, beifügen **IV WSD**, 65
end [end] Ende **I**
ending [ˈendɪŋ] Ende, Schluss *(bei Geschichten)* **I**
enemy [ˈenəmɪ] Feind/in **II**
energy [ˈenədʒɪ] Energie **III**
engine [ˈendʒɪn] Motor **III**
engineer [ˌendʒɪˈnɪə] Ingenieur/in **IV 5**, 72
English [ˈɪŋglɪʃ] englisch, Englisch **I**
to **enjoy** [ɪnˈdʒɔɪ] genießen, gern tun **II**
enjoyable [ɪnˈdʒɔɪəbl] nett; unterhaltsam, amüsant **IV WSA**, 19
enormous [ɪˈnɔːməs] riesig **III**
enough [ɪˈnʌf] genug **I**
to **enter** [ˈentə] eintreten **III**
entry [ˈentrɪ] Eingang, Einfahrt **IV WSA**, 17
environment [ɪnˈvaɪərənmənt] Umwelt **III**
equipment [ɪˈkwɪpmənt] Ausstattung, Ausrüstung **IV WSA**, 19
error [ˈerə] Fehler **IV 5**, 71
escalator [ˈeskəleɪtə] Rolltreppe **II**
especially [ɪˈspeʃəlɪ] insbesondere **III**
etc. [ɪtˈsetərə] usw. **III**
European [ˌjʊərəˈpiːən] europäisch, Europäer/in **III**
even [ˈiːvn] sogar **II**
evening [ˈiːvnɪŋ] Abend **I**
in the evening [ɪn‿ðiː‿ˈiːvnɪŋ] abends, am Abend **I**
event [ɪˈvent] Veranstaltung **III**
ever [ˈevə] jemals **II**
every [ˈevrɪ] jede/jeder/jedes **I**
everybody [ˈevrɪbədɪ] jede/jeder **II**
everyone [ˈevrɪwʌn] jede/jeder **I**
everything [ˈevrɪθɪŋ] alles **I**
everywhere [ˈevrɪweə] überall **IV 3**, 40
exact [ɪgˈzækt] genau, exakt **IV WSB**, 33
exam [ɪgˈzæm] Prüfung **III**
to **examine** [ɪgˈzæmɪn] untersuchen **I**
example [ɪgˈzɑːmpl] Beispiel **I**
excellent [ˈeksələnt] ausgezeichnet, hervorragend **IV WSA**, 19
exchange [ɪksˈtʃeɪnʒ] Austausch **III**
excited [ɪkˈsaɪtɪd] aufgeregt **II**
exciting [ɪkˈsaɪtɪŋ] aufregend, spannend **I**
excuse [ɪkˈskjuːs] Ausrede **III**

Excuse me, please. [ɪk'skju:z mɪ pli:z] Entschuldigung., Entschuldigen Sie bitte. **I**
exercise ['eksəsaɪz] Übung, Aufgabe **I**
exercise book ['eksəsaɪz ˌbʊk] Heft **I**
to **exist** [ɪg'zɪst] existieren **IV WSA**, 18
to **expect** [ɪk'spekt] erwarten **IV WSC**, 49
expensive [ɪk'spensɪv] teuer **II**
experience [ɪk'spɪərɪəns] Erfahrung, Erlebnis **III**
⟨experienced rafter⟩ [ɪk'spɪərɪənst ˌrɑ:ftə] erfahrener Floßfahrer, erfahrene Floßfahrerin **IV WSA**, 19
experiment [ɪk'sperɪmənt] Experiment, Versuch **III**
to **explain** [ɪk'spleɪn] erklären **II**
express (train) [ɪk'spres] Schnellzug **III**
extra ['ekstrə] zusätzlich **I**
extract ['ekstrækt] Auszug **IV WSB**, 35
eye [aɪ] Auge **I**

F

face [feɪs] Gesicht **II**
face to face [ˌfeɪs tə 'feɪs] von Angesicht zu Angesicht **III**
fact [fækt] Tatsache, Fakt **II**
factory ['fæktərɪ] Fabrik **III**
⟨to fade⟩ [feɪd] nachlassen, schwächer werden **IV 3**, 43
fair [feə] Volksfest, Jahrmarkt **II**
to **fall*** [fɔ:l] fallen **III**
⟨to fall apart⟩ [ˌfɔ:l ə'pɑ:t] sich entspannen **IV 3**, 44
to fall down [ˌfɔ:l 'daʊn] umfallen, hinfallen, herunterfallen **III**
to fall off [ˌfɔ:l‿'ɒf] (von etwas) herunterfallen **III**
to fall over [fɔ:l‿'əʊvə] hinfallen **I**
false friends [ˌfɔ:ls 'frendz] „falsche Freunde" **III**
family ['fæməlɪ] Familie **I**
famous ['feɪməs] berühmt **III**
fan [fæn] Fan **II**
⟨fancy⟩ ['fænsɪ] fein, toll, schick **IV 3**, 44
fantastic [fæn'tæstɪk] fantastisch, toll **II**
far [fɑ:] weit **II**
farm [fɑ:m] Bauernhof **I**
farmer ['fɑ:mə] Bauer/Bäuerin **III**
farmland ['fɑ:mlænd] Ackerland **IV 3**, 40
farther ['fɑ:ðə] weiter **IV WSC**, 53
fascinating ['fæsɪneɪtɪŋ] faszinierend **III**
fast [fɑ:st] schnell **II**
father ['fɑ:ðə] Vater **I**
favorite (*AE*) ['feɪvərɪt] Lieblings- **IV 1**, 8
favourite ['feɪvərɪt] Lieblings- **I**
fax [fæks] Telefax **IV 5**, 70
fear [fɪə] Angst, Furcht **IV WSB**, 35
feather ['feðə] Feder **IV WSC**, 53
February ['febrʊərɪ] Februar **I**
to **feed*** [fi:d] füttern **I**
to **feel*** [fi:l] fühlen, sich fühlen **I**
to feel sick [ˌfi:l 'sɪk] sich schlecht, krank fühlen **II**
to feel well [ˌfi:l 'wel] sich wohl fühlen **II**
feeler ['fi:lə] Fühler **I**
feeling ['fi:lɪŋ] Gefühl **III**
foot, **feet** (= **ft.**) [fʊt, fi:t] Fuß (*Maßeinheit*) **IV 1**, 12
ferry ['ferɪ] Fähre **I**
⟨fertile⟩ ['fɜ:taɪl] fruchtbar **IV WSC**, 51
festival ['festəvl] Fest, Festival **IV 2**, 28
fete [feɪt] Schulfest, Stadtfest **II**

a **few** [ə 'fju:] [(einige) wenige] **II**; ein paar **III**
field [fi:ld] Feld, Wiese **III**
to **fight*** [faɪt] kämpfen **III**
figure ['fɪgə] Figur, Gestalt **III**
to **figure out** ['fɪgər‿aʊt] (heraus)finden **IV WSB**, 34
to **fill** [fɪl] stopfen **IV WSC**, 52
to fill in [ˌfɪl‿'ɪn] ausfüllen **III**
film [fɪlm] Film **II**
to **film** [fɪlm] filmen **II**
financial [faɪ'nænʃəl] finanziell **IV 4**, 59
to **find*** [faɪnd] finden **I**
to find out [faɪnd‿'aʊt] herausfinden **I**
⟨fine⟩ [faɪn] schön **IV 1**, 14
I'm fine. [aɪm 'faɪn] Mir geht's gut. **I**
finger ['fɪŋgə] Finger **II**
to **finish** ['fɪnɪʃ] beenden, aufhören **I**
fire ['faɪə] Feuer **IV 2**, 27
fire brigade ['faɪə brɪˌgeɪd] Feuerwehr **I**
firefighter ['faɪəˌfaɪtə] Feuerwehrmann/-frau **IV 2**, 27
fireman ['faɪəmən] Feuerwehrmann **I**
fireworks (*pl*) ['faɪəwɜ:ks] Feuerwerk **IV WSD**, 64
firm [fɜ:m] Firma **I**
firm [fɜ:m] fest **IV WSC**, 53
first [fɜ:st] erste/erster/erstes **I**; zuerst, als Erste/r/s **II**
at first [ət 'fɜ:st] zuerst **II**
fish [fɪʃ] Fisch **I**
fish finger [fɪʃ 'fɪŋgə] Fischstäbchen **I**
fish tank ['fɪʃ ˌtæŋk] Aquarium **II**
fishing ['fɪʃɪŋ] Fischen, Fischfang, Angeln **III**
° **flag** ['flæg] Fahne, Flagge **IV WSB**, 32
flame [fleɪm] Flamme **IV 2**, 26
flat [flæt] Wohnung **I**
flat [flæt] flach, platt **I**
flat tyre [ˌflæt 'taɪə] platter Reifen, Platten **I**
flight [flaɪt] Flug **III**
⟨to float⟩ [fləʊt] treiben, schweben **IV 5**, 76
floor [flɔ:] Boden **I**; Stockwerk, Etage **II**
flour ['flaʊə] Mehl **IV 1**, 11
to **flow** [fləʊ] fließen **IV WSD**, 66
flower ['flaʊə] Blume **II**
flowerpot ['flaʊəpɒt] Blumentopf **I**
flu [flu:] Grippe **II**
to **fly*** [flaɪ] fliegen **II**
° to fly high ['flaɪ ˌhaɪ] gute Laune haben **IV WSB**, 34
to **fold** [fəʊld] falten **II**
folder ['fəʊldə] Mappe, Hefter **I**
folk [fəʊk] Folk (*Musikrichtung*) **III**
to **follow** ['fɒləʊ] folgen, verfolgen **III**
⟨to be fond of s.o./s.th.⟩ [fɒnd] jdn./etw. (sehr) gern haben **IV 3**, 44
food [fu:d] Nahrung, Essen **II**
⟨fool⟩ [fu:l] Dummkopf **IV 2**, 28
foot, feet (*pl*) [fʊt] Fuß, Füße **II**
football ['fʊtbɔ:l] Fußball **I**; American Football **IV WSB**, 32
for [fɔ:, fə] für **I**
for ages [fɔ: 'eɪdʒɪz] seit langem, schon ewig **IV 1**, 10
for sale [fə 'seɪl] zu verkaufen **II**
to ask for ['ɑ:sk fɔ:] bitten um **I**
force [fɔ:s] Kraft, Macht **III**
to **force** [fɔ:s] zwingen **IV WSC**, 48
to force s.o. to do s.th. [fɔ:s] jdn. zwingen etw. zu tun **IV WSA**, 19
foreigner ['fɒrənə] Ausländer/in **IV 2**, 20
forest ['fɒrɪst] Wald **II**
⟨forever⟩ [fə'revə] ewig, für immer **IV RI**, 31
to **forget*** [fə'get] vergessen **II**
fork [fɔ:k] Gabel **II**

form [fɔ:m] Art **III**; Form **I**
application form [ˌæplɪˈkeɪʃn ˈfɔ:m] Anmeldeformular; Bewerbungsformular **IV WSD**, 65
to **form** [fɔ:m] bilden, formen **IV WSC**, 50
formal [ˈfɔ:ml] formell, förmlich **IV WSD**, 65
fortunately [ˈfɔ:tʃnətlɪ] glücklicherweise, zum Glück **IV WSD**, 66
fortune [ˈfɔ:tʃu:n] Schicksal **IV 2**, 26
°fortune cookie [ˈfɔ:tʃu:n ˌkʊkɪ] *Keks, der eine Art Lebensweisheit enthält* **IV 2**, 26
⟨Forward Motion⟩ [ˌfɔ:wəd ˈməʊʃn] Vorwärtsbewegung **IV 5**, 75
fourteen-year-old [fɔ:ˈti:n jɪər‿ˌəʊld] vierzehnjährig **III**
free [fri:] frei **I**; kostenlos **I**
freedom [ˈfri:dəm] Freiheit **III**
French [frentʃ] französisch, Französisch **III**
⟨freshly christened⟩ [freʃlɪ ˈkrɪsnd] gerade getauft **IV 2**, 24
Friday [ˈfraɪdeɪ] Freitag **I**
fridge (= **refrigerator**) [frɪdʒ] Kühlschrank **IV WSA**, 16
friend [frend] Freund/in **I**
friendly [ˈfrendlɪ] freundlich **II**
to get **frightened** [ˈfraɪtnd] Angst bekommen **IV 3**, 39
frightening [ˈfraɪtnɪŋ] erschreckend, Furcht erregend **II**
frog [frɒg] Frosch **I**
from [frɒm] aus, von **I**
from behind [frɒm bɪˈhaɪnd] von hinten **II**
from time to time [frəm ˈtaɪm tə ˈtaɪm] von Zeit zu Zeit **IV 1**, 11
from top to bottom [frəm ˈtɒp tə ˌbɒtəm] von oben bis unten **III**
from ... to [frəm ... tu:] von ... nach **I**
at the **front** [ət ðə ˈfrʌnt] vorn **II**
front door [ˈfrʌnt ˈdɔ:] Haustür **I**
in **front of** [ɪn ˈfrʌnt əv] vor **I**
fruit (*sg* + *pl*) [fru:t] Frucht, Früchte, Obst **II**
full [fʊl] voll **II**
⟨full-day⟩ [ˈfʊl deɪ] Ganztags-, ganztags **IV WSA**, 19
fun [fʌn] Spaß **I**
funny [ˈfʌnɪ] lustig, komisch **I**
further [ˈfɜ:ðə] weiter **IV WSC**, 50
future [ˈfju:tʃə] Zukunft **II**

G

gallery [ˈgælərɪ] Kunstgalerie **IV 4**, 54
gallows [ˈgæləʊz] Galgen **II**
game [geɪm] Spiel **I**
gameboy [ˈgeɪmbɔɪ] *Computerspiel* **III**
gang [gæŋ] Bande, Gang **IV 2**, 23
garage [ˈgærɑ:dʒ] Garage **I**
garbage (*AE*) [ˈgɑ:bɪdʒ] Abfall **IV 1**, 11
garbage can (*AE*) [ˈgɑ:bɪdʒ kæn] Abfalleimer **IV 3**, 39
garden [ˈgɑ:dən] Garten **I**
⟨to gasp⟩ [gɑ:sp] nach Luft schnappen **IV WSC**, 52
GCSE (= **General Certificate of Secondary Education**) [ˌdʒi: si: es i:, ˌdʒenərəl səˈtɪfɪkət‿əv ˈsekəndərɪ ˌedʒʊˈkeɪʃn] Abschlussprüfung (*entspricht in etwa Mittlerer Reife*) **III**
genitive [ˈdʒenɪtɪv] Genitiv **III**
°**geographical** [dʒɪəˈgræfɪkəl] geografisch **IV WSC**, 48
Geography [dʒɪˈɒgrəfɪ] Erdkunde **II**
⟨geology⟩ [dʒɪˈɒlədʒɪ] Geologie **IV WSA**, 19
German [ˈdʒɜ:mən] deutsch, Deutsch, Deutsche/r **I**
to **get*** [get] bekommen **I**; holen **I**
to get + adj. [get] werden **III**
to get around [əˈraʊnd] sich fortbewegen **III**
to get at s.th. [ˈget æt] auf etw. hinauswollen **IV WSB**, 35
to get bored [bɔ:d] Langeweile haben/bekommen **IV 2**, 23
to get frightened [ˈfraɪtnd] Angst bekommen **IV 3**, 39
to get in line (*AE*) [ˌget ɪn ˈlaɪn] sich anstellen **IV 1**, 13
to get into the mood [get‿ˌɪntə ðə ˈmu:d] sich einstimmen **III**
to get lost [get ˈlɒst] verloren gehen, sich verirren **I**
to get off [ˌget‿ˈɒf] aussteigen **III**
to get on with s.o. [get‿ˈɒn wɪð] sich mit jdm. gut verstehen **III**
Get out! [get ˈaʊt] Hinaus mit dir!, Hinaus mit euch! **I**
to get ready [get ˈredɪ] (sich) vorbereiten **I**
to get s.th. ready [get ˈsʌmθɪŋ ˈredɪ] etw. fertig machen, vorbereiten **II**
to get stuck [get ˈstʌk] stecken bleiben **I**
to get the bus [ˌget ðə ˈbʌs] den Bus nehmen **I**
to get there [ˈget ðeə] hinkommen **I**
[to get tired] [get ˈtaɪəd] müde werden **II**
to get up [get‿ˈʌp] aufstehen **I**
Get well soon! [ˈget wel ˈsu:n] Gute Besserung! **I**
ghost [gəʊst] Geist, Gespenst **II**
ghost train [ˈgəʊst ˈtreɪn] Geisterbahn **II**
giant [ˈdʒaɪənt] Riese; riesig, Riesen- **IV 3**, 36
girl [gɜ:l] Mädchen **I**
gist [dʒɪst] Wesentliches **IV WSB**, 32
to **give*** [gɪv] geben **I**
to give a talk [ˌgɪv‿ə ˈtɔ:k] eine Rede/ein Referat halten **III**
to give away [gɪv əˈweɪ] weggeben **II**
give my love to ... [ˌgɪv maɪ ˈlʌv tə] grüß/grüßt ... recht herzlich **I**
to give s.o. a message [gɪv ə ˈmesɪdʒ] jdm. etw. ausrichten **III**
to give up [ˌgɪv‿ˈʌp] aufgeben **III**
to give ... a lift [lɪft] ... im Auto mitnehmen **I**
glad [glæd] froh **I**
glass [glɑ:s] Glas **II**
glasses [ˈglɑ:sɪz] Brille **III**
to **go*** [gəʊ] gehen, fahren **I**
to go across [ˈgəʊ əˌkrɒs] überqueren **III**
to go down on one's knees [gəʊ ˌdaʊn‿ɒn wʌnz ˈni:z] sich hinknien **III**
to go for a walk [ˌgəʊ fər‿ə ˈwɔ:k] spazieren gehen **I**
to go home [gəʊ ˈhəʊm] nach Hause gehen **I**
to go on [gəʊ‿ˈɒn] weitermachen **I**
to go (out) with s.o. [gəʊ ˈaʊt wɪð] mit jdm. (aus)gehen **IV 2**, 24
to go shopping [gəʊ ˈʃɒpɪŋ] einkaufen gehen **II**
to go swimming [gəʊ ˈswɪmɪŋ] schwimmen gehen **I**
[to be going to] [bi: ˈgəʊɪŋ tu:] vorhaben zu ... **II**
to go to bed [gəʊ tə ˈbed] ins Bett gehen, schlafen gehen **I**
to go to the shops [gəʊ tə ðə ˈʃɒps] einkaufen gehen **I**
to go together [gəʊ təˈgeðə] zusammenpassen **I**
to go wrong [gəʊ ˈrɒŋ] schief gehen **II**; sich verfahren **II**
goal [gəʊl] Tor (*beim Sport*) **I**
goalkeeper [ˈgəʊlˌki:pə] Torwart **III**
God [gɒd] Gott **III**
God bless you! [ˌgɒd ˈbles‿ju:] Gott segne Dich/Euch! (*veraltete Grußform*) **III**
gold [gəʊld] (aus) Gold **III**; [Gold] **II**
golf [gɒlf] Golf **IV WSB**, 32
⟨Gonna (= I'm going to)⟩ [gɒnə] Ich werde ... **IV 1**, 14

good [gʊd] gut **I**
Good afternoon. [gʊd ɑːftə'nuːn] Guten Tag. (*Anrede am Nachmittag*) **I**
Good morning. [gʊd 'mɔːnɪŋ] Guten Morgen. **I**
It's good to see you. [ɪts ˌgʊd tə 'siː juː] Schön, dich/euch zu sehen. **I**
It's no good … [ɪts nəʊ 'gʊd] Es bringt nichts, …, Es hat keinen Sinn, … **II**
to be good at [bɪ 'gʊd‿ət] gut sein in … **I**
Goodbye. [gʊd'baɪ] Auf Wiedersehen., Tschüs. **I**
Thank **goodness!** [θæŋk 'gʊdnɪs] Gott sei Dank! **IV 1**, 14
⟨Goodness!⟩ ['gʊdnɪs] Meine Güte! **IV WSC**, 52
goose, geese (*pl*) [guːs] Gans, Gänse **II**
⟨gorge⟩ [gɔːdʒ] Schlucht **IV WSA**, 19
Gosh! [gɒʃ] *Ausruf des Erstaunens* **II**
gotten (*AE*) ['gɒtn] bekommen **IV WSB**, 35
government ['gʌvnment] Regierung **IV WSC**, 50
to **grab** [græb] greifen, schnappen **IV 3**, 42
grade (*AE*) [greɪd] Note (*in der Schule*); Klasse **IV WSB**, 33
gradually ['grædʒʊəlɪ] nach und nach, allmählich **IV WSC**, 48
graffiti [grə'fiːtɪ] Wandmalereien, Graffiti **IV 4**, 58
grammar ['græmə] Grammatik **III**
⟨Gran⟩ [græn] Oma, Omi **IV 5**, 75
Grandma ['grænmɑː] Oma **I**
Grandpa ['grænpɑː] Opa **I**
⟨Granny⟩ ['grænɪ] Oma **IV 5**, 74
graphics (*pl*) ['græfɪks] Bilder, Grafik **III**
grass [grɑːs] Gras **IV 4**, 54
great [greɪt] toll, großartig **I**
Greek [griːk] griechisch, Griechisch **I**
green [griːn] grün **I**
grid [grɪd] Tabelle **IV 3**, 36
ground [graʊnd] Boden **III**
⟨ground control⟩ ['graʊnd kən'trəʊl] Bodenstation **IV 5**, 76
group [gruːp] Gruppe **I**
tutor group ['tjuːtə ˌgruːp] Klasse (*in einer englischen Schule*) **I**
to **group** [gruːp] gruppieren, in Gruppen einteilen **IV WSC**, 48
to **grow*** [grəʊ] (an)pflanzen, wachsen **II**
⟨to grow up⟩ [ˌgrəʊ 'ʌp] aufwachsen **IV 2**, 28
[grumpy] ['grʌmpɪ] mürrisch, schlecht gelaunt **II**
to **guess** [ges] raten **III**
guest [gest] Gast **I**
guest house ['gest haʊs] Pension, Gästehaus **I**
guide [gaɪd] Führer/in **IV WSA**, 19; Reiseführer (*Buch*) **IV WSA**, 17
guided tour [ˌgaɪdɪd 'tʊə] Führung **IV WSA**, 17
guitar [gɪ'tɑː] Gitarre **I**
gun [gʌn] Schusswaffe, Pistole, Gewehr **IV WSC**, 52
guy (*AE*) [gaɪ] Mann, Kerl **IV 3**, 42
gym [dʒɪm] Turnhalle, Sporthalle **III**; Fitnessstudio **IV 1**, 8

H

hair [heə] Haar(e) **II**
haircut ['heəkʌt] Haarschnitt, Frisur **II**
half [hɑːf] halb; Hälfte **I**
⟨half-day⟩ ['hɑːf deɪ] Halbtags-, halbtags **IV WSA**, 19
hall [hɔːl] Diele, Flur **I**
°**Halloween** [ˌhæləʊ'iːn] *Halloween* **IV WSD**, 64
ham [hæm] gekochter Schinken **I**
hammer ['hæmə] Hammer **III**
hamster ['hæmstə] Hamster **II**
hand [hænd] Hand **I**
to give s.o. a hand [gɪv‿ə 'hænd] jdm. helfen **IV WSA**, 16
⟨a handful⟩ [hændfʊl] eine Hand voll **IV WSA**, 19
handwriting ['hændˌraɪtɪŋ] Handschrift **IV WSD**, 66
hangman ['hæŋmən] Henker **II**
to **happen** ['hæpən] passieren, geschehen **II**
happy ['hæpɪ] fröhlich, glücklich **I**
Happy birthday! [ˌhæpɪ 'bɜːθdeɪ] Herzlichen Glückwunsch zum Geburtstag! **I**
hard [hɑːd] schwer **IV 1**, 7
hard [hɑːd] hart **III**
harmless ['hɑːmles] harmlos **IV 5**, 75
harvest ['hɑːvɪst] Ernte **IV WSD**, 64
hat [hæt] Hut **II**
to **hate** [heɪt] hassen, nicht leiden können **II**
to **have*** [hæv] haben **I**
have got ['hæv gɒt] haben, besitzen **I**
haven't got … ['hævnt gɒt] nicht haben **I**
Let's have a go. [hæv‿ə 'gəʊ] Probieren wir es mal. **II**
So have you. ['səʊ hæv‿juː] Du auch. **II**
to have a bath [hæv‿ə 'bɑːθ] baden **I**
to have a good time [hæv‿əˌgʊd 'taɪm] Spaß haben **II**
to have a ride [hæv‿ə 'raɪd] fahren **II**
to have a word with s.o. [ˌhæv‿ə'wɜːd‿wɪð] mit jdm. sprechen **III**
to have an argument [ˌhæv‿ən 'ɑːgjʊmənt] einen Streit, eine Auseinandersetzung haben **II**
to have to ['hæv tə] müssen **III**
he [hiː] er **I**
head [hed] Kopf **I**
headache ['hedeɪk] Kopfschmerzen **II**
heading ['hedɪŋ] Überschrift **IV WSC**, 48
[headline] ['hedlaɪn] Titel, Schlagzeile **IV 3**, 41
headphones ['hedfəʊnz] Kopfhörer **III**
headteacher [ˌhed'tiːtʃə] Schuldirektor/in **I**
°**headword** ['hedwɜːd] Stichwort **IV WSA**, 17
healthy living ['helθɪ 'lɪvɪŋ] gesunde Lebensweise **I**
to **hear*** [hɪə] hören **II**
heart [hɑːt] Herz **IV 2**, 26
heating ['hiːtɪŋ] Heizung **III**
heavy ['hevɪ] schwer **III**
heavy metal [hevɪ 'metl] Heavy Metal (*Musikrichtung*) **III**
heavy traffic [ˌhevɪ 'træfɪk] viel Verkehr **III**
height [haɪt] Höhe **IV 5**, 75
helicopter ['helɪkɒptə] Hubschrauber **IV 4**, 60
⟨hell⟩ [hel] Hölle **IV 4**, 62
Hello. [hə'ləʊ] Hallo., Guten Tag. **I**
to say hello ['seɪ hə'ləʊ] grüßen **I**
helmet ['helmɪt] Helm **II**
to **help** [help] Hilfe **III**
Help! [help] Hilfe! **I**
to help [help] helfen **I**
helper ['helpə] Helfer/in **II**
helpful ['helpfʊl] hilfsbereit **III**
helpless ['helplɪs] hilflos **III**
hen [hen] Henne **I**
her [hɜː] ihr/ihre **I**; ihr/sie **I**
here [hɪə] hier **I**
Here we come! ['hɪə wiː ˌkʌm] Jetzt kommen wir! **IV 1**, 12
Here you are. ['hɪə jʊ‿ɑː] Hier, bitte schön. **I**
hero, heroes (*pl*) ['hɪərəʊ] Held, Helden **III**
herself [hɜː'self] (sie/ihr) selbst **III**
Hey! [heɪ] He! **I**
Hi! [haɪ] Hallo! **I**

Hi there! ['haɪ ˌðeə] Hallo! **II**
to **hide*** [haɪd] (sich) verstecken **II**
high [haɪ] hoch **II**
high jump ['haɪdʒʌmp] Hochsprung **III**
high school (*AE*) ['haɪ ˌsku:l] Gesamtschule **IV 2**, 20
hiker ['haɪkə] Wanderer/Wanderin **IV 3**, 42
to go **hiking** [ˌgəʊ 'haɪkɪŋ] wandern gehen **IV 1**, 7
hill [hɪl] Hügel **I**
him [hɪm] ihm/ihn **I**
himself [hɪm'self] (ihn/ihm) selbst **III**
Hindu ['hɪndu:] hinduistisch, Hindu **III**
his [hɪz] sein/seine **I**
°**Hispanic** [hɪ'spænɪk] hispanisch, *Amerikaner/in lateinamer. Herkunft* **IV 2**, 28
History ['hɪstərɪ] Geschichte **II**
to **hit*** [hɪt] treffen, schlagen **II**
to hit the trail [hɪt ðə 'treɪl] *umg.:* sich auf den Weg machen **IV 3**, 42
Hmm. [hm] Hm., Tja. **I**
hobby ['hɒbɪ] Hobby **II**
hockey ['hɒkɪ] Rasenhockey **I**
to **hold*** [həʊld] halten **III**
Hold on! [ˌhəʊld‿'ɒn] Halt dich fest!, Halten Sie sich fest! **III**
to hold up [ˌhəʊld‿'ʌp] (hoch)halten **III**
hole [həʊl] Loch **I**
holiday ['hɒlədeɪ] Urlaub, Ferien **III**
on holiday [ˌɒn 'hɒlədeɪ] im Urlaub, in den Ferien **III**
home [həʊm] Heim, Zuhause **I**
at home [ət 'həʊm] zu Hause **I**
to come home [kʌm 'həʊm] nach Hause kommen **I**
to go home [gəʊ 'həʊm] nach Hause gehen **I**
hometown [ˌhəʊm'taʊn] Heimatstadt **IV 1**, 8
homework ['həʊmwɜ:k] Hausaufgaben **I**
honey ['hʌnɪ] Honig; Liebling (*Kosename*) **IV 1**, 11
hood [hʊd] Kapuze **II**
to **hope** [həʊp] hoffen **I**
horrible ['hɒrəbl] grauenhaft, schrecklich **IV 1**, 11
horror ['hɒrə] Horror **III**
horse [hɔ:s] Pferd **II**
hospital ['hɒspɪtl] Krankenhaus **I**
host [həʊst] Gastgeber; Moderator/in **IV 3**, 40
hot dog [ˌhɒt 'dɒg] Hot dog (*heißes Würstchen in einem Brötchen*) **II**
hot [hɒt] heiß **I**
hotel [həʊ'tel] Hotel **II**
hotline ['hɒtˌlaɪn] Hotline, „heißer Draht“ **IV 5**, 72
hour ['aʊə] Stunde **I**
house [haʊs] Haus **I**
housekeeper ['haʊsˌki:pə] Haushälter/in **II**
housework ['haʊswɜ:k] Hausarbeit **I**
°**housing unit** ['haʊzɪŋ‿ˌju:nɪt] Wohneinheit **IV 5**, 74
hovercraft ['hɒvəkrɑ:ft] Luftkissenboot **I**
how [haʊ] wie **I**
How about ...? [haʊ‿ə'baʊt] Wie steht's mit ...?, Wie wär's mit ...? **II**
How are you? [haʊ‿'ɑ: ju:] Wie geht es dir/euch/Ihnen? **I**
How are you doing? Wie geht es dir/euch/Ihnen? **IV 1**, 8
How many? [haʊ 'menɪ] Wie viele? **I**
How much? [haʊ 'mʌtʃ] Wie viel? **I**
⟨How!⟩ ['haʊ] *indianischer Gruß* **IV WSC**, 52
hug [hʌg] Umarmung **II**
huge [hju:dʒ] riesig **IV 3**, 40
human ['hju:mən] Mensch **III**
human ['hju:mən] menschlich **IV 3**, 43
Humanities (*pl*) [hju:'mænətɪz] Erdkunde und Geschichte (*in der Schule*) **II**
hungry ['hʌŋgrɪ] hungrig **I**
to **hunt** [hʌnt] jagen **III**
hunter ['hʌntə] Jäger/in **IV WSC**, 50
hurricane ['hʌrɪkən] Wirbelsturm **IV 3**, 38
to **hurry** ['hʌrɪ] (sich) (be)eilen **II**
to be in a **hurry** [bɪ ɪn‿ə'hʌrɪ] in Eile sein **III**
to **hurt*** [hɜ:t] weh tun, schmerzen **I**
husband ['hʌzbənd] Ehemann **III**
⟨Hydroponic Facility⟩ [ˌhaɪdrə'pɒnɪk fə'sɪlətɪ] *Anlage zur Aufzucht von Bäumen* **IV 5**, 74
hyphen ['haɪfn] Bindestrich **IV WSA**, 18

I

I [aɪ] ich **I**
⟨I don't give a damn.⟩ [ˌaɪ dəʊnt gɪv‿ə 'dæm] Das ist mir piepegal. **IV 2**, 24
I'd like ... [aɪd laɪk] Ich hätte gern ... **II**
I've got ... ['aɪv gɒt] Ich habe ... **I**
ice cream [ˌaɪs 'kri:m] Eiskrem **I**
ice rink ['aɪs ˌrɪŋk] Eisbahn **II**
ice-skating ['aɪs'skeɪtɪŋ] Schlittschuhlaufen **II**
idea [aɪ'dɪə] Idee **I**
ideal [aɪˌdɪəl] ideal, besonders geeignet **II**
idiot ['ɪdɪət] Idiot/in, Dummkopf **III**
if [ɪf] ob **IV WSA**, 17
if [ɪf] wenn, falls **II**
⟨ignition⟩ [ɪg'nɪʃn] Zündung **IV 5**, 76
ill [ɪl] krank **II**
illegal [ɪ'li:gəl] illegal, ungesetzlich **IV 2**, 21
image ['ɪmɪdʒ] Bild, Figur **IV 5**, 74
to **imagine** [ɪ'mædʒɪn] sich vorstellen **III**
immigrant ['ɪmɪgrənt] Einwanderer/Einwanderin **IV 2**, 20
important [ɪm'pɔ:tnt] wichtig **II**
impression [ɪm'preʃn] Eindruck **IV WSC**, 53
to **improve** [ɪm'pru:v] verbessern **IV WSD**, 65
in [ɪn] in **I**
in a fun way [ɪn‿ə fʌn 'weɪ] auf unterhaltsame Art **III**
in front of [ɪn 'frʌnt əv] vor **I**
in the afternoon [ɪn ði:‿ ɑ:ftə'nu:n] nachmittags, am Nachmittag **I**
in the evening [ɪn‿ði:‿'i:vnɪŋ] abends, am Abend **I**
in the morning [ɪn ðə 'mɔ:nɪŋ] morgens, am Vormittag **I**
in turn [ɪn 'tɜ:n] der Reihe nach, abwechselnd **IV WSB**, 35
in ... days [ɪn ... 'deɪz] in ... Tagen **I**
°**incident** ['ɪnsɪdent] Vorfall, Ereignis **IV 4**, 62
⟨to include⟩ [ɪn'klu:d] einschließen **IV WSA**, 19
indeed [ɪn'di:d] (*nachgestellt*) sehr **III**
indefinite article [ɪn'defɪnət ˌɑ:tɪkl] unbestimmter Artikel **IV 5**, 72
°**Independence Day** [ˌɪndɪ'pendəns deɪ] *Unabhängigkeitstag* **IV WSD**, 64
index ['ɪndeks] Inhaltsverzeichnis **IV 5**, 71
Indian ['ɪndjən] indianisch, Indianer/in **IV WSC**, 48
Indian ['ɪndjən] indisch, Inder/in **II**
⟨indication⟩ [ˌɪndɪ'keɪʃn] Anzeige **IV 5**, 71
⟨individual⟩ [ˌɪndɪ'vɪdzʊəl] Einzelne/r, Individuum **IV WSA**, 19
°**indivisible** [ˌɪndɪ'vɪzəbl] unteilbar **IV WSB**, 32
industry ['ɪndəstrɪ] Industrie **III**
infinitive [ɪn'fɪnətɪv] Infinitiv, Grundform **II**
to **inform** [ɪn'fɔ:m] benachrichtigen, informieren **IV WSA**, 18

information (*sg* + *pl*) [ˌɪnfəˈmeɪʃn] Information(en), Auskunft/Auskünfte **II**
-ing-form [ˈɪŋ fɔːm] -ing-Form, Gerundium **IV 2**, 25
to **input** [ˈɪnpʊt] eingeben **IV 5**, 71
inside [ɪnˈsaɪd] drinnen **I**
to **install** [ɪnˈstɔːl] installieren **IV WSA**, 16
instead [ɪnˈsted] statt **III**
instructions (*pl*) [ɪnˈstrʌkʃnz] Betriebsanleitung, Anweisungen **IV 5**, 71
⟨interactive⟩ [ˌɪntərˈæktɪv] interaktiv **IV RI**, 31
interest [ˈɪntrəst] Interesse **III**
to be **interested in s.th.** [bɪ ˈɪntrəstɪd ɪn] interessiert sein an **IV 2**, 25
interesting [ˈɪntrɪstɪŋ] interessant **II**
°to **interfere** (with) [ˌɪntəˈfɪə wɪð] sich einmischen (in) **IV WSC**, 48
international [ˌɪntəˈnæʃənl] international **III**
⟨Internet⟩ [ˈɪntənet] Internet **IV 3**, 37
interview [ˈɪntəvjuː] Interview, Gespräch **III**
to **interview** [ˈɪntəvjuː] interviewen **IV 2**, 27
into [ˈɪntʊ] in, hinein **I**
to **introduce** (-self) [ɪntrəˈdjuːs] (sich) vorstellen **III**
introduction [ˌɪntrəˈdʌkʃn] Einführung, Einleitung **III**
invitation [ˌɪnvɪˈteɪʃn] Einladung **I**
to **invite** [ɪnˈvaɪt] einladen **I**
to **involve** [ɪnˈvɒlv] beteiligen **IV WSA**, 18
involvement [ɪnˈvɒlvmənt] Engagement, Mitarbeit **IV WSA**, 19
Irish [ˈaɪrɪʃ] irisch, Irisch **III**
irregular [ɪˈregjʊlə] unregelmäßig **I**
is [ɪz] ist **I**
island [ˈaɪlənd] Insel **II**
it [ɪt] es/er/sie **I**; ihn/sie/es; ihm/ihr **I**
Italian [ɪtˈæljən] italienisch, Italienisch, Italiener/in **I**
⟨item⟩ [ˈaɪtəm] Gegenstand, Stück **IV 3**, 43
its [ɪts] sein, seine/ihr, ihre **I**
it's [ɪts] er, sie, es ist **I**
It's no good … [ɪts nəʊ ˈgʊd] Es bringt nichts, …; Es hat keinen Sinn, … **II**
It's up to you. [ɪts‿ˌʌp tə ˈjuː] Es liegt an dir., Du entscheidest. **III**
itself [ɪtˈself] (sich) selbst **III**

J

jacket [ˈdʒækɪt] Jacke **II**
January [ˈdʒænjʊərɪ] Januar **I**
Japanese [ˌdʒæpəˈniːz] japanisch, Japanisch, Japaner/in **III**
jazz [dʒæz] Jazz **III**
jealous [ˈdʒeləs] eifersüchtig **III**
jeans (*sg* + *pl*) [dʒiːnz] Jeans **I**
job [dʒɒb] Beruf, Arbeit **I**
to **jog** [dʒɒg] joggen **IV 4**, 54
to **join** [dʒɔɪn] eintreten, sich anschließen **II**
joke [dʒəʊk] Witz **II**
journey [ˈdʒɜːnɪ] (lange) Reise **IV 2**, 20
July [dʒuːˈlaɪ] Juli **I**
to **jump** [dʒʌmp] springen **II**
junction [ˈdʒʌŋkʃn] Straßenkreuzung **III**
June [dʒuːn] Juni **I**
junior [ˈdʒuːnjə] Unterstufen- **II**
just [dʒʌst] eben, gerade, nur **I**
⟨just in time⟩ [dʒʌst ɪn ˈtaɪm] gerade (noch) rechtzeitig **IV WSC**, 52
°**justice** [ˈdʒʌstɪs] Gerechtigkeit **IV WSB**, 32

K

to **keep*** [kiːp] halten, behalten **II**
kettle [ˈketl] Kessel **II**
key [kiː] Schlüssel **III**
key word [ˌkiː ˈwɜːd] Schlüsselwort, wichtigster Begriff **III**
to **kick** [kɪk] treten, mit dem Fuß stoßen **I**
kid [kɪd] Kind **III**
to **kill** [kɪl] töten **IV 3**, 42
kilt [kɪlt] Schottenrock **II**
kind [kaɪnd] Art **III**
king [kɪŋ] König **III**
kiss [kɪs] Kuss **IV 2**, 27
kit [kɪt] Kätzchen **II**
kitchen [ˈkɪtʃɪn] Küche **I**
kite [kaɪt] Drachen **I**
knee [niː] Knie **II**
knife, knives (*pl*) [naɪf] Messer **I**
knight [naɪt] Ritter **III**
to **knit** [nɪt] stricken **IV 5**, 75
to **knock over** [ˈnɒk ˌəʊvə] umwerfen, umstoßen **III**
to **know*** [nəʊ] wissen, kennen **I**
°**Korean** [kəˈrɪən] koreanisch, Koreanisch, Koreaner/in **IV 2**, 24

L

lace [leɪs] Spitze (*Gewebeart*) **II**
ladder [ˈlædə] Leiter **I**
lady [ˈleɪdɪ] Dame **II**
lake [leɪk] (der) See, Teich **I**
lamb [læm] Lamm **I**
lambing time [ˈlæmɪŋ taɪm] Zeit, in der Lämmer geboren werden **I**
lance [lɑːns] Lanze **III**
land [lænd] Boden, Grundstück, Land **III**
landscape [ˈlænskeɪp] Landschaft **IV 3**, 36
language [ˈlæŋgwɪdʒ] Sprache **III**
large [lɑːdʒ] groß **III**
last [lɑːst] letzter/letzte/letztes **I**
last but not least [ˌlɑːst bʌt nɒt ˈliːst] nicht zuletzt **IV 4**, 54
late [leɪt] spät, zu spät **I**
to work late [ˈwɜːk leɪt] länger arbeiten **I**
⟨Lateral Hold⟩ [ˈlætərəl ˌhəʊld] *etwa:* seitliche Kontrolle **IV 5**, 75
to **laugh** [lɑːf] lachen **I**
to laugh at s.o. [ˈlɑːf ət] lachen über jdn. **II**
⟨to be a laugh⟩ [lɑːf] ein Witz sein **IV WSD**, 67
to **lay*** [leɪ] legen **I**
lb (= **pound**) [paʊnd] *Abkürzung für* pound (*Gewicht*) **I**
to **lead*** [liːd] führen **IV WSB**, 35
leader [ˈliːdə] Führer/in **III**
leaflet [ˈliːflɪt] Prospekt, Informationsblatt **II**
to **learn*** [lɜːn] lernen **I**
at **least** [ət ˈliːst] wenigstens, mindestens **II**
⟨leather⟩ [ˈleðə] Leder **IV 3**, 39
to **leave*** [liːv] abfahren **I**; verlassen **II**
to leave on [ˌliːv‿ˈɒn] anlassen, laufen lassen **III**
to leave s.o. alone [liːv əˈləʊn] jdn. in Ruhe lassen **II**
[to leave s.th. open] [liːv ˈəʊpən] etw. offen lassen **II**
left [left] (nach) links **I**
on the left/right [ɒn ðə ˈleft, ɒn ðə ˈraɪt] links/rechts, auf der linken/rechten Seite **I**
leg [leg] Bein **I**

legend [ˈledʒənd] Legende **III**
⟨leisure time⟩ [ˈleʒə ˌtaɪm] Freizeit **IV 2**, 28
lemonade [leməˈneɪd] Limonade **I**
to **lend*** [lend] leihen, verleihen **I**
less [les] weniger **IV 2**, 21
lesson [lesn] Unterrichtsstunde **I**
private lesson [ˌpraɪvɪt ˈlesn] Nachhilfeunterricht **IV WSB**, 35
to **let*** [let] lassen, erlauben **III**
let's [lets] lasst uns **I**
to let s.o. know [let ˈnəʊ] jdm. Bescheid geben/sagen; wissen lassen **IV WSD**, 65
°to let the dirt fly [let ðə ˈdɜːt flaɪ] Spaß haben **IV WSB**, 34
letter [ˈletə] Brief **I**; Buchstabe **I**
level [ˈlevl] Niveau, Stufe **III**
°**liberty** [ˈlɪbətɪ] Freiheit **IV WSB**, 32
library [ˈlaɪbrərɪ] Bibliothek, Bücherei **III**
lie [laɪ] Lüge **III**
to **lie*** [laɪ] liegen **I**
life [laɪf] Leben **III**
way of life [ˌweɪ‿əv ˈlaɪf] Lebensstil **IV WSC**, 50
life-sized [ˌlaɪfˈsaɪzd] lebensgroß **IV 5**, 74
lifeboat [ˈlaɪfbəʊt] Seenotrettungsboot **III**
lifeboatman/woman [ˈlaɪfbəʊtmæn/wʊmən] Seenotrettungsmann/-frau **III**
lifelike [ˈlaɪflaɪk] lebensecht **III**
lifestyle [laɪfˌstaɪl] Lebensstil **IV WSC**, 51
lift [lɪft] Aufzug, Fahrstuhl **II**
to **lift** [lɪft] (hoch)heben **IV WSC**, 49
to give … **a lift** [lɪft] … im Auto mitnehmen **I**
light [laɪt] Licht **III**
to **light** [laɪt] anzünden; beleuchten **IV WSC**, 52
lightning [ˈlaɪtnɪŋ] Blitz **II**
⟨lightweight⟩ [ˈlaɪtweɪt] leicht(gewichtig) **IV WSA**, 19
to **like** [laɪk] mögen, gern haben **I**
like [laɪk] (so) wie **I**
What's … like? [wɒts … laɪk] Wie ist …? **I**
to **limit** [ˈlɪmɪt] begrenzen, limitieren **IV 5**, 73
limo [ˈlɪməʊ] Stretchlimousine **IV 4**, 60
line [laɪn] Zeile **II**; Linie **III**
to get in line (*AE*) [ˌget ɪn ˈlaɪn] sich anstellen **IV 1**, 13
lion [ˈlaɪən] Löwe **II**
lipstick [ˈlɪpstɪk] Lippenstift **III**
list [lɪst] Liste **I**
to **listen** [ˈlɪsn] zuhören **I**
listening practice [ˈlɪsnɪŋ ˌpræktɪs] Hörverstehensübung **I**
little [lɪtl] klein **I**
⟨little britches⟩ [ˌlɪtl ˈbrɪtʃɪz] Dreikäsehoch **IV 3**, 44
to **live** [lɪv] leben, wohnen **I**
to live on [ˌlɪv‿ˈɒn] weiterleben **III**
live [laɪv] live, direkt **II**
living-room [ˈlɪvɪŋrʊm] Wohnzimmer **I**
to **lock** [lɒk] abschließen, verschließen **III**
locked [lɒkt] abgeschlossen **I**
locker [ˈlɒkə] Schließfach **IV WSB**, 32
long [lɒŋ] lang **I**
°**longhouse** [ˈlɒŋhaʊs] *langes Holzhaus der Indianer des amer. Nordwestens* **IV WSC**, 49
look [lʊk] Blick **IV 1**, 12
to **look** [lʊk] aussehen **I**; sehen, anschauen **I**
to look after s.o. [ˌlʊk‿ˈɑːftə ˈsʌmwʌn] sich um jdn. kümmern **II**
to look at [ˈlʊk‿ət] anschauen **I**
to look for [ˈlʊk ˌfɔː] etw. suchen **II**
to look forward to s.th. [lʊk ˈfɔːwəd] sich auf etw. freuen **IV 2**, 25
to look nice [lʊk ˈnaɪs] nett, schön aussehen **II**
to look s.o. up [lʊk‿ˈʌp] bei jdm. vorbeischauen **IV 4**, 58
to look up [lʊk‿ʌp] hochschauen, aufsehen **IV WSC**, 52; nachschlagen **III**
lorry [ˈlɒrɪ] Lastwagen **II**
to **lose*** [luːz] verlieren **III**
to lose s.o. [luːz] jdn. abhängen **IV 5**, 75
lots of [lɒts‿əv] eine Menge, viel(e) **II**
a lot of [əˈlɒt‿əv] viel/viele, eine Menge **I**
loud [laʊd] laut **II**
love [lʌv] alles Liebe (*als Briefschluss*) **I**
to **love** [lʌv] lieben **II**
lovely [ˈlʌvlɪ] schön, herrlich **II**
⟨lover⟩ [ˈlʌvə] Liebhaber/in **IV WSC**, 48
low rate [ləʊ ˈreɪt] günstig **IV 5**, 75
⟨low-riding Chicano⟩ [ˌləʊ raɪdɪŋ tʃɪˈkɑːnəʊ] *Fahrer mexikanischer Herkunft mit tiefergelegtem Auto* **IV 2**, 28
lower [ˈləʊə] der/die/das untere **II**
luck [lʌk] Glück **IV 3**, 38
lucky [ˈlʌkɪ] glücklich, Glücks- **I**
to be lucky [bɪ ˈlʌkɪ] Glück haben **I**
lunch [lʌntʃ] Mittagessen **I**
lunch box [ˈlʌntʃ bɒks] *Dose für belegte Brote zum Mittagessen* **I**
⟨to lurch⟩ [lɜːtʃ] sich ruckartig bewegen; taumeln, torkeln **IV 5**, 75

M

⟨Ma⟩ [mɑː] Mutter, Mama **IV WSC**, 52
machine [məˈʃiːn] Maschine, Gerät **III**
mad [mæd] verrückt; böse, verärgert **IV WSC**, 53
Madam [ˈmædəm] *Anrede für eine Dame* **IV WSD**, 65
magazine [ˌmægəˈziːn] Zeitschrift **I**
⟨magic⟩ [ˈmædʒɪk] magisch, Zauber- **IV 2**, 24
mail [meɪl] Post **IV 4**, 54
main [meɪn] Haupt- **III**
mainly [ˈmeɪnlɪ] hauptsächlich **III**
to **make*** [meɪk] machen **I**
made in Wales [ˌmeɪd‿ɪn ˈweɪlz] hergestellt in Wales **III**
to make friends with s.o. [ˌmeɪk ˈfrendz‿wɪð] sich mit jdm. anfreunden **III**
to make it [ˈmeɪk‿ɪt] Erfolg haben; es rechtzeitig schaffen **IV 4**, 60
[to make money] [meɪk ˈmʌnɪ] Geld verdienen **II**
to make notes [meɪk ˈnəʊts] sich Notizen machen **II**
⟨to make sure⟩ [meɪk ˈsʊə] sich vergewissern **IV 3**, 43
man, men (*pl*) [mæn] Mann, Männer **I**
to **manage to do s.th.** [ˈmænɪdʒ] schaffen etw. zu tun **IV WSC**, 50
management [ˈmænɪdʒmənt] Führung, Leitung, Management **IV WSA**, 19
manager [ˈmænɪdʒə] Geschäftsführer/in, Manager/in **IV 2**, 23
How **many?** [haʊ ˈmenɪ] Wie viele? **I**
map [mæp] Landkarte **I**
marathon [ˌmærəθn] Marathon **III**
March [mɑːtʃ] März **I**
mark [mɑːk] Note **III**
marked [mɑːkt] markiert **III**
market [ˈmɑːkɪt] Markt **I**
mascot [ˈmæskət] Maskottchen **I**
match [mætʃ] Spiel **III**
to **match s.th. with s.th.** [mætʃ] das Passende zu etw. finden **IV 5**, 71

material [mə'tɪərɪəl] Material, Stoff **IV WSB**, 32
Math (*AE*) [mæθ] Mathe, Mathematikunterricht **IV WSB**, 32
Maths [mæθs] Mathe **II**
it doesn't **matter** [ɪt ˌdʌznt 'mætə] es macht nichts, es ist egal **II**
May [meɪ] Mai **I**
may [meɪ] dürfen **III**; vielleicht tun **III**
maybe ['meɪbi:] vielleicht **I**
me [mi:] mir/mich **I**
meal [mi:l] Mahlzeit, Essen **II**
to **mean*** [mi:n] bedeuten, meinen **II**; wollen **IV 1**, 13
meaning ['mi:nɪŋ] Bedeutung **III**
What's it **meant to do?** [ment tʊ] Was soll er/sie/es eigentlich tun/machen? **IV 5**, 74
meat [mi:t] Fleisch **II**
mechanic [mɪ'kænɪk] Mechaniker/in **I**
medal ['medəl] Orden, Medaille **III**
medicine ['medsɪn] Medizin **II**
to **meet*** [mi:t] (sich) treffen **I**; sich kennen lernen **IV 1**, 7
meeting [mi:tɪŋ] Treffen, Besprechung **II**; Begegnung **III**
⟨to melt away⟩ [melt‿ə'weɪ] wegschmelzen **IV 4**, 59
⟨melting pot⟩ ['meltɪŋ pɒt] Schmelztiegel **IV 2**, 24
member ['membə] Mitglied, Angehörige/r **III**
memory ['memərɪ] Gedächtnis **II**
to **mend** [mend] reparieren, flicken **III**
mess [mes] Unordnung **I**
message ['mesɪdʒ] Botschaft, Nachricht **III**
to give s.o. a message [gɪv ə 'mesɪdʒ] jdm. etw. ausrichten **III**
meter (*AE*) ['mi:tə] Meter **IV 3**, 40
metre ['mi:tə] Meter **III**
°**Mexican** ['meksɪkn] mexikanisch, Mexikaner/in **IV 2**, 29
micro ['maɪkrəʊ] Mikro- **IV WSA**, 16
microwave (oven) ['maɪkrəweɪv] Mikrowelle(nherd) **IV WSA**, 16
middle ['mɪdl] Mitte **IV 1**, 11
midnight ['mɪdnaɪt] Mitternacht **IV WSA**, 16
might [maɪt] könnte **III**
mile [maɪl] Meile **III**
milk [mɪlk] Milch **I**
milkman ['mɪlkmən] Milchmann **II**
milkshake ['mɪlkʃeɪk] Milchmixgetränk **I**
million ['mɪljən] Million **III**
millionaire [ˌmɪljə'neə] Millionär/in **IV 5**, 72
mince [mɪns] Hackfleisch **II**
to **mind** [maɪnd] jdm. etw. ausmachen **II**
Do you mind if …? [də‿ju: maɪnd‿ɪf] Macht es dir/Ihnen etwas aus, wenn …? **III**
Never mind. ['nevə ˌmaɪnd] Mach dir nichts daraus., Macht euch nichts daraus. **I**
mind map ['maɪnd ˌmæp] Wörternetz **IV WSB**, 34
mine [maɪn] Mine, Bergwerk **III**
⟨minerals⟩ ['mɪnərəlz] Mineralien, Bodenschätze **IV WSC**, 51
minute ['mɪnɪt] Minute **I**
In a minute. [ɪn‿ə 'mɪnɪt] Augenblick noch!, Warte/t mal einen Moment. **I**
mirror ['mɪrə] Spiegel **II**
to **miss** [mɪs] verpassen, vermissen, übersehen **III**
missing ['mɪsɪŋ] fehlend **III**
mistake [mɪ'steɪk] Fehler **III**
⟨to mix⟩ [mɪks] mischen **IV 2**, 24
⟨mode⟩ [məʊd] Modus, Funktionsweise **IV 5**, 71
model ['mɒdl] Modell **III**
modern ['mɒdən] modern **III**
mom (*AE*) [mɑ:m] Mutter, Mutti, Mama **IV 1**, 7
moment ['məʊmənt] Moment, Augenblick **II**
Monday ['mʌndeɪ] Montag **I**
money ['mʌnɪ] Geld **I**
monkey ['mʌŋkɪ] Affe **II**
monster ['mɒnstə] Ungeheuer, Monster **II**
month [mʌnθ] Monat **I**
mood [mu:d] Stimmung **III**
more [mɔ:] mehr, weitere **I**
more interesting [mɔ: 'ɪntrəstɪŋ] interessanter **II**
more … than ever [ˌmɔ: ðən‿'evə] mehr …/…-er denn je **III**
morning ['mɔ:nɪŋ] Morgen **I**
Good morning. [gʊd 'mɔ:nɪŋ] Guten Morgen. **I**
in the morning [ɪn ðə 'mɔ:nɪŋ] morgens, am Vormittag **I**
most [məʊst] am meisten **II**
most exciting [məʊst ɪk'saɪtɪŋ] am aufregendsten **II**
motel [məʊ'tel] Motel **IV 5**, 75
mother ['mʌðə] Mutter **I**
motorbike ['məʊtəbaɪk] Motorrad **III**
motorhome ['məʊtəhəʊm] Wohnmobil **IV WSA**, 16
motorway ['məʊtəweɪ] Autobahn **III**
mountain ['maʊntɪn] Berg **II**
mountain biking ['maʊntɪn ˌbaɪkɪŋ] Mountainbike fahren **III**
mountain rescue ['maʊntɪn 'reskju:] Bergwacht **II**
⟨mountaineering⟩ [ˌmaʊntɪ'nɪərɪŋ] Bergsteigen, Klettern **IV WSA**, 19
mouse, mice (*pl*) [maʊs] Maus, Mäuse **II**
mouth [maʊθ] Mund **I**
to **move** [mu:v] (sich) bewegen **III**; umziehen **III**
⟨to be on the move⟩ [ɒn ðə 'mu:v] unterwegs sein **IV WSC**, 50
movie (*AE*) ['mu:vɪ] Film **IV WSA**, 16
Mr ['mɪstə] Herr *(Anrede für Männer)* **I**
Mrs ['mɪsɪz] Frau *(Anrede für verheiratete Frauen)* **I**
Mt. (= **Mount**) [ˌmaʊnt] Berg (*bei Namen*) **IV 1**, 10
°**mud ball** ['mʌd bɔ:l] Schlammball **IV WSB**, 34
°**mugger** ['mʌgə] Straßenräuber/in **IV 4**, 60
multi- ['mʌltɪ] multi- **IV 4**, 54
multi-cultural [ˌmʌltɪ‿'kʌltʃərəl] multikulturell **IV 4**, 54
multi-ethnic [ˌmʌltɪ‿'eθnɪk] multiethnisch, Vielvölker- **IV 4**, 54
Mum [mʌm] Mama, Mutti **I**
mummy ['mʌmɪ] Mumie **III**
museum [mju:'zɪəm] Museum **II**
music ['mjʊzɪk] Musik **I**
pop music ['pɒp 'mju:zɪk] Popmusik **I**
musical ['mju:zɪkəl] Musical **IV 4**, 54
Muslim ['mʊslɪm] islamisch, Moslem/Moslime **III**
must [mʌst] müssen **I**
my [maɪ] mein/meine **I**
myself [maɪ'self] (mich/mir) selbst **III**
°**mystery** ['mɪstrɪ] Geheimnis, Rätsel **IV WSB**, 35

N

°**nacho** ['nʌtʃəʊ] *mexikanische Vorspeise* **IV 4**, 57
⟨to nag⟩ [næg] herumnörgeln **IV 1**, 14
name [neɪm] Name **I**
My name is … ['maɪ neɪm‿ɪz] Ich heiße … **I**
named [neɪmd] namens, mit dem Namen **IV WSB**, 33
nasty ['nɑ:stɪ] scheußlich, übel, gemein **II**
⟨nation⟩ ['neɪʃn] Nation **IV 2**, 24
national ['næʃənl] national **III**

national park ['næʃənl 'pɑ:k] Nationalpark **IV 3**, 36
⟨nationality⟩ [ˌnæʃə'næləti] Nationalität **IV 2**, 22
° **Native American** ['neɪtɪv ə'merɪkən] indianisch, *amer. Ureinwohner/in* **IV 2**, 20
⟨natural⟩ ['nætʃrəl] natürlich, angeboren **IV 3**, 43
naturally ['nætʃrəlɪ] natürlich; selbstverständlich **IV WSC**, 50
nature ['neɪtʃə] Natur **IV WSB**, 32
⟨navigation⟩ [ˌnævɪ'geɪʃn] Navigation **IV WSA**, 19
near [nɪə] in der Nähe von **I**
nearly ['nɪəlɪ] fast **III**
to **need** [ni:d] brauchen, benötigen **I**
negative ['negətɪv] verneinter Satz **III**
neighbor (*AE*) ['neɪbə] Nachbar/in **IV 1**, 15
neighborhood (*AE*) ['neɪbəhʊd] Nachbarschaft, Wohnviertel **IV WSA**, 16
neighborhood watch (*AE*) [ˌneɪbəhʊd 'wɒtʃ] *Nachbarschaftshilfe zum Schutz vor Kriminalität* **IV WSA**, 16
neighbour ['neɪbə] Nachbar/in **I**
neither ['naɪðə] auch nicht **IV 2**, 25
° **neon sign** [ˌnɪɒn 'saɪn] Leuchtreklame **IV 4**, 54
nervous ['nɜ:vəs] aufgeregt, nervös **II**
never ['nevə] nie **I**
Never mind. ['nevə ˌmaɪnd] Mach dir nichts daraus., Macht euch nichts daraus. **I**
new [nju:] neu **I**
news (*sg + pl*) [nju:z] Nachricht(en) **II**
newsagent's ['nju:z ˌeɪdʒənts] Laden für Zeitungen, Zeitschriften, Tabakwaren, Süßigkeiten, etc. **II**
newspaper ['nju:sˌpeɪpə] Zeitung **III**
next [nekst] nächste/r/s **I**
next to [nekst tʊ] neben **II**
nice [naɪs] nett, schön **I**
(the) **nicest** [ðə 'naɪsɪst] am schönsten, der/die/das schönste **II**
night [naɪt] Nacht **I**
nightmare ['naɪtmeə] Alptraum **III**
no [nəʊ] nein **I**
⟨no U turns⟩ [nəʊ 'ju:‿tɜ:nz] nicht wenden **IV 4**, 62
nobody ['nəʊbədɪ] niemand, keiner **I**
to **nod** [nɒd] nicken **IV WSB**, 35
noise [nɔɪz] Lärm, Krach, Geräusch **I**
noisy ['nɔɪzɪ] laut, lärmend **II**
non-swimmers ['nɒnˌswɪmməz] Nichtschwimmer **II**
[non-uniform day] [nɒn 'ju:nɪfɔ:m deɪ] *Tag, an dem keine Uniform getragen werden muss* **II**
nonsense ['nɒnsəns] Quatsch, Unsinn **III**
normal ['nɔ:ml] normal **III**
north [nɔ:θ] nördlich, Nord-, Norden **II**
nose [nəʊz] Nase **II**
nosy ['nəʊzɪ] neugierig **I**
not [nɒt] nicht **I**
not ... any more [nɒt 'enɪˌmɔ:] nicht mehr **IV 2**, 24
not ... either ['aɪðə] auch nicht **IV WSD**, 66
not ... yet [nɒt ... jet] noch nicht **I**
note [nəʊt] Zettel **III**
notebook (*AE*) ['nəʊtbʊk] (Übungs-)Heft **IV WSB**, 35
to make **notes** [meɪk 'nəʊts] sich Notizen machen **II**
to take notes [teɪk 'nəʊts] Notizen machen **II**
nothing ['nʌθɪŋ] nichts **I**
notice ['nəʊtɪs] Aushang, Schild **II**
to **notice** ['nəʊtɪs] bemerken **III**
noun [naʊn] Substantiv **II**
November [nəʊ'vembə] November **I**
now [naʊ] jetzt, nun **I**
number ['nʌmbə] Nummer, Zahl **I**
nurse [nɜ:s] Krankenschwester/Krankenpfleger **I**
nursery school ['nɜ:sərɪ ˌsku:l] Kindergarten **I**

O

o [əʊ] null (*bei Telefonnummern*) **I**
oak [əʊk] Eiche **II**
⟨to occupy⟩ ['ɒkjʊpaɪ] bewohnen; besetzen **IV WSC**, 48
⟨to occur⟩ [ə'kɜ:] auftreten, vorkommen **IV 5**, 71
at ... o'clock [ət ... ə'klɒk] um ... Uhr **I**
October [ɒk'təʊbə] Oktober **I**
of [ɒv , əv] von **I**
of course [əv‿'kɔ:s] natürlich, selbstverständlich **I**
Off you go! [ˌɒf ju: 'gəʊ] Fort mit dir/euch! **II**
to **offer** ['ɒfə] (an)bieten **IV 2**, 23
office ['ɔfɪs] Büro, Amt **I**
police **officer** [pə'li:s‿ˌɒfɪsə] Polizist/in **I**
often ['ɒfn] oft **I**
oh [əʊ] oh **I**
Oh dear! [əʊ 'dɪə] Oh je! **I**
oil [ɔɪl] Öl **III**
oil rig ['ɔɪl rɪg] Ölplattform, Ölbohrinsel **III**
OK [əʊ'keɪ] OK, in Ordnung **I**
old [əʊld] alt **I**
on [ɒn] auf **I**
on (the radio) [ɒn] im (Rundfunk) **I**
on business [ɒn 'bɪznɪs] geschäftlich **IV 2**, 21
on foot [ɒn 'fʊt] zu Fuß **IV 2**, 21
⟨on my mind⟩ [ɒn maɪ 'maɪnd] im Kopf **IV 1**, 14
on the coast [ˌɒn ðə 'kəʊst] an der Küste **III**
on the left/right [ɒn ðə 'left, ɒn ðə 'raɪt] links/rechts, auf der linken/rechten Seite **I**
on the phone [ɒn ðə 'fəʊn] am Telefon **IV 1**, 10
on the seventh of [ɒn ðə 'sevnθ‿əv] am siebten **I**
on the telephone [ɒn ðə 'telɪfəʊn] am Telefon **I**
to be on [bɪ‿'ɒn] eingeschaltet sein **I**
⟨once⟩ [wʌns] sobald **IV 3**, 43
at **once** [ˌət 'wʌns] sofort **II**
one [wʌn] ein/eine/eins **I**
the **one** [ðə wʌn] derjenige/diejenige/dasjenige **III**
only ['əʊnlɪ] nur, erst **I**
Oops! [u:ps] Hoppla! **I**
to **open** ['əʊpən] öffnen, aufmachen **I**
open ['əʊpən] offen, geöffnet **I**
⟨open-air concert⟩ [ˌəʊpn‿eə 'kɒnsət] Freiluftkonzert **IV RII**, 46
open-air museum [ˌəʊpn‿'eə mju:'zɪəm] Freilichtmuseum **IV WSC**, 49
operation [ˌɒpə'reɪʃn] Operation **II**; Arbeitsgang; Bedienung **IV 5**, 71
opinion [ə'pɪnjən] Meinung **III**
in my opinion [ɪn 'maɪ əˌpɪnjən] meiner Meinung (nach) **III**
opponent [ə'pəʊnənt] Gegner/in **III**
opposite ['ɒpəzɪt] Gegenteil **I**
opposite ['ɒpəzɪt] gegenüber **II**
or [ɔ:] oder **I**
orange ['ɒrɪndʒ] Orange **II**
orchestra ['ɔ:kɪstrə] Orchester **III**
order ['ɔ:də] Reihenfolge; Ordnung **I**
word order ['wɜ:d ˌɔ:də] Satzstellung **I**
organization [ˌɔ:gənaɪ'zeɪʃn] Organisation **IV WSD**, 66
to **organize** ['ɔ:gənaɪz] organisieren **III**
origin ['ɒrɪdʒɪn] Ursprung, Herkunft **IV 2**, 20
⟨original⟩ [ə'rɪdʒənl] Original **IV WSA**, 19
other ['ʌðə] andere, weitere **I**

Ouch! [aʊtʃ] Aua! **II**
ought to [ˈɔːt‿tʊ] sollte, solltest, solltet, sollten **IV WSB**, 33
our [ˈaʊə] unser/unsere **I**
ourselves [ˌaʊəˈselvz] (uns) selbst **III**
out [aʊt] draußen, heraus **I**
out of [ˈaʊt‿əv] aus **II**
out of action [aʊt‿əv ˈækʃn] außer Betrieb **IV 5**, 75
⟨out of sight⟩ [aʊt‿əv ˈsaɪt] außer Sichtweite, nicht zu sehen **IV 1**, 14
out of work [ˌaʊt‿əv ˈwɜːk] arbeitslos **III**
to find out [faɪnd‿ˈaʊt] herausfinden **I**
outdoor [ˈaʊtdɔː] draußen, im Freien, Freiluft- **IV WSA**, 19
outlaw [ˈaʊtlɔː] Gesetzlose/r, Vogelfreie/r, Bandit/in **II**
outside [ˌaʊtˈsaɪd] draußen **I**
over [ˈəʊvə] über **I**
over there [əʊvə ˈðeə] da drüben, dort **I**
to be over at … [biː‿ˈəʊvər‿æt] bei … sein **IV WSA**, 16
"Over 60s" [ˌəʊvə ˈsɪkstɪz] Über Sechzigjährige **II**
⟨overnight trip⟩ [ˌəʊvəˈnaɪt trɪp] zweitägige Fahrt **IV WSA**, 19
own [əʊn] eigen **II**

P

⟨Pa⟩ [pɑː] Vater, Papa **IV WSC**, 52
P.A. system (= **public address system**) [piː eɪ ˈsɪstəm = ˈpʌblɪk əˈdres sɪstəm] Lautsprecheranlage **IV WSB**, 34
package [ˈpækɪdʒ] Paket **IV 4**, 54
packed lunch [ˌpækt ˈlʌntʃ] Lunchpaket **III**
packet [ˈpækɪt] Päckchen **I**
⟨packing list⟩ [ˈpækɪŋ lɪst] Checkliste beim Kofferpacken **IV WSA**, 19
page [peɪdʒ] Seite **I**
paint [peɪnt] Farbe, Lack **III**
to **paint** [peɪnt] (be)malen, streichen **II**
painting [ˈpeɪntɪŋ] Bild, Gemälde **IV 4**, 58
pair [peə] Paar **I**
⟨pan⟩ [pæn] Pfanne **IV 2**, 28
pants (*AE*) (*sg + pl*) [pænts] Hose, Hosen **IV WSA**, 19
paper [ˈpeɪpə] Papier **II**; Zeitung **IV WSB**, 32
test paper (*AE*) [test ˈpeɪpə] Klassenarbeit **IV WSB**, 35
parade [pəˈreɪd] Umzug, Parade **IV WSD**, 64
paragraph [ˈpærəgrɑːf] Absatz, Abschnitt **IV WSC**, 51
Pardon? [ˈpɑːdn] Wie bitte? **III**
parents (*pl*) [ˈpeərənts] Eltern **I**
park [pɑːk] Park **I**
national park [ˈnæʃənl ˈpɑːk] Nationalpark **IV 3**, 36
park-and-ride [ˌpɑːk‿ənˈraɪd] „Park-and-Ride"-System **III**
to **park** [pɑːk] parken **III**
part [pɑːt] Teil, Rolle **II**
part-time job [ˌpɑːt taɪm ˈdʒɒb] Teilzeitstelle **IV 1**, 8
partner [ˈpɑːtnə] Partner/in **I**
party [ˈpɑːtɪ] Party, Feier **I**
to **pass** [pɑːs] reichen, weitergeben **I**; ⟨überqueren⟩ **IV 2**, 24; vorbeigehen; bestehen **IV WSC**, 52
passenger [ˈpæsɪndʒə] Passagier/in; Beifahrer/in **IV 4**, 56
[passive] [ˈpæsɪv] Passiv- **IV 3**, 41
passport [ˈpɑːspɔːt] Reisepass **IV 4**, 60
past tense [ˈpɑːst tens] *Vergangenheitsform im Englischen* **II**
past participle [pɑːst ˈpɑːtɪsɪpl] Partizip Perfekt **II**
[past progressive] [ˈpɑːst prəʊˈgresɪv] Verlaufsform der Vergangenheit **II**
past [pɑːst] nach (*bei Uhrzeiten*) **I**
°**pastrami** [pəˈstrɑːmɪ] *Wurstsorte* **IV 4**, 57
patchwork quilt [ˌpætʃˌwɜːk ˈkwɪlt] aus bunten Flicken zusammengesetzte Decke **IV 2**, 20
path [pɑːθ] Pfad, Weg **II**
patient [ˈpeɪʃnt] Patient/in **II**
paved [peɪvd] gepflastert **IV 2**, 21
⟨paw⟩ [pɔː] Pfote **IV 3**, 44
⟨paw-paw⟩ [ˈpɔː pɔː] *Obstsorte* **IV 3**, 44
to **pay*** [peɪ] (be)zahlen **III**; [zahlen, bezahlen] **II**
⟨payment⟩ [ˈpeɪmənt] Bezahlung **IV WSA**, 19
PE (= **Physical Education**) [ˌpiː ˈiː = ˈfɪzɪkl ˌedjuːˈkeɪʃn] Sportunterricht **II**
⟨peaceable⟩ [ˈpiːsəbl] friedlich **IV WSC**, 52
peaceful [ˈpiːsfʊl] friedlich **IV WSC**, 50
⟨peculiar⟩ [pɪˈkjuːljə] eigenartig, komisch **IV 5**, 76
to **peel** [piːl] schälen **II**
pen [pen] Füller **I**
pence (= **p**) (*pl*) [pens] Pfennige (*britisches Geld*) **I**
pencil [ˈpensl] Bleistift **I**
pencil case [ˈpensl keɪs] Federmäppchen **I**
penfriend [ˈpenfrend] Brieffreund/in **III**
people (*pl*) [ˈpiːpl] Leute **I**
pepper [ˈpepə] Pfeffer **III**
per [pɜː] pro **III**
percent [pəˈsent] Prozent **IV WSB**, 35
perfect [ˈpɜːfɪkt] vollkommen **IV WSC**, 52
perhaps [pəˈhæps] vielleicht **II**
period (*AE*) [ˈpɪərɪəd] Unterrichtsstunde **IV WSB**, 32
person [ˈpɜːsn] Person **I**
⟨personal⟩ [ˈpɜːsnl] persönlich **IV WSA**, 19
personalized [ˈpɜːsnəlaɪzd] auf eine bestimmte Person bezogen **IV 5**, 74
pet [pet] Haustier **I**
petrol [ˈpetrəl] Benzin **III**
petrol station [ˈpetrəl ˌsteɪʃn] Tankstelle **III**
phone booth (*AE*) [ˈfəʊn ˌbuːð] Telefonzelle **IV 1**, 12
to **phone** [fəʊn] anrufen **I**
photo [ˈfəʊtəʊ] Foto **I**
to take a photo of [teɪk‿əˈfəʊtəʊ‿əv] ein Foto machen von **I**
phrase [freɪz] Ausdruck, Satzteil **II**
⟨physical condition⟩ [ˈfɪzɪkl kənˈdɪʃn] Kondition, körperliche Verfassung **IV WSA**, 19
piano [pɪˈænəʊ] Klavier **II**
⟨to pick⟩ [pɪk] pflücken **IV 3**, 44
to **pick up** [ˈpɪk‿ʌp] aufheben, aufnehmen, abholen **II**
to pick up (*AE*) [pɪk‿ˈʌp] kaufen, holen **IV 1**, 11
picnic [ˈpɪknɪk] Picknick **III**
picture [ˈpɪktʃə] Bild **I**
pie [paɪ] Kuchen; Pastete **IV WSD**, 66
piece [piːs] Stück **II**
pig [pɪg] Schwein **I**
pigeon [ˈpɪdʒɪn] Taube **III**
⟨pill⟩ [pɪl] Pille, Tablette **IV 5**, 76
pillow [ˈpɪləʊ] Kopfkissen **II**
pink [pɪŋk] rosa, pink **II**
pint [paɪnt] *etwa 0,5l* **I**
pipe [paɪp] Pfeife **IV WSC**, 51
pitch [pɪtʃ] Feld (*für Sport*) **III**
pizza [ˈpiːtsə] Pizza **II**
place [pleɪs] Ort, Stelle **II**
to go places [ˌgəʊ ˈpleɪsɪz] herumfahren, herumreisen **IV 1**, 11
⟨plainly⟩ [ˈpleɪnlɪ] eindeutig **IV WSC**, 52
plan [plæn] Plan **I**

to **plan** [plæn] planen **IV WSB**, 35
plane [pleɪn] Flugzeug **I**
⟨planet⟩ ['plænɪt] Planet **IV 5**, 76
plant [plɑ:nt] Pflanze **IV 3**, 39
plastic ['plæstɪk] Plastik, Kunststoff **III**
plate [pleɪt] Teller **II**
play [pleɪ] Theaterstück **II**
to **play** [pleɪ] spielen **I**
to play tricks on [ˌpleɪ 'trɪks] jdm. einen Streich spielen **II**
player ['pleɪə] Spieler/in **III**
playground ['pleɪgraʊnd] Schulhof, Spielplatz **I**
please [pli:z] bitte **I**
pleased [pli:zd] erfreut **III**
°to **pledge allegiance** [pledʒ ə'li:dʒns] Treue geloben **IV WSB**, 32
pm [ˌpi:'em] 12.00–24.00 Uhr **III**
pocket ['pɒkɪt] Tasche (*bei Kleidung*) **I**
pocket money ['pɒkɪt ˌmʌnɪ] Taschengeld **I**
poem ['pəʊɪm] Gedicht **III**
point [pɔɪnt] Punkt **III**
to **point s.th. at s.o.** [pɔɪnt] etw. auf jdn. richten **IV WSC**, 53
police [pə'li:s] Polizei **I**
police officer [pə'li:s‿ˌɒfɪsə] Polizist/in **I**
Polish ['pəʊlɪʃ] polnisch, Polnisch **III**
polite [pə'laɪt] höflich **II**
to **pollute** [pə'lu:t] verschmutzen **III**
pond [pɒnd] Teich **I**
pony ['pəʊnɪ] Pony **II**
poor [pɔ:] arm **I**; schlecht **III**
pop music ['pɒp 'mju:zɪk] Popmusik **I**
pop star ['pɒp 'stɑ:] Popstar **III**
popcorn ['pɒpkɔ:n] Popcorn **II**
popular ['pɒpjʊlə] beliebt **I**
porridge ['pɒrɪdʒ] Haferbrei **II**
possible ['pɒsəbl] möglich **III**
post office ['pəʊst ˌɒfɪs] Post, Postamt **I**
postcard ['pəʊstkɑ:d] Postkarte **I**
poster ['pəʊstə] Poster, Plakat **I**
⟨pot⟩ [pɒt] Topf **IV 2**, 28
potato, potatoes (*pl*) [pə'teɪtəʊ] Kartoffel, Kartoffeln **I**
pound (= **lb**) [paʊnd] Pfund *(Gewicht)* **I**
pound (= **£**) [paʊnd] Pfund *(britisches Geld)* **I**
Word **power** ['wɜ:d ˌpaʊə] Die Kraft der Wörter **I**
powerful ['paʊəfʊl] stark, kraftvoll, kräftig **IV 3**, 43
practice ['præktɪs] Übung, Training **I**
listening practice ['lɪsnɪŋ ˌpræktɪs] Hörverstehensübung **I**
sound practice ['saʊnd ˌpræktɪs] Ausspracheübung **I**
to **practise** ['præktɪs] üben **II**
prairie ['preərɪ] Prärie **IV WSC**, 48
to **prefer** [prɪ'fɜ:] lieber haben, vorziehen **III**
°**prejudice** ['predʒʊdɪs] Vorurteil **IV 2**, 26
preposition [ˌprepə'zɪʃn] Präposition **III**
prescription [prɪ'skrɪpʃn] Rezept (*vom Arzt*) **II**
present ['prezənt] Geschenk **I**
⟨present-day⟩ ['preznt ˌdeɪ] heutig **IV WSC**, 48
present perfect ['preznt 'pɜ:fɪkt] *englische Vergangenheitsform* **II**
present progressive [ˌpreznt prəʊ'gresɪv] *Verlaufsform* **IV 3**, 38
present tense ['preznt tens] Präsens **II**
⟨president⟩ ['prezɪdənt] Präsident **IV 2**, 28
to **press** [pres] drücken **IV 2**, 23
pretty [prɪtɪ] hübsch **II**
price [praɪs] Preis **III**
⟨to prick⟩ [prɪk] stechen **IV 3**, 44
⟨prickly pear⟩ ['prɪklɪ peə] Kaktusfeige **IV 3**, 44
primary school ['praɪmərɪ ˌsku:l] Grundschule **III**
°**principal** (*AE*) ['prɪnsəpl] Schuldirektor/in **IV WSB**, 35
prisoner ['prɪznə] Gefangene/r **II**
private ['praɪvɪt] ⟨privat⟩ **IV RI**, 31; ⟨Privat-⟩ **IV 2**, 24
private lesson [ˌpraɪvɪt 'lesn] Nachhilfeunterricht **IV WSB**, 35
prize [praɪz] Preis, Gewinn **I**
°**probability** [ˌprɒbə'bɪlətɪ] Wahrscheinlichkeit **IV WSB**, 35
probably ['prɒbəblɪ] wahrscheinlich **II**
problem ['prɒbləm] Aufgabe **IV WSB**, 35; Problem **I**
°**producer** [prə'dju:sə] Produzent/in **IV 4**, 61
program (*AE*) ['prəʊgræm] Sendung (*im Radio oder TV*); Programm **IV 3**, 40
to **program** ['prəʊgræm] programmieren **IV 5**, 75
programme ['prəʊgræm] [Programm] **II**; Sendung **III**
progress (*sg + pl*) ['prəʊgres] Fortschritt **III**
project ['prɒdʒekt] Projekt **III**
⟨to project⟩ [prə'dʒekt] projizieren **IV RII**, 46
promenade [ˌprɒmə'nɑ:d] Promenade **I**
to **promise** ['prɒmɪs] versprechen **III**
prompter ['prɒmptə] Souffleur/Souffleuse (*Stichwortgeber/in beim Theater*) **II**
pronoun ['prəʊnaʊn] Pronomen **III**
to **pronounce** [prə'naʊns] aussprechen **IV WSA**, 17
⟨properly⟩ ['prɒpəlɪ] richtig, ordentlich **IV 3**, 43
to **protect** [prə'tekt] schützen, beschützen **IV 3**, 36
⟨protein⟩ ['prəʊti:n] Eiweiß **IV 5**, 76
to **protest** [prəʊ'test] protestieren **IV 1**, 12
proud [praʊd] stolz **II**
to be proud of [bɪ 'praʊd‿əv] stolz sein auf **II**
PS (= **postscript**) [pi: 'es] PS, Postskriptum **IV 1**, 7
public [ˌpʌblɪk] öffentlich **III**
to **pull** [pʊl] ziehen **II**
pullover ['pʊlˌəʊvə] Pullover **I**
pump [pʌmp] Luftpumpe **I**
⟨pumpkin⟩ ['pʌmpkɪn] Kürbis **IV WSC**, 50
pupil ['pju:pl] Schüler/in **I**
puppet ['pʌpɪt] Marionette **II**
purse [pɜ:s] Geldbeutel, Portmonee **II**
to **push** [pʊʃ] schieben **III**
to **put*** [pʊt] setzen, stellen, legen **I**
to put down [pʊt 'daʊn] hinlegen, hinstellen; auflegen (*Telefon*) **IV 1**, 11
to put in ['pʊt‿ɪn] einsetzen, hineintun **I**
to put on ['pʊt‿ɒn] anziehen, aufsetzen **II**
to put up [ˌpʊt‿'ʌp] aufhängen, montieren **III**
puzzle ['pʌzl] Rätsel **II**

Q

quality ['kwɒlətɪ] Qualität **III**
quarter ['kwɔ:tə] Viertel **I**
queen [kwi:n] Königin **III**
question ['kwestʃən] Frage **I**
queue [kju:] Schlange **III**
quick [kwɪk] schnell **II**
quickly ['kwɪklɪ] schnell *(Adverbialform)* **III**
quiet ['kwaɪət] still, ruhig **I**
quite [kwaɪt] ganz **II**
quite a [kwaɪt‿ə] ziemlich, ein/e ziemliche/r/s **IV 5**, 72
quiz [kwɪz] Quiz, Ratespiel **I**

R

rabbit ['ræbɪt] Kaninchen **II**
race [reɪs] Rennen **III**
to **race** [reɪs] rennen, rasen **IV 4**, 60
racket ['rækɪt] Schläger **III**
radio ['reɪdɪəʊ] Radio **I**
raffle ['ræfl] Verlosung, Tombola **II**
railroad (*AE*) ['reɪlrəʊd] Eisenbahn **IV WSC**, 50
⟨railroad worker⟩ ['reɪlrəʊd 'wɜ:kə] Eisenbahnarbeiter/in **IV WSC**, 50
railway ['reɪlweɪ] Eisenbahn **III**
rain [reɪn] Regen **II**
to **rain** [reɪn] regnen **I**
[to rain hard] [reɪn 'hɑ:d] heftig regnen **II**
⟨raingear⟩ [reɪn'gɪə] Regenkleidung **IV WSA**, 19
rainstorm ['reɪnstɔ:m] heftiger Regenguss, Wolkenbruch **III**
ranger ['reɪndʒə] Aufseher/in, Ranger/in **IV 3**, 38
rap [ræp] Rap (*Musikrichtung*) **III**
[to rap] [ræp] „rappen" **II**
rapids (*sg + pl*) ['ræpɪds] Stromschnellen **IV WSA**, 19
rare [reə] selten, rar **IV 3**, 39
rather than ['rɑ:ðə] eher **IV 4**, 58
would rather ['rɑ:ðə] lieber **IV WSB**, 34
raw [rɔ:] ⟨nackt⟩ **IV 3**, 44; roh **IV 4**, 57
RE (= Religious Education) [ˌɑ: r‿i: = rɪ'lɪdʒəs ˌedju:'keɪʃn] Religionsunterricht **II**
⟨to re-enter⟩ [ˌri:'entə] nochmals eingeben **IV 5**, 71
to **reach** [ri:tʃ] erreichen, greifen (nach) **IV 1**, 12
to reach for s.th. ['ri:tʃ fɔ:] nach etw. greifen **IV 1**, 13
to **react** [rɪ'ækt] reagieren **IV 3**, 43
to **read*** [ri:d] lesen **I**
to read out [ˌri:d‿'aʊt] vorlesen **III**
reader ['ri:də] Leser/in **III**
ready ['redɪ] fertig, bereit **I**
to get ready [get 'redɪ] (sich) vorbereiten **I**
real [rɪəl] echt, wirklich **III**
really ['rɪəlɪ] wirklich **I**
reason ['ri:zn] Grund, Ursache **IV WSA**, 18
reasonable ['ri:znəbl] vernünftig, angemessen **IV WSA**, 19
reception [rɪ'sepʃn] Rezeption **IV 4**, 56
receptionist [rɪ'sepʃənɪst] Empfangschef/-dame **IV 4**, 60
recipe ['resɪpɪ] (Koch-)Rezept **II**
to **recognize** ['rekəgnaɪz] erkennen **III**
to **recommend** [ˌrekə'mend] empfehlen **IV WSD**, 66
to **record** [rɪ'kɔ:d] aufnehmen **III**
recording [rɪ'kɔ:dɪŋ] Aufnahme **II**
recycling bin [ˌri:'saɪklɪŋ bɪn] Recyclingtonne **IV 3**, 39
red [red] rot **I**
°**red-eye-flight** (*AE*) ['red‿aɪ‿flaɪt] *umg.:* Nachtflug **IV WSA**, 16
reduced in size [rɪˌdju:st‿ɪn 'saɪz] verkleinert **I**
redwood ['redwʊd] *Baumart* **IV 3**, 36
region ['ri:dʒən] Region **IV WSC**, 48
register ['redʒɪstə] Klassenbuch **III**
regular ['regjʊlə] regelmäßig **II**
related [rɪ'leɪtɪd] verwandt; zusammenhängend **IV WSA**, 17
relative ['relətɪv] Verwandte/r **IV 1**, 7
relative clause [ˌrelətɪv 'klɔ:z] Relativsatz **III**
⟨to relax⟩ [rɪ'læks] (sich) entspannen **IV 3**, 44
religion [rɪ'lɪdʒən] Religion **IV WSC**, 51
to **remember** [rɪ'membə] behalten, sich merken, sich erinnern **I**
⟨remote control⟩ [rɪ'məʊt kən'trəʊl] Fernbedienung **IV 5**, 71
remote [rɪ'məʊt] entfernt, abgelegen **IV 3**, 40
to **rent** (*AE*) [rent] mieten **IV 1**, 13
⟨rental (AE)⟩ ['rentl] Miet- **IV WSA**, 19
to **repair** [rɪ'peə] reparieren **I**
to **repeat** [rɪ'pi:t] wiederholen **III**
to **reply** [rɪ'plaɪ] antworten **IV WSC**, 52
report [rɪ'pɔ:t] Bericht, Reportage **II**; Zeugnis **III**
to **report** [rɪ'pɔ:t] berichten **IV 4**, 62
reporter [rɪ'pɔ:tə] Reporter/in, Journalist/in **III**
°**republic** [rɪ'pʌblɪk] Republik **IV WSB**, 32
request [rɪ'kwest] Bitte, Wunsch **I**
⟨to request⟩ [rɪ'kwest] anfordern, wünschen, fragen nach **IV 5**, 71
to **require** [rɪ'kwaɪə] benötigen, brauchen; erfordern **IV WSA**, 19
rescue ['reskju:] Rettung **III**
rescue service ['reskju: sɜ:vɪs] Rettungsdienst **III**
to **rescue** ['reskju:] retten, bergen **II**
reservation [ˌrezə'veɪʃn] Reservat **IV WSC**, 48; Reservierung **IV WSA**, 19
to **respond** [rɪ'spɒnd] antworten, reagieren auf **IV 5**, 74
rest [rest] Rest **IV WSA**, 19
⟨to rest at ease⟩ ['rest‿ət 'i:z] sich zurücklehnen, sich wohl fühlen **IV 3**, 44
restaurant ['restərɒnt] Restaurant **I**
result [rɪ'zʌlt] Ergebnis, Resultat; Folge **IV 3**, 43
to **retell** [ˌri:'tel] nacherzählen **III**
⟨to return⟩ [rɪ'tɜ:n] zurückgehen, zurückkehren **IV 5**, 71
review [rɪ'vju:] Kritik, Besprechung (eines Buches, Filmes, einer CD) **III**
to **revise** [rɪ'vaɪz] wiederholen **III**
rhyme [raɪm] Reim **I**
rich [rɪtʃ] reich **IV 2**, 20
ride [raɪd] Fahrt **II**
to **ride*** [raɪd] reiten, fahren **II**
riding school ['raɪdɪŋ ˌsku:l] Reitschule **II**
right [raɪt] (nach) rechts **I**
on the left/right [ɒn ðə 'left, ɒn ðə 'raɪt] links/rechts, auf der linken/rechten Seite **I**
right [raɪt] richtig **I**
right away ['raɪt‿ə'weɪ] sofort **I**
⟨right through the very heart of it⟩ [raɪt θru: ðə 'verɪ hɑ:t‿əv‿ɪt] mitten durch sein Herz **IV 4**, 59
ring [rɪŋ] Ring **I**
to **ring*** [rɪŋ] klingeln (lassen) **III**
⟨R.I.P. (= Rest in Peace)⟩ [ɑ:‿aɪ‿pi: = rest‿ɪn pi:s] Ruhe in Frieden **IV 3**, 43
to **rise up*** ['raɪz‿ʌp] aufstehen **IV WSC**, 52
⟨ritual⟩ ['rɪtʃʊəl] Ritual, Zeremoniell **IV WSC**, 51
river [rɪvə] Fluss **IV WSA**, 16
river-rafting ['rɪvə‿ˌrɑ:ftɪŋ] Schlauchboot fahren (*auf einem Fluss*) **IV WSA**, 16
road (= **Rd.**) [rəʊd] Straße **I**
roadworks ['rəʊdwɜ:ks] Baustelle **III**
⟨to roam⟩ [rəʊm] streifen durch **IV 3**, 44
roast beef ['rəʊst ˌbi:f] Rinderbraten **II**
⟨robot⟩ ['rəʊbɒt] Roboter/in **IV RI**, 31
rock [rɒk] Fels **I**
⟨rock 'n' roll⟩ [ˌrɒkn'rəʊl] Rock 'n' Roll (*Musikrichtung*) **IV 2**, 28
role play ['rəʊl pleɪ] Rollenspiel **I**
Roman ['rəʊmən] Römer/in, römisch **III**
room [ru:m] Platz **I**; Raum, Zimmer **I**
rope [rəʊp] Seil **III**
⟨rose⟩ [rəʊz] Rose **IV WSD**, 67

rough [rʌf] rau, aufgewühlt **III**; grob **IV WSB**, 32
round [raʊnd] rund **III**
round [raʊnd] in ... herum **III**; um ... herum **I**
roundabout ['raʊndəbaʊt] Karussell **II**; Kreisverkehr **III**
route [ru:t] Weg, Route **IV WSC**, 50
to **row** [rəʊ] rudern **II**
rubbish ['rʌbɪʃ] Abfall, Müll **I**
rude [ru:d] unhöflich, grob **IV 1**, 13
rugby ['rʌgbɪ] Rugby **III**
rule [ru:l] Regel **III**
⟨run⟩ [rʌn] Strecke, Fahrt **IV WSA**, 19
to **run** [rʌn] ⟨betreiben⟩ **IV RII**, 46; rennen, laufen **II**
⟨to run (tours)⟩ [rʌn] anbieten, organisieren; betreiben **IV WSA**, 19
to run off, ran off [ræn ɒf] rannte weg **II**
Russian ['rʌʃən] russisch, Russisch **III**

S

sack [sæk] Sack **II**
sad [sæd] traurig **IV WSD**, 65
safe [seɪf] sicher **III**
safely [seɪflɪ] sicher **III**
to **sail** [seɪl] segeln **IV WSA**, 17
salad ['sæləd] gemischter Salat **I**
[sale] [seɪl] Verkauf **II**
same [seɪm] gleich **I**; gleichzeitig **III**
sandcastle ['sændkɑ:sl] Sandburg **I**
sandwich ['sænwɪdʒ] belegtes Brot **I**
⟨satellite station⟩ ['sætəlaɪt ˌsteɪʃn] Satellitensender **IV 2**, 28
Saturday ['sætədeɪ] Samstag, Sonnabend **I**
sauerkraut ['saʊəkraʊt] Sauerkraut **II**
sausage ['sɒsɪdʒ] Würstchen, Wurst **I**
° **savage** ['sævɪdʒ] Wilde/r **IV WSC**, 50
to **save** [seɪv] retten **I**; sparen **I**
to **say*** [seɪ] sagen **I**
It doesn't say. [ɪt ˌdʌznt 'seɪ] Das wird nicht gesagt., Das steht nicht darauf. **II**
to say hello ['seɪ hə'ləʊ] grüßen **I**
⟨scalplock⟩ [skælp'lɒk] Skalplocke **IV WSC**, 53
to be **scared of** [bɪ 'skeəd əv] Angst haben vor **II**
scarf, scarves (*pl*) [skɑ:f] Schal, Schals **III**
⟨scary⟩ ['skærɪ] unheimlich, gruselig, gespenstisch **IV WSD**, 67
scene [si:n] Szene **II**
schedule (*AE*) ['ʃedju:l] Stundenplan; Fahrplan **IV WSB**, 32
school [sku:l] Schule **I**
boarding school ['bɔ:dɪŋ ˌsku:l] Internat **III**
Science ['saɪəns] Naturwissenschaft(en) **II**
to **score** [skɔ:] ein Tor erzielen **III**
⟨Scot⟩ [skɒt] Schotte/Schottin **IV 2**, 24
Scottish ['skɒtɪʃ] schottisch **II**
to **scowl** [skaʊl] ein böses Gesicht machen **IV 5**, 72
scream [skri:m] Schrei **IV 3**, 42
⟨to be a scream⟩ [skri:m] zum Schreien sein **IV WSD**, 67
to **scream** [skri:m] schreien **III**
screen [skri:n] Bildschirm, Leinwand **III**
sea [si:] Meer **I**
at the **seaside** [si:saɪd] an der See **I**
seal [si:l] Robbe **II**
seaside ['si:saɪd] an der Küste, am Meer **III**
season ['si:zn] Jahreszeit **I**
seat [si:t] Sitz, Sitzplatz **I**
second ['sekənd] Sekunde **III**
secondary school ['sekəndərɪ ˌsku:l] weiterführende Schule **III**
section ['sekʃn] Abteilung, Teil **III**
to **see*** [si:] sehen **I**
You only see the fun side. [jʊ 'əʊnlɪ si: ðə 'fʌn saɪd] Du siehst nur dein Vergnügen. **IV 1**, 11
See you! *umg.*: Tschüs!, Bis bald!, Bis dann! **IV 1**, 8
⟨to seek out⟩ [si:k‿aʊt] aussuchen **IV 3**, 43
to **seem** [si:m] scheinen **II**
to **select** [sɪ'lekt] auswählen **IV 5**, 71
to **sell*** [sel] verkaufen **I**
to **send*** [send] schicken **II**
⟨Senior Citizen⟩ ['si:njə 'sɪtɪzn] Senior/in **IV 5**, 75
⟨sense⟩ [sens] Sinn **IV 3**, 43
sentence ['sentəns] Satz **I**
° **separate entry** ['seprət‿ˌentrɪ] eigener Eintrag **IV WSA**, 17
September [sep'tembə] September **I**
serious ['sɪərɪəs] ernsthaft **III**
service ['sɜ:vɪs] Dienst, Dienstleistung **III**
service station ['sɜ:vɪs ˌsteɪʃn] Raststätte **III**
to **settle** ['setl] (be)siedeln, sich niederlassen **IV 2**, 20
settlement ['setlmənt] Siedlung **IV WSC**, 48
settler ['setlə] Siedler/in **IV 2**, 20
several ['sevrl] mehrere, einige **IV 3**, 43
to **shake*** ['ʃeɪk] zittern, schütteln **IV 3**, 43
⟨shark⟩ [ʃɑ:k] Schlitzohr **IV 2**, 28
she [ʃi:] sie **I**
shed [ʃed] Stall, Schuppen **I**
sheep (*sg + pl*) [ʃi:p] Schaf, Schafe **I**
sheepdog ['ʃi:pdɒg] Hirtenhund **I**
shelf, shelves (*pl*) [ʃelf] Regal, Regale **I**
sheriff ['ʃerɪf] Sheriff **II**
ship [ʃɪp] Schiff **III**
shirt [ʃɜ:t] Hemd(bluse) **I**
shock [ʃɒk] [Schock] **II**; Schock(zustand) **IV 5**, 72
to be **shocked** [ʃɒkt] schockiert sein **IV 1**, 13
shoe [ʃu:] Schuh **I**
to **shoot*** [ʃu:t] schießen **II**
shop [ʃɒp] Geschäft, Laden **I**
shop assistant ['ʃɒp‿əˌsɪstənt] Verkäufer/in **I**
to go to the shops [gəʊ tə ðə 'ʃɒps] einkaufen gehen **I**
shopping ['ʃɒpɪŋ] Einkaufs-, Einkaufen **I**
shopping centre ['ʃɒpɪŋ ˌsentə] Einkaufszentrum **I**
shopping list ['ʃɒpɪŋ lɪst] Einkaufsliste **I**
short cut ['ʃɔ:t kʌt] Abkürzung **II**
short [ʃɔ:t] kurz **I**
shorts (*sg + pl*) [ʃɔ:ts] Shorts, kurze Hose, kurze Hosen **IV WSA**, 19
shotgun ['ʃɒtgʌn] Schrotflinte **IV WSC**, 49
should [ʃʊd] sollte, sollten, solltest, solltet **III**
shoulder ['ʃəʊldə] Schulter **II**
shout [ʃaʊt] Schrei **IV 5**, 75
to **shout** [ʃaʊt] rufen **II**
⟨Shove your old pot.⟩ [ʃʌv] *etwa:* Steckt euch euren blöden Topf an den Hut. **IV 2**, 24
show [ʃəʊ] Vorstellung, Vorführung **III**
to **show*** [ʃəʊ] zeigen **I**
to show s.th. off [ʃəʊ‿'ɒf] mit etw. protzen, mit etw. angeben **IV WSB**, 35
to **shut*** [ʃʌt] schließen **II**
to be **sick** [bɪ 'sɪk] sich übergeben **IV 2**, 23
to feel sick [ˌfi:l 'sɪk] sich schlecht, krank fühlen **II**
side [saɪd] Seite **II**
sight [saɪt] Sehenswürdigkeit **III**
sign [saɪn] Schild, Zeichen **II**
⟨sign language⟩ [saɪn 'læŋgwɪdʒ] Zeichensprache **IV WSC**, 51

signal [ˈsɪgnl] Signal, Zeichen **II**
silence [ˈsaɪləns] Ruhe, Stille **IV 5**, 75
silent [ˈsaɪlənt] still, stumm, geräuschlos; schweigsam **IV WSC**, 52
silly [ˈsɪlɪ] dumm, albern **I**
⟨simple⟩ [ˈsɪmpl] einfach **IV 3**, 44
[simple past] [ˈsɪmpl ˌpɑːst] einfache Vergangenheit **II**
simple present [ˌsɪmpl ˈpreznt] Präsens **III**
since [sɪns] seit **IV 1**, 10
Sincerely, [sɪnˈsɪəlɪ] Mit freundlichen Grüßen (*Schlussformel in Briefen*) **IV WSD**, 65
Sincerely yours, (*AE*) [sɪnˈsɪəlɪ jɔːz] Mit freundlichen Grüßen (*Schlussformel in Briefen*) **IV WSD**, 65
to **sing*** [sɪŋ] singen **I**
singer [ˈsɪŋə] Sänger/in **III**
Sir [sɜː] *Anrede/Titel eines Ritters* **III**
sister [ˈsɪstə] Schwester **I**
to **sit*** [sɪt] sitzen **I**
Sit down. [sɪt ˈdaʊn] Setz dich., Setzt euch. **I**
to sit down [sɪt ˈdaʊn] sich hinsetzen **I**
situation [ˌsɪtjʊˈeɪʃn] Situation, Lage **III**
size [saɪz] Größe **I**
to **skate** [skeɪt] Rollschuh/Schlittschuh laufen **IV 4**, 54
skateboard [ˈskeɪtbɔːd] Skateboard **I**
skater [ˈskeɪtə] Schlitt-/Rollschuhläufer/in, Skateboardfahrer/in **II**
skates [skeɪts] Schlittschuhe **II**
⟨ski touring⟩ [ˈskiː ˌtɔːrɪŋ] Skiwandern **IV WSA**, 19
skill [skɪl] Fertigkeit, Fähigkeit **IV WSA**, 18
skin [skɪn] Haut **I**
skirt [skɜːt] Rock **II**
skyscraper [ˈskaɪˌskreɪpə] Wolkenkratzer **IV 4**, 54
slave [sleɪv] Sklave/Sklavin **IV 2**, 20
to **sleep*** [sliːp] schlafen **I**
⟨to go to sleep⟩ [gəʊ tʊ ˈsliːp] einschlafen **IV WSC**, 53
sleeping bag [ˈsliːpɪŋ bæg] Schlafsack **IV WSA**, 19
sleepless [ˈsliːplɪs] schlaflos **III**
⟨sleeve⟩ [sliːv] Ärmel **IV WSA**, 19
slippery [ˈslɪpərɪ] rutschig, glatt **II**
slow [sləʊ] langsam **III**
slow-moving traffic [ˌsləʊmuːvɪŋ ˈtræfɪk] zähfließender Verkehr **III**
small [smɔːl] klein **I**
to **smell*** [smel] riechen **IV 3**, 38
smile [smaɪl] Lächeln **IV 1**, 12
to **smile** [smaɪl] lächeln **II**
smoke [sməʊk] Rauch **III**
⟨smoke signal⟩ [sməʊk ˈsɪgnl] Rauchzeichen **IV WSC**, 51
to **smoke** [sməʊk] rauchen **IV 2**, 20
no **smoking** [nəʊ ˈsməʊkɪŋ] Rauchen verboten **II**
snack bar [ˈsnæk bɑː] Imbissstube **I**
snake [sneɪk] Schlange **I**
snow [snəʊ] Schnee **I**
so [səʊ] also **I**
so (much) [səʊ] so (viel) **II**
so (that) [ˈsəʊ ðæt] damit **IV WSD**, 65
So what? [səʊ ˈwɒt] Na und? **IV 2**, 20
soap [səʊp] Seife **I**
soccer [ˈsɒkə] Fußball **IV WSB**, 32
sock [sɒk] Socke **II**
software [ˈsɒftweə] Software **IV WSA**, 16
soldier [ˈsəʊldʒə] Soldat/in **IV 5**, 74
some [sʌm] einige, etwas **II**
somebody [ˈsʌmbədɪ] jemand **II**
someone [ˈsʌmwʌn] jemand **III**
something [ˈsʌmθɪŋ] etwas **II**
sometimes [ˈsʌmtaɪmz] manchmal **I**
somewhere [ˈsʌmweə] irgendwo **II**
son [sʌn] Sohn **II**
song [sɒŋ] Lied **I**
soon [suːn] bald **I**
as soon as possible [əz‿suːn‿əz ˈpɒsəbl] so bald wie möglich **IV WSD**, 65
sore [sɔː] schmerzend **II**
Sorry. [ˈsɒrɪ] Entschuldigung., Tut mir Leid. **I**
to be **sorry about s.th.** [bɪ ˈsɒrɪ əbaʊt] Leid tun, dass ..., Leid tun wegen **II**
to be sorry for s.o. [bɪ ˈsɒrɪ fə] Mitleid haben mit jdm. **II**
⟨soul (= soul music)⟩ [səʊl] Soul (*Musikrichtung*) **IV 2**, 28
sound [ˈsaʊnd] Geräusch, Laut **II**
sound effect [ˈsaʊnd ɪˌfekt] Geräuscheffekt **II**
sound practice [ˈsaʊnd ˌpræktɪs] Ausspracheübung **I**
to **sound** [saʊnd] klingen, sich anhören **III**
soup [suːp] Suppe **III**
south [saʊθ] südlich, Süd-, Süden **II**
souvenir [ˌsuːvəˈnɪə] Souvenir, Andenken, Mitbringsel **I**
⟨space oddity⟩ [speɪs ˈɒdɪtɪ] *etwa:* seltsamer Zwischenfall im Weltall **IV 5**, 76
⟨spaceship⟩ [ˈspeɪsʃɪp] Raumschiff **IV 5**, 76
spade [speɪd] Spaten **I**
Spanish [ˈspænɪʃ] spanisch, Spanisch **I**
to **speak*** [spiːk] sprechen **I**
to speak up [spiːk ˈʌp] sich äußern, die Meinung sagen; lauter sprechen **IV WSB**, 35
special [ˈspeʃl] besondere/r/s; Spezialität des Hauses **I**
speech [spiːtʃ] Rede **IV WSC**, 49
speed [spiːd] Geschwindigkeit, Schnelligkeit, Tempo **IV 4**, 60
to **spell*** [spel] buchstabieren **I**
spelling [ˈspelɪŋ] Rechtschreibung **III**
to **spend*** [spend] verbringen, ausgeben **II**
spoon [spuːn] Löffel **I**
sports [spɔːts] Sport(arten) **II**
Sports Day [ˈspɔːtsdeɪ] Sportfest **III**
sportsfield [ˈspɔːtsfiːld] Sportplatz **III**
sportsperson [ˈspɔːtsˌpɜːsn] Sportler/in **III**
spot [spɒt] Fleck, Pickel **II**
to **spray** [spreɪ] sprühen **IV 4**, 58
⟨to spread the news⟩ [spred] weitersagen **IV 4**, 59
spring [sprɪŋ] Frühling **I**
⟨to spring*⟩ [sprɪŋ] springen **IV WSC**, 52
square [ˈskweə] Platz **I**
⟨to squat⟩ [skwɒt] hocken **IV WSC**, 52
stable [ˈsteɪbl] Stall **IV WSC**, 52
stack [stæk] Stapel **IV WSD**, 66
staff [stɑːf] Mitarbeiterteam, Personal **IV WSB**, 34
stage [steɪdʒ] Bühne **II**
to be on the **stage** [bɪ ɒn ðə ˈsteɪdʒ] auf der Bühne sein, stehen **II**
⟨stain⟩ [steɪn] Klecks, Fleck **IV 2**, 24
stairs [steəz] Treppe, Treppenhaus **III**
stall [stɔːl] Bude **II**
stamp [stæmp] Briefmarke **II**
to **stand*** [stænd] stehen **I**
I can't stand ... [aɪ ˈkɑːnt ˈstænd] ich kann ... nicht leiden, ausstehen **II**
to stand back [ˌstænd ˈbæk] zurückbleiben **III**
star [stɑː] Star; Stern **IV 2**, 29
to **start** [stɑːt] anfangen, beginnen **I**
Let's start. [ˌlets ˈstɑːt] Lasst uns anfangen. **I**
⟨starvation⟩ [stɑːˈveɪʃn] Hunger, Hungersnot **IV WSC**, 51

Vocabulary

Vocabulary

state [steɪt] (Bundes-)Staat **IV 3**, 37
statement [ˈsteɪtmənt] Aussage, Aussagesatz **II**
station [ˈsteɪʃn] Bahnhof **I**; ⟨Sender⟩ **IV 5**, 71
statue [ˈstætʃuː] Statue, Denkmal **I**
to **stay** [steɪ] (zu Besuch) wohnen **I**; bleiben **I**
steak [steɪk] Steak **IV 1**, 11
to **steal*** [stiːl] stehlen **III**
steep [stiːp] steil **II**
step [step] Schritt, Stufe **I**
to **step** [step] treten **III**
to step between [step bɪˈtwiːn] dazwischen treten **IV WSC**, 53
⟨to step in⟩ [step ˈɪn] hineingehen, hineinsteigen **IV 2**, 24
to step on s.o.'s toes [ˈstep‿ɒn …ˈtəʊz] jdm. auf die Füße treten; jdn. beleidigen **III**
⟨to step out⟩ [step ˈaʊt] hinausgehen, hinaussteigen **IV 2**, 24
⟨stiff⟩ [stɪf] steif **IV WSC**, 52
still [stɪl] regungslos **IV WSC**, 52
still [stɪl] (immer) noch **II**
stomach [ˈstʌmək] Magen **II**
stomach-ache [ˈstʌməkeɪk] Bauchschmerzen **II**
stone [stəʊn] Stein **I**
to **stop** [stɒp] anhalten **I**; aufhören **II**
Stop it! [ˈstɒp‿ɪt] Hör/Hört auf! **II**
store (*AE*) [stɔː] Geschäft, Laden **IV 1**, 11
⟨to store⟩ [stɔː] lagern **IV 3**, 43
storm [stɔːm] Sturm **III**
stormy [ˈstɔːmɪ] stürmisch **III**
story [ˈstɔːrɪ] Geschichte, Erzählung **I**
storyline [ˈstɔːrɪlaɪn] (Verlauf einer) Geschichte **III**
straight on [streɪt‿ˈɒn] geradeaus **I**
strange [streɪndʒ] seltsam, merkwürdig **II**
⟨strap⟩ [stræp] Band **IV WSA**, 19
straw [strɔː] Strohhalm, Trinkhalm **IV 1**, 11
street [striːt] Straße **I**
⟨strife⟩ [straɪf] Unfriede, Streit **IV 3**, 44
string [strɪŋ] Saite, Bindfaden **III**
strong [strɒŋ] stark **III**
⟨structure⟩ [ˈstrʌktʃə] Aufbau, Struktur **IV WSC**, 51
to be **stuck** [bɪ ˈstʌk] klemmen **IV 5**, 75
to be stuck with [bɪ ˈstʌk wɪð] etw. am Hals haben **IV 5**, 75
student (*AE*) [ˈstjuːdnt] Schüler/in; Student/in **IV 2**, 20
Student Council (*AE*) [ˌstjuːdnt ˈkaʊnsl] Schülermitverwaltung **IV WSB**, 32
to **study** [stʌdɪ] studieren; beobachten; lesen **IV 4**, 56
stuff [stʌf] Zeug; Stoff **IV 4**, 58
stupid [ˈstjuːpɪd] dumm **II**
style [staɪl] Stil, Richtung **III**
subject [ˈsʌbdʒɪkt] Fach **II**; Thema **III**
subway (*AE*) [ˈsʌbweɪ] U-Bahn **IV 4**, 54
success [səkˈses] Erfolg **III**
such a [sʌtʃ‿ə] solch ein/e, ein/e solche/r **IV 5**, 72
⟨such as …⟩ [ˈsʌtʃ‿æz] wie (zum Beispiel) … **IV WSC**, 50
suddenly [ˈsʌdnlɪ] plötzlich **II**
sugar [ˈʃʊgə] Zucker **I**
to **suggest** [səˈdʒest] vorschlagen; andeuten, hindeuten auf **IV 1**, 12
suggestion [səˈdʒestʃn] Vorschlag **IV WSB**, 34
suit [suːt] Anzug, Kostüm **III**
suitable [ˈsuːtəbl] geeignet, passend **IV WSA**, 19
summary [ˈsʌmərɪ] Zusammenfassung **II**
summer [ˈsʌmə] Sommer **I**
sun [sʌn] Sonne **III**
⟨sunburn⟩ [ˈsʌnbɜːn] Sonnenbrand **IV WSA**, 19
° **sundae** [ˈsʌndeɪ] Eisbecher **IV 4**, 57
Sunday [ˈsʌndeɪ] Sonntag **I**
sunglasses (*sg + pl*) [ˈsʌnglɑːsɪz] Sonnenbrille, Sonnenbrillen **IV WSA**, 19
sunny [ˈsʌnɪ] sonnig **I**
[sunroof] [ˈsʌnruːf] Schiebedach **II**
⟨sunscreen⟩ [ˈsʌnskriːn] Sonnenschutzmittel **IV WSA**, 19
sunshine [ˈsʌnʃaɪn] Sonnenschein **III**
supermarket [ˈsuːpəˌmɑːkɪt] Supermarkt **I**
superstar [ˌsuːpəˈstɑː] Superstar **III**
sure [ʃɔː] sicher **I**
I'm not sure. [aɪm nɒt ˈʃɔː] Ich bin mir nicht sicher. **I**
to **surf** [sɜːf] surfen, Wellen reiten **III**
surprise [səˈpraɪz] Überraschung **I**
surprised [səˈpraɪzd] überrascht **III**
to **survive** [səˈvaɪv] überleben **IV WSC**, 50
° **sushi** [ˈsuːʃɪ] *japanisches Fischgericht* **IV 4**, 57
swampland [ˈswɒmplænd] Sumpf(gebiet) **IV 3**, 36
to **swear*** [sweə] schwören; fluchen **IV WSC**, 50
sweater [ˈswetə] Pullover **IV WSA**, 19
sweatshirt [ˈswetʃɜːt] Sweatshirt **I**
sweet [swiːt] Bonbon **I**
sweet [swiːt] süß, niedlich **II**
to **swim*** [swɪm] schwimmen **II**
swimmer [ˈswɪmə] Schwimmer/in **III**
to go **swimming** [gəʊ ˈswɪmɪŋ] schwimmen gehen **I**
swimming pool [ˈswɪmɪŋpuːl] Schwimmbad **II**
° **Swiss** [swɪs] schweizerisch **IV 2**, 29
to **switch on** [swɪtʃ‿ˈɒn] einschalten **III**

T

T-shirt [ˈtiːʃɜːt] T-Shirt **I**
table [ˈteɪbl] Tisch **I**
to **tackle** [ˈtækl] angreifen (*beim Sport*) **III**
to **take*** [teɪk] nehmen **I**; bringen **I**; erfordern; dauern **IV 2**, 21
⟨to take a glance at⟩ [glɑːns] einen Blick werfen auf **IV 3**, 44
to take a photo of [teɪk‿əˈfəʊtəʊ‿əv] ein Foto machen von **I**
to take care of s.th. [teɪk ˈkeər‿ɒv ˌsʌmθɪŋ] etw. erledigen; nach etw. schauen; sich um etw. kümmern **IV WSB**, 35
to take home [teɪk ˈhəʊm] nach Hause bringen **I**
to take notes [teɪk ˈnəʊts] Notizen machen **II**
to take off, took off [ˈteɪk ɒf, ˈtʊk ɒf] ausziehen, wegnehmen **II**
⟨to take one's pick⟩ [ˌteɪk wʌnz ˈpɪk] sich etw. heraussuchen **IV WSC**, 53
to take out [teɪk ˈaʊt] hinaustragen **IV 1**, 11
to take part in s.th. [ˌteɪk ˈpɑːt‿ɪn] an etw. teilnehmen **III**
to take place [ˌteɪk ˈpleɪs] stattfinden **III**
takeaway [ˈteɪkəweɪ] *Imbissstube, Schnellgaststätte mit Straßenverkauf* **II**
tale [teɪl] Geschichte, Sage **II**
talk [tɔːk] Referat, Rede, Gespräch **III**
talk-radio program (*AE*) [tɔːk ˈreɪdɪəʊ prəʊgræm] *Radiosendung, bei der die Hörer und Hörerinnen anrufen können* **IV 3**, 40
to give a talk [ˌgɪv‿ə ˈtɔːk] eine Rede/ein Referat halten **III**

to **talk about** ['tɔːk‿əˌbaʊt] reden über, sprechen über **I**
tall story [tɔːl 'stɔːrɪ] Lügengeschichte **IV 3**, 38
tall [tɔːl] groß; hoch **IV 3**, 38
tape [teɪp] Band, Kassette **IV 1**, 7
to **taste** [teɪst] schmecken, probieren **II**
taxi ['tæksɪ] Taxi **III**
tea [tiː] Mahlzeit am frühen Abend **I**; Tee **I**
tea-cosy [ˌtiː'kəʊzɪ] Teewärmer **II**
to **teach*** [tiːtʃ] lehren, unterrichten **III**
teacher ['tiːtʃə] Lehrer/in **I**
team [tiːm] Mannschaft **I**
techno [tek'nəʊ] Techno (*Musikrichtung*) **III**
Technology [tek'nɒlədʒɪ] Informatik (*Computerunterricht*) **II**; Technologie **III**
teddy ['tedɪ] Teddybär **II**
⟨teenage⟩ ['tiːnˌeɪdʒ] Jugend-, Teenager- **IV RII**, 46
teenager ['tiːnˌeɪdʒə] Jugendliche/r; Teenager **IV 1**, 12
°**teepee** [tiː'piː] Tipi (*kegelförmiges Zelt der Prärie-Indianer*) **IV WSC**, 49
tel. [tel] Telefonnummer (*Abkürzung*) **III**
telephone ['telɪfəʊn] Telefon **I**
(telephone) call [kɔːl] Anruf **III**
on the telephone [ɒn ðə 'telɪfəʊn] am Telefon **I**
telephone bill ['telɪfəʊn ˌbɪl] Telefonrechnung **IV 5**, 72
to **telephone** ['telɪfəʊn] telefonieren, anrufen **III**
teletext ['telɪtekst] Videotext **IV 5**, 70
to **tell*** [tel] erzählen **I**; sagen, mitteilen **I**
to tell lies [ˌtel 'laɪz] lügen **III**
to tell the time ['tel ðə 'taɪm] die Uhrzeit angeben **I**
to have a **temperature** [ˌhæv‿ə 'temprətʃə] Fieber haben **II**
temple ['templ] Tempel **III**
tennis ['tenɪs] Tennis **I**
tennis court ['tenɪskɔːt] Tennisplatz **III**
tense [tens] Zeit **III**
term [tɜːm] Schuljahresabschnitt **III**
terrible ['terəbl] schrecklich, furchtbar **I**
⟨territory⟩ ['terətərɪ] Gebiet, Territorium **IV WSC**, 51
test [test] Prüfung, Klassenarbeit **III**
test paper (*AE*) [test 'peɪpə] Klassenarbeit **IV WSB**, 35
to **test** [test] prüfen **III**
text [tekst] Text **I**
than [ðən] als (*bei Vergleichen*) **II**
to **thank s.o.** [θæŋk] jdm. danken **IV 4**, 60
Thank goodness! [θæŋk 'gʊdnɪs] Gott sei Dank! **IV 1**, 14
Thank you. ['θæŋk‿jʊ] Danke schön. **I**
Thanks! [θæŋks] Danke! **I**
°**Thanksgiving** ['θænksˌgɪvɪŋ] Erntedankfest **IV WSD**, 64
that [ðæt] dass **II**
that [ðæt] der/die/das **III**
that well [ðæt 'wel] besonders gut **IV WSB**, 35
the [ðiː] der/die/das **I**
theater (*AE*) [θɪ'etə] Theater **IV 4**, 55
theatre ['θɪətə] Theater **II**
their [ðeə] ihr/ihre (*Pl.*) **I**
them [ðem] sie/ihnen **I**
theme park ['θiːm ˌpɑːk] Freizeitpark, Erlebnispark **III**
themselves [ðəm'selvz] (sich) selbst **III**
then [ðen] dann **I**
there [ðeə] da, dort **I**
over there [əʊvə 'ðeə] da drüben, dort **I**
there are [ðeər‿'ɑː] es gibt, es sind **I**
there is [ðeər‿'ɪz] es gibt, es ist **I**
these [ðiːz] diese hier **I**
⟨these little town blues⟩ [ðiːz lɪtl taʊn 'bluːz] *etwa:* diese Kleinstadtdepressionen **IV 4**, 59

they [ðeɪ] sie (*Pl.*) **I**
⟨Indians are getting so thick around here.⟩ *etwa.:* Hier wimmelt es langsam von Indianern. **IV WSC**, 52
thief, thieves (*pl*) [θiːf] Dieb/Diebin, Diebe/Diebinnen **II**
thing [θɪŋ] Ding, Sache **I**
to **think*** [θɪŋk] denken, glauben **I**
to think of ['θɪnk‿əv] ausdenken **I**
I think so. [aɪ 'θɪŋk səʊ] Ich denke schon. **II**
thirsty ['θɜːstɪ] durstig **II**
this [ðɪs] dies/dieser/diese/dieses **I**
this afternoon [ðɪs‿ɑːftə'nuːn] heute Nachmittag **I**
this suggests … [ðɪs sə'dʒests] das legt den Schluss nahe **IV WSB**, 35
those [ðəʊz] die da drüben **I**
though [ðəʊ] jedoch; aber **IV WSB**, 35
a **thousand** ['θaʊznd] (ein)tausend **II**
throat [θrəʊt] Hals, Rachen **II**
through [θruː] durch **I**
throw [θrəʊ] Wurf **II**
to **throw*** [θrəʊ] werfen **I**
to throw off [θrəʊ ɒf] abwerfen, wegwerfen **II**
thunder ['θʌndə] Donner **II**
thunderstorm ['θʌndəstɔːm] Gewitter **III**
Thursday ['θɜːzdeɪ] Donnerstag **I**
ticket ['tɪkɪt] Fahrkarte **I**
the **tide**(s) [taɪd] Gezeiten, Ebbe, Flut **III**
to **tidy** ['taɪdɪ] aufräumen **II**
to tidy up ['taɪdɪ‿ʌp] aufräumen **I**
tidy ['taɪdɪ] ordentlich, aufgeräumt **I**
to **tie** [taɪ] (fest)binden, anbinden **IV WSC**, 52
tiger ['taɪgə] Tiger **II**
tights (*sg +pl*) [taɪts] Strumpfhose, Strumpfhosen **II**
till (= **until**) [tɪl] bis **IV WSA**, 16
time [taɪm] Mal **III**; Zeit **I**
all the time [ɔːl θə‿'taɪm] die ganze Zeit **IV 2**, 25
from time to time [frəm 'taɪm tə 'taɪm] von Zeit zu Zeit **IV 1**, 11
ten times [ˌten 'taɪmz] zehnmal **II**
to tell the time ['tel ðə 'taɪm] die Uhrzeit angeben **I**
What time is it? [ˌwɒt 'taɪm‿ɪz‿ɪt] Wie spät ist es?, Wie viel Uhr ist es? **I**
timetable ['taɪmteɪbl] Fahrplan **I**; Stundenplan **II**
°**tin** [tɪn] Zinn, Blech **IV WSC**, 52
⟨tin can⟩ [tɪn 'kæn] Blechdose **IV 5**, 76
tip [tɪp] Tipp, Hinweis **III**; Trinkgeld **IV 4**, 54
tired ['taɪəd] müde **I**
to be tired of s.th. [bɪ 'taɪəd‿əv] von etw. genug haben **IV 2**, 25
title ['taɪtl] Titel **II**
to [tʊ] vor **I**; zu **I**
from … to [frəm … tə] von … nach **I**
°**tobacco** [tə'bækəʊ] Tabak **IV WSC**, 52
today [tə'deɪ] heute **I**
toe [təʊ] Zehe **II**
together [tə'geðə] zusammen **I**
toilet ['tɔɪlɪt] Toilette **I**
tomato, tomatoes (*pl*) [tə'mɑːtəʊ] Tomate, Tomaten **I**
tomorrow [tə'mɒrəʊ] morgen **I**
tone [təʊn] Ton **III**
tonight [tə'naɪt] heute Abend, heute Nacht **III**
too [tuː] allzu, zu **I**; auch **I**
tooth, teeth (*pl*) [tuːθ] Zahn, Zähne **III**
top [tɒp] oberer Teil; Gipfel **III**
⟨top of the heap⟩ [hiːp] der/die Beste **IV 4**, 59
at the **top of** [ət ðə 'tɒp‿əv] ganz oben **I**
⟨to be tossed out⟩ [biː tɒst 'aʊt] hinausgeworfen werden **IV 2**, 24

⟨to touch⟩ [tʌtʃ] anfassen, berühren **IV 4**, 62
tour ['tʊə] Rundfahrt, Rundgang **III**
guided tour [ˌgaɪdɪd 'tʊə] Führung **IV WSA**, 17
to **tour around** [tʊə ə'raʊnd] eine Tour/(Rund-)Reise machen, herumreisen **IV WSA**, 16
tourist ['tʊərɪst] Tourist/in **III**
tournament ['tɔ:nəmənt] Turnier **III**
towards [tə'wɔ:dz] auf ... zu **II**
tower ['taʊə] Turm **III**
town [taʊn] Stadt **I**
toy [tɔɪ] Spielzeug **III**
tractor ['træktə] Traktor, Trecker **I**
tradition [trə'dɪʃn] Tradition, Brauch **IV WSC**, 50
traffic ['træfɪk] Verkehr **III**
traffic lights (*sg + pl*) ['træfɪk ˌlaɪts] Verkehrsampel, Verkehrsampeln **III**
heavy traffic [ˌhevɪ 'træfɪk] viel Verkehr **III**
slow-moving traffic [ˌsləʊmu:vɪŋ 'træfɪk] zähfließender Verkehr **III**
traffic jam ['træfɪk ˌdʒæm] Stau **III**
trail (*AE*) [treɪl] Spur; Weg, Pfad **IV 1**, 12
to hit the trail [hɪt ðə 'treɪl] *umg.:* sich auf den Weg machen **IV 3**, 42
train [treɪn] Zug **I**
to **train** [treɪn] trainieren **III**
trainers ['treɪnəz] Turnschuhe **II**
to **translate** [træns'leɪt] übersetzen **III**
transport ['trænspɔ:t] Verkehrsmittel, Transport **III**
⟨transportation⟩ [ˌtrænspɔ:'teɪʃn] Verkehrsmittel, Transport **IV RI**, 31
trap [træp] Falle **III**
to be **trapped** [bɪ 'træpt] in der Falle sein, abgeschnitten sein **III**
° **trapper** ['træpə] Fallensteller/in, Trapper/in **IV WSC**, 50
⟨travel agent's⟩ ['trævl ˌeɪdʒənts] Reisebüro **IV 3**, 37
travel diary ['trævl ˌdaɪərɪ] Reisetagebuch **II**
to **travel** ['trævl] reisen **II**
traveled (*AE*) ['trævld] reiste, reistest, reisten **IV 2**, 21
to **treat** [tri:t] behandeln **IV WSC**, 52
tree [tri:] Baum **I**
° **tribal land** [ˌtraɪbl 'lænd] Stammesland **IV WSC**, 51
tribe [traɪb] Stamm **IV WSC**, 48
trick [trɪk] Trick, Kunstgriff **I**
trick-or-treat [trɪk‿ɔ:‿'tri:t] *etwa:* „Streich-oder-Leckerei" **IV WSD**, 64
to **trick** [trɪk] austricksen **I**
tricky ['trɪkɪ] schwierig **IV 2**, 23
trip [trɪp] Ausflug, Reise **II**
to **trip** ['trɪp] stolpern **I**
trouble ['trʌbl] Schwierigkeiten **I**
to be in trouble [bɪ‿ɪn 'trʌbl] Schwierigkeiten haben **I**
trousers (*sg +pl*) ['traʊzəz] Hose, Hosen **I**
truck (*AE*) [trʌk] Lkw, Lastwagen **IV 2**, 21
true [tru:] wahr **IV 2**, 26
[trumpet] ['trʌmpɪt] Trompete **II**
truth [tru:θ] Wahrheit **IV 2**, 26
to **try** [traɪ] (aus)probieren, versuchen **II**
to try harder [traɪ 'hɑ:də] sich mehr anstrengen **III**
to try on [traɪ‿'ɒn] anprobieren **I**
to try out for [ˌtraɪ 'aʊt fɔ:] vorsingen, vorspielen **IV 4**, 54
the **tube** [ðə tju:b] *gängiger Ausdruck für die Londoner U-Bahn* **III**
Tuesday ['tju:zdeɪ] Dienstag **I**
tune [tju:n] Melodie **III**
tunnel ['tʌnl] Tunnel **I**
turkey ['tɜ:kɪ] Pute/r, Truthahn/Truthenne **IV WSD**, 64
Turkish ['tɜ:kɪʃ] türkisch, Türkisch **I**
Your **turn.** ['jɔ: tɜ:n] Du bist an der Reihe. **I**
to **turn** [tɜ:n] abbiegen **I**
to turn down [ˌtɜ:n 'daʊn] herrunterschalten **III**
to turn off [ˌtɜ:n‿'ɒf] ausschalten **III**
to turn over [ˌtɜ:n 'əʊvə] umkippen, umdrehen **III**
to turn up [tɜ:n 'ʌp] lauter drehen, hoch drehen **IV 1**, 11
tutor ['tju:tə] Klassenlehrer/in, Betreuungslehrer/in **I**
tutor group ['tju:tə ˌgru:p] Klasse (*in einer englischen Schule*) **I**
TV [ti:'vi:] Fernsehen **I**
twice [twaɪs] zweimal **II**
twin [twɪn] Zwilling **I**
twin town ['twɪn 'taʊn] Partnerstadt **I**
Twinning Office ['twɪnɪŋ ˌɒfɪs] Städtepartnerschaftsbüro **I**
type [taɪp] Typ; Art, Sorte **IV WSA**, 19
to **type** [taɪp] tippen **IV 5**, 71
⟨typical⟩ ['tɪpɪkl] typisch **IV RII**, 46
tyre ['taɪə] Reifen **I**

U

ugly ['ʌglɪ] hässlich **IV 3**, 42
umbrella [ʌm'brelə] Regenschirm **III**
⟨unbreakable⟩ [ʌn'breɪkəbl] unzerbrechlich **IV RII**, 47
uncle ['ʌŋkl] Onkel **I**
great uncle ['greɪt ˌʌŋkl] Großonkel **II**
under ['ʌndə] unter **I**
the **underground** [ðɪ 'ʌndəgraʊnd] U-Bahn **III**
to **understand*** [ʌndə'stænd] verstehen **I**
unfriendly [ʌn'frendlɪ] unfreundlich **III**
unhappy [ʌn'hæpɪ] unglücklich **II**
uniform ['ju:nɪfɔ:m] Uniform **I**
unit ['ju:nɪt] Lektion, Kapitel **I**
to be **unlucky** [bɪ ʌn'lʌkɪ] Pech haben **III**
untidy [ʌn'taɪdɪ] unordentlich **I**
until [ʌn'tɪl] bis **II**
up to ['ʌp ˌtʊ] bis **III**
It's up to you. [ɪts‿ˌʌp tə 'ju:] Es liegt an dir., Du entscheidest. **III**
upper ['ʌpə] der/die/das obere **II**
upstairs [ˌʌp'steəz] oben (im Gebäude) **I**
⟨upstream⟩ [ˌʌp'stri:m] flussaufwärts **IV WSA**, 19
us [ʌs] uns **I**
use of s.th. [ju:s‿ɒv] Gebrauch von etw. **IV WSC**, 51
to **use** [ju:z] benutzen **I**
to be **used to s.th.** [bɪ 'ju:st tʊ] gewöhnt sein an **IV 2**, 25
useful ['ju:sfʊl] nützlich **II**
useless ['ju:slɪs] nutzlos **III**
usually ['ju:ʒʊəlɪ] gewöhnlich, normalerweise **I**

V

vacation (*AE*) [və'keɪʃn] Ferien, Urlaub **IV 3**, 38
⟨vagabond⟩ ['vægəbɒnd] Vagabund/in **IV 4**, 59
Valentine ['væləntaɪn] *Freund/in, dem/der man am Valentinstag einen Gruß schickt* **IV WSD**, 64
° **Valentine's card** ['væləntaɪnz kɑ:d] Valentinskarte **IV WSD**, 64
° **Valentine's Day** ['væləntaɪnz deɪ] Valentinstag **IV WSD**, 64
valley ['vælɪ] Tal **III**
van [væn] Lieferwagen, Transporter **II**
vanilla [və'nɪlə] Vanille **IV 1**, 11

vegetable ['vedʒtəbl] Gemüse **II**
verb [vɜ:b] Verb **I**
very ['verɪ] sehr **I**
vet [vet] Tierarzt/Tierärztin **I**
vet's assistant ['vets‿ə'sɪstənt] Tierarzthelfer/in **I**
⟨via⟩ ['vaɪə] über **IV 5**, 71
video ['vɪdɪəʊ] Video **I**
view [vju:] Blick, Aussicht **IV 2**, 22
to **view** [vju:] anschauen, betrachten **IV 5**, 71
village ['vɪlɪdʒ] Dorf **III**
violence ['vaɪələns] Gewalt **III**
to **visit** ['vɪzɪt] besuchen, besichtigen **II**
visitor ['vɪzɪtə] Besucher/in **III**
vocabulary [vəʊ'kæbjʊlərɪ] Wortschatz, Vokabular **III**
voice [vɔɪs] Stimme **II**
volleyball ['vɒlɪbɔ:l] Volleyball **II**
⟨Volume Control⟩ ['vɒlju:m 'kəntrəʊl] Lautstärkeregler **IV 5**, 75
vowel ['vaʊəl] Vokal **II**

W

wagon ['wægən] Planwagen **IV WSC**, 48
° covered wagon ['kʌvəd ˌwægən] Planwagen **IV WSC**, 48
° wagon train ['wægən ˌtreɪn] Planwagentreck **IV WSC**, 50
to **wait** [weɪt] warten **I**
to wait for ['weɪt fɔ:] warten auf **I**
° **wake boarding** (*AE*) ['weɪk ˌbɔ:dɪŋ] *Wassersportart* **IV WSB**, 34
to **wake up*** ['weɪk‿ʌp] aufwachen **II**
walk [wɔ:k] Spaziergang **I**
to go for a walk [ˌgəʊ fər‿ə 'wɔ:k] spazieren gehen **I**
to **walk** [wɔ:k] (zu Fuß) gehen **I**
to walk down [wɔ:k 'daʊn] hinuntergehen **IV 1**, 12
walkway ['wɔ:kweɪ] Fußweg **IV 5**, 74
wall [wɔ:l] Wand, Mauer **IV 2**, 29
⟨wall display⟩ ['wɔ:l dɪ'spleɪ] Wandzeitung **IV 3**, 44
wallet (*AE*) ['wɒlɪt] Geldbeutel, Portmonee **IV 1**, 13
⟨to wander⟩ ['wɒndə] umherwandern **IV 3**, 44
to **want** [wɒnt] (haben) wollen **I**
ward [wɔ:d] Station (*in einem Krankenhaus*) **II**
warden ['wɔ:dn] Jugendherbergsvater/mutter **III**
to **warm up** [wɑ:m‿'ʌp] aufwärmen **IV WSA**, 16
warm [wɔ:m] warm **I**
to **warn** [wɔ:n] warnen **II**
⟨warpath⟩ ['wɔ:pɑ:θ] Kriegspfad **IV WSC**, 51
warrior ['wɒrɪə] Krieger/in **IV WSC**, 51
to **wash** [wɒʃ] waschen **IV WSA**, 18
to **wash up** [wɒʃ‿'ʌp] abwaschen, (Geschirr) spülen **I**
washable ['wɒʃəbl] waschbar **IV WSA**, 18
washing-up [ˌwɒʃɪŋ'ʌp] Abwasch **I**
waste [weɪst] Müll, Abfall **III**
watch [wɒtʃ] Armbanduhr **IV 3**, 45
to **watch** [wɒtʃ] (zu)schauen, gucken **I**
Watch out! [ˌwɒtʃ‿'aʊt] Pass auf! **III**
water ['wɔ:tə] Wasser **I**
waterfall ['wɔ:təfɔ:l] Wasserfall **IV 1**, 12
wave [weɪv] Welle **III**
to **wave** [weɪv] wehen; winken **IV WSC**, 53
waxwork ['wækswɜ:k] Wachs- **III**
way [weɪ] Weg **I**; Weise **III**
in different ways [ɪn ˌdɪfrənt 'weɪz] auf verschiedene Weise **III**
[no way] [nəʊ 'weɪ] auf keinen Fall **II**
way of life [ˌweɪ‿əv 'laɪf] Lebensstil **IV WSC**, 50

we [wi:] wir **I**
weak [wi:k] schwach **III**
weapon ['wepən] Waffe **III**
to **wear*** [weə] tragen, anhaben **I**
weather ['weðə] Wetter **I**
weather forecast ['weðə ˌfɔ:kɑ:st] Wettervorhersage **II**
Wednesday ['wenzdeɪ] Mittwoch **I**
week [wi:k] Woche **I**
weekend [ˌwi:k'end] Wochenende **II**
weight [weɪt] Gewicht **IV WSA**, 18
Welcome to ... ['welkəm tʊ] Willkommen in ... **I**
Welcome back. [ˌwelkəm 'bæk] Willkommen zurück. **II**
well [wel] gut, nun, na ja **I**
well [wel] gut *(Adverbialform)* **III**
Get well soon! ['get wel 'su:n] Gute Besserung! **I**
to do well [ˌdu: 'wel] gut sein, gut abschneiden **III**
to feel well [ˌfi:l 'wel] sich wohl fühlen **II**
Well done! [wel 'dʌn] Gut gemacht!, Bravo! **I**
Welsh [welʃ] walisisch, Walisisch **II**
⟨werewolf⟩ ['wɪəwʊlf] Werwolf **IV WSD**, 67
west [west] westlich, West-, Westen **II**
West Indian [ˌwest‿'ɪndjən] westindisch, Westinder/in **III**
wet [wet] nass **I**
⟨wetsuit⟩ ['wetsu:t] Neopren-, Taucheranzug **IV WSA**, 19
what [wɒt] was **I**
So what? [səʊ 'wɒt] Na und? **IV 2**, 20
What a ... ['wɒt‿ə] Was für ein/e ... **I**
What about ...? ['wɒt‿əˌbaʊt] Wie wär's mit ...? **II**
What if ...? ['wɒt‿ɪf] Was wäre, wenn ...? **II**
What on earth ...? [ˌwɒt‿ɒn 'ɜ:θ] Was um alles in der Welt ...? **II**
What's ... like? [wɒts ... 'laɪk] Wie ist ...? **I**
whatever [wɒt'evə] was (auch immer), egal was **IV 4**, 54
What's up? Was gibt's Neues?, Was ist los? **IV 1**, 8
whatsit ['wɒtsɪt] Wieheißtesnochmal, Dingsda **III**
wheel [wi:l] Rad **II**
when [wen] wann **I**
where [weə] wo **I**
⟨Where there's a will, there's a way.⟩ [weə ðeəz‿ə 'wɪl ðeəz‿ə 'weɪ] Wo eine Wille ist, ist auch ein Weg. **IV RI**, 30
wherever [weər'evə] wo auch immer, egal wo **IV 3**, 42
which [wɪtʃ] der/die/das **III**; welche/welcher/welches **II**
while [waɪl] Weile **III**
while [waɪl] während **II**
to **whisper** ['wɪspə] flüstern **III**
white [waɪt] weiß **I**
° **whitewater rafting** [ˌwaɪt'wɔ:tə 'rɑ:ftɪŋ] Wildwasser Rafting **IV WSA**, 18
who [hu:] der/die/das **III**; wen/wem **I**; wer **I**
° Who's a pretty boy, then? *etwa:* Ach, bist du niedlich! **IV 5**, 75
on the **whole** [ˌɒn ðə 'həʊl] im Großen und Ganzen **III**
whole [həʊl] ganz **III**
(to) **whom** [(tə) hu:m] (an) wen **III**
whose [hu:z] dessen, deren **III**; wessen **III**
why [waɪ] warum **I**
wide [waɪd] weit, breit **IV WSC**, 48
wife, wives (*pl*) [waɪf] Ehefrau, Ehefrauen **II**
wig [wɪg] Perücke **II**
wild [waɪld] wild, unberührt **III**
wilderness ['wɪldənes] Wildnis **IV WSC**, 50
will [wɪl] werden **II**
to **win*** [wɪn] gewinnen **II**
wind [wɪnd] Wind **III**

window ['wɪndəʊ] Fenster **I**
window-shopping ['wɪndəʊʃɒpɪŋ] Schaufensterbummel **II**
windy ['wɪndɪ] windig **I**
wine [waɪn] Wein **II**
winner ['wɪnə] Gewinner/in **I**
winter ['wɪntə] Winter **I**
⟨to wish⟩ [wɪʃ] wünschen **IV 5**, 71
⟨witch⟩ [wɪtʃ] Hexe **IV WSD**, 67
with [wɪð] bei, mit **I**
within [wɪ'ðɪn] innerhalb **IV 3**, 45
without [wɪð'aʊt] ohne **I**
woman, women (*pl*) ['wʊmən] Frau, Frauen **I**
wonderful ['wʌndəfl] wunderbar **III**
⟨wood⟩ [wʊd] Holz; Wald **IV 3**, 39
wool [wʊl] Wolle **IV 5**, 75
word [wɜːd] Wort **I**
word order ['wɜːd ˌɔːdə] Satzstellung **I**
Word power ['wɜːd ˌpaʊə] Die Kraft der Wörter **I**
work [wɜːk] Arbeit **III**
All in a day's work. [ɔːl ɪn‿ə 'deɪz wɜːk] *etwa:* Das gehört zu meiner täglichen Arbeit. **IV 4**, 60
work of art [wɜːk‿əv 'ɑːt] Kunstwerk **IV 4**, 58
to **work** [wɜːk] arbeiten **I**; funktionieren, klappen **III**
to work hard [wɜːk 'hɑːd] hart, schwer arbeiten **II**
worksheet ['wɜːkʃiːt] Arbeitsblatt **III**
workshop ['wɜːkʃɒp] Kurs, Schulung, Werkstatt **III**
world [wɜːld] Welt **II**
worried ['wʌrɪd] besorgt, beunruhigt **I**
worry ['wʌrɪ] Sorge **IV 2**, 26
to **worry** ['wʌrɪ] sich Sorgen machen **II**
Don't worry. [ˌdəʊnt 'wʌrɪ] Mach dir/Macht euch keine Sorgen. **II**
worse [wɜːs] schlechter, schlimmer **III**
(the) **worst** [ðə wɜːst] am schlechtesten, am schlimmsten **III**
to be **worth + gerund** [bɪ 'wɜːθ] sich lohnen etw. zu machen **III**
would rather ['rɑːðə] lieber **IV WSB**, 34
Would you like …? ['wʊd‿jʊ laɪk] Hättest du/Hätten Sie gern …? **II**
Wow! [waʊ] Toll!, Super! (*Ausruf der Begeisterung*) **II**
wrestling ['reslɪŋ] Ringen **IV WSB**, 32
to **write*** [raɪt] schreiben **I**
writer ['raɪtə] Autor/in, Schriftsteller/in **III**
wrong [rɒŋ] falsch **I**
to be wrong about [biː 'rɒŋ ə'baʊt] Unrecht haben mit **II**
S.th. is wrong. [rɒŋ] Es stimmt etw. nicht. **IV 2**, 26
What's wrong with you? [wɒts 'rɒŋ wɪð 'juː] Was fehlt dir/Ihnen? **II**

Y

Yeah! [jeə] *umg.:* Ja! **IV 1**, 12
year [jɪə] Jahr, Jahrgang **I**
yearbook (*AE*) ['jɪəbʊk] Jahrbuch *(einer Schule)* **IV WSB**, 32
yellow ['jeləʊ] gelb **I**
yes [jes] ja **I**
yesterday ['jestədɪ] gestern **II**
yet [jet] schon **III**
not … yet [nɒt … jet] noch nicht **I**
YHA (= **Youth Hostel Association**) [waɪ eɪtʃ‿'eɪ] Jugendherbergsverband **III**
you [jʊ] dich/euch/Sie; dir/euch/Ihnen **I**; du, Sie **I**; ihr/Sie **I**; man, einen **II**
Thank you. ['θæŋk‿jʊ] Danke schön. **I**
⟨You've really made the grade.⟩ [juːv 'rɪəlɪ meɪd ðə 'greɪd] Du hast es wirklich geschafft. **IV 5**, 76
young [jʌŋ] jung **II**
your [jɔː] dein/deine; Ihr/Ihre; euer/eure; Ihr/Ihre **I**
yourself [jɔː'self] dich selbst **II**
do it yourself [ˌduː ɪt jɔː'self] heimwerken **III**
youth centre ['juːθ sentr] Jugendzentrum **II**
youth hostel ['juːθ ˌhɒstl] Jugendherberge **III**
youth [juːθ] Jugend **III**
Yuck! [jʌk] Igitt!, Pfui!, Bäh! (*Ausruf des Ekels*) **IV 2**, 23

Z

zero ['zɪərəʊ] Null **IV WSB**, 35
zipper (*AE*) ['zɪpə] Reißverschluss **IV 1**, 13
zoo [zuː] Zoo **II**

Boys' names

Alan ['ælən]
Alex ['æˌlɪks]
Arthur ['ɑ:θə]
Asim ['æzi:m]
Barry ['bærɪ]
Bill [bɪl]
Bruce [bru:s]
Colin ['kɒlɪn]
Daniel ['dænjəl]
Darren ['dærən]
Daryl ['dærɪl]
David ['deɪvɪd]
Eddy ['edɪ]
Edward ['edwəd]
Florian ['flɔ:rɪən]
Fred [fred]
George [dʒɔ:dʒ]
Herbert ['hɜ:bət]
Hugh [hju:]
Ike [aɪk]
Jack [dʒæk]
Jackie ['dʒækɪ]
James [dʒeɪmz]
Jerry ['dʒerɪ]
Jim [dʒɪm]
John [dʒɒn]
Jonah ['dʒəʊnə]
Josh [dʒɒʃ]
Kevin ['kevɪn]
Lee [li:]
Lenny ['lenɪ]
Leo ['li:əʊ]
Mal [mæl]
Mark [mɑ:k]
Michael ['maɪkəl]
⟨Mick⟩ [mɪk]
Mike [maɪk]
Nick [nɪk]
Percival ['pɜ:sɪvl]
Pete [pi:t]
Peter ['pi:tə]
Rajiv ['rɑ:dʒi:v]
Rick [rɪk]
Robert ['rɒbət]
Ryan ['raɪən]
Sam [sæm]
Seymour ['si:mɔ:]
Shane [ʃeɪn]
Simon ['saɪmən]
Stan [stæn]
Steve [sti:v]
Tim [tɪm]
Tom [tɒm]
°**Tony** ['təʊnɪ]
Washington ['wɒʃɪŋtən]
Wayne [weɪn]
William ['wɪljəm]

Girls' names

Anna ['ænə]
Annabel ['ænəbel]
Anne ['æn]
Audrey [ɔ:drɪ]
Becky ['bekɪ]
Betsy ['betsɪ]
Candy ['kændɪ]
Cathy [kæθɪ]
Cindy ['sɪndɪ]
Claudia ['klɔ:djə]
Daisy ['deɪzɪ]
Debbie ['debɪ]
Dee [di:]
Ed ['ed]
Ellen ['elɪn]
Emma ['emə]
Gwen [gwen]
Helen ['helɪn]
Holly ['hɒlɪ]
Isi (= **Isadorella**) [ɪzɪ]
Jackie ['dʒækɪ]
Jane [dʒeɪn]
Janet ['dʒænɪt]
Janine [dʒəni:n]
Jenny ['dʒenɪ]
Jill [dʒɪl]
Joanna [dʒəʊ'ænə]
⟨Joanne⟩ [dʒəʊ'æn]
Judy ['dʒu:dɪ]
Karen [kə'ren]
Kate [keɪt]
Kim [kɪm]
Kittie ['kɪtɪ]
Kristy ['krɪstɪ]
Lucy ['lu:sɪ]
Lynn [lɪn]
Margaret ['mɑ:grɪt]
Mary ['meərɪ]
Megan ['megən]
Nina ['ni:nə]
Nora ['nɔ:rə]
Pam [pæm]
Pat [pæt]
Patricia [pə'trɪʃə]
Polly ['pɒlɪ]
Rachel ['reɪtʃl]
Sally [ˌsælɪ]
Samira [sə'mɪərə]
Sarah ['seərə]
Shabina [ʃə'bɪnə]
Shawna [ʃɔ:nə]
Shelley ['ʃelɪ]
Soo [su:]
Sue [su:]
Sukey ['su:kɪ]
Susan ['su:zn]
⟨Susie⟩ ['su:zɪ]
Suvina [sə'vi:nə]
Tammy ['tæmɪ]
Tori ['tɔ:rɪ]
Trudi ['tru:dɪ]
Victoria [vɪk'tɔ:rɪə]
Virginia [və'dʒɪnjə]
Wilma ['wɪlmə]
Yasmin ['jæzmɪn]

Surnames

Abbott [ˈæbət]
Adib [əˈdɪb]
Alburg [ˈælˌbɜ:rg]
Barker [ˈbɑ:kə]
Benson [ˈbensn]
Blackwell [blækwəl]
Braddock [ˈbrædək]
Broadwood [ˈbrɔ:dwʊd]
Brown [braʊn]
Burton [ˈbɜ:tn]
Cameron [ˈkæmərən]
Campbell [ˈkæmbl]
Canterville [ˈkæntəvɪl]
Carlson [ˈkɑ:lsən]
Chang [tʃæŋ]
Cho [tʃɔ:]
Chung [tʃʌng]
Clark [klɑ:k]
Cooper [ˈku:pə]
Crane [kreɪn]
Croft [krɒft]
Dane [deɪn]
Davis [ˈdeɪvɪs]
Dixon [ˈdɪksn]
Duncan [ˈdʌŋkən]
Gibson [ˈgɪbsn]
Grant [grɑ:nt]
Hilton [ˈhɪltən]
Hunt [ˈhʌnt]
Ismaili [ɪzˈmeɪlɪ]
Jackson [ˈdʒæksən]
Jenkins [ˈdʒeŋkɪnz]
Jessop [ˈdʒesəp]
Jonker [ˈjɒŋkə]
Kishi [kɪʃɪ]
Lomu [ˈləʊmu:]
MacTavish [məkˈtævɪʃ]
Martin [ˈmɑ:tɪn]
Mason [ˈmeɪsn]
Matthews [ˈmæθju:z]
Mc Carthy [məˈkɑ:θɪ]
McLean [məˈkleɪn]
Mikhailovich [ˈmɪkhæləvɪtʃ]
Miller [ˈmɪlə]
Moreno [mɒri:nəʊ]
Morgan [ˈmɔ:gən]
Mushnick [ˈmʌʃnɪk]
Nosy [ˈnəʊzɪ]
O'Hara [əˈhɑ:rə]
O'Reilly [əʊ‿ˈraɪlɪ]
Otis [ˈəʊtɪs]
Parker [ˈpɑ:kə]
Patel [pəˈtəl]
Patterson [ˈpætəsn]
Penrose [ˈpenrəʊz]
Percy [ˈpɜ:sɪ]
Price [praɪs]
Pritchard [ˈprɪtʃəd]
Reynolds [ˈrenldz]
Richards [ˈrɪtʃədz]
Ross [rɒs]
Schweitzer [ˈʃwaɪtsə]
Sheikh [ʃeɪk]
Singh [sɪŋ]
Smith [smɪθ]
Smyth [smɪθ]
Stevenson [ˈsti:vnzn]
Stuart [ˈstju:ət]
Taylor [ˈteɪlə]
Umney [ˈʌmnɪ]
Underwood [ˈʌndəwʊd]
Walker [ˈwɔ:kə]
Wall [wɔ:l]
Weston [westən]
White [waɪt]
Wilder [ˈwaɪldə]
Wood [wʊd]
Zorzi [zɔ:zɪ]

Geographical names

Aberystwyth [ˌæbəˈrɪstwɪθ]
Africa [ˈæfrɪkə]
Alaska [əˈlæskə]
Alaska Range [əˈlæskə reɪndʒ]
the **Alps** [ælps]
Ambleside [ˈæmblsaɪd]
America [əˈmerɪkə]
Antarctica [æntˈɑ:ktɪkə]
Arkansas River [ˈɑ:kənsɔ: ˌrɪvə]
Asia [ˈeɪʃə]
Australia [ɒˈstreɪljə]
Baker Street [ˈbeɪkə ˌstri:t]
The **Bakerloo Line** [ðə ˌbeɪkəˈlu: ˌlaɪn]
Belfast [ˌbelˈfɑ:st]
Belgium [ˈbeldʒəm]
Ben Nevis [ˌben ˈnevɪs]
Berlin [bɜ:ˈlɪn]
Big Ben [ˌbɪg ˈben]
The **Big Apple** [ðə ˌbɪg ˈæpl]
Birmingham [ˈbɜ:mɪŋəm]
Britain [ˈbrɪtn]
Great **Britain** [ˌgreɪt ˈbrɪtn]
the **British Isles** [ðə ˌbrɪtɪʃ‿ˈaɪlz]
Broad Haven [ˈbrɔ:d heɪvn]
the **Bronx** [ðə ˈbrɒŋks]
Brooklyn [ˈbrʊklɪn]
Buckingham Palace [ˌbʌkɪŋəm ˈpælɪs]
Caerleon [kɑ:ˈli:ən]
California [ˌkælɪˈfɔ:njə]
Camden Market [ˌkæmdən ˈmɑ:kɪt]
Camelot [ˈkæmɪlɒt]
Cardiff [ˈkɑ:dɪf]
The **Caribbean** [ðə ˌkærɪˈbi:ən]
Castleton [ˈkɑ:sltən]
Central Park [ˌsentrl ˈpɑ:k]
Channel Tunnel [ˈtʃænl ˈtʌnl]
Chelsea [ˈtʃelsɪ]
Chester [ˈtʃestə]
Chicago [ʃi:ˈkɑ:gəʊ]
China [ˈtʃaɪnə]
Chinatown [ˈtʃaɪnəˌtaʊn]
The **Circle Line** [ðə ˈsɜ:kl ˌlaɪn]
Colorado [ˌkɒləˈrɑ:dəʊ]
Conway [ˈkɒnweɪ]
Cornwall [ˈkɔ:nwəl]
Covent Garden [ˌkɒvənt ˈgɑ:dn]
Coventry [ˈkɒvəntrɪ]
Cowden [ˈkaʊden]

Denali [de'nɑ:lɪ]
Denmark ['denmɑ:k]
Denver ['denvə]
Dover ['dəʊvə]
Druidston ['dru:ɪdstən]
East Cheam [ˌi:st 'tʃi:m]
Edinburgh ['edɪnbrə]
Elf Row [ˌelf 'rəʊ]
England ['ɪŋglənd]
Europe ['jʊərəp]
Everglades ['evəgleɪdz]
Fishguard ['fɪʃgɑ:d]
Florida ['flɒrɪdə]
Fort William [ˌfɔ:t 'wɪljəm]
France [frɑ:ns]
Germany ['dʒɜ:mənɪ]
Gilman Village [ˌgɪlmən 'vɪlɪdʒ]
Glenarm [glen'ɑ:m]
Golden ['gəʊldən]
Grand Canyon [ˌgrænd 'kænjən]
Greece [gri:s]
Greenwich Village [ˌgrenɪdʒ 'vɪlɪdʒ]
Harlem ['hɑ:ləm]
Harrod's ['hærədz]
Hastings ['heɪstɪŋs]
Heathrow [ˌhi:θ'rəʊ]
Holyhead ['hɒlɪhed]
The **Houses of Parliament** [ðə ˌhaʊzɪz‿əv 'pɑ:ləmənt]
Hull [hʌl]
Humberside ['hʌmbəsaɪd]
Hyde Park [ˌhaɪd 'pɑ:k]
India ['ɪndjə]
Northern **Ireland** ['nɔ:θən‿'aɪələnd]
the Republic of **Ireland** [ðə rɪˌpʌblɪk‿ɒv‿'aɪələnd]
Isle of Wight [ˌaɪl‿əv 'waɪt]
Issaquah ['ɪzəˌkwɑ:]
Italy ['ɪtəlɪ]
Jamaica [dʒə'meɪkə]
Japan [dʒə'pæn]
Kansas ['kænzəs]
Kings Canyon [ˌkɪŋz 'kænjən]
Korea [kə'rɪə]
Lake District ['leɪk ˌdɪstrɪkt]
Lake View Drive [ˌleɪk vju: 'draɪv]
Lake Windermere [ˌleɪk 'wɪndəˌmɪə]
Latin America [ˌlætɪn ə'merɪkə]
Leeds [li:dz]
Leicester Square [ˌlestə 'skweə]
Little Italy [ˌlɪtl 'ɪtəlɪ]
Little Ukraine [ˌlɪtl ju:'kreɪn]
Loch Lomond [lɒk 'ləʊmənd]
Loch Ness [lɒk 'nes]
London ['lʌndən]
London Bridge [ˌlʌndən 'brɪdʒ]
London Zoo [ˌlʌndən 'zu:]
The **London Dungeon** [ðə ˌlʌndən 'dʌnʒən]
Luton ['lu:tn]
Madame Tussaud's [ˌmædəm tə'sɔ:dz]
Malham ['mæləm]
Malibu ['mælɪbʊ]
Manchester ['mæntʃɪstə]
Manhattan [mæn'hætn]
Mesa Verde [ˌmesə 'vədɪ]
The **Metropolitan Line** [ðə ˌmetrə'pɒlɪtən ˌlaɪn]
Mexico ['meksɪkəʊ]
Milford Haven [ˌmɪlfəd 'heɪvn]
Mississippi [ˌmɪsɪ'sɪpɪ]
Mt. McKinley [ˌmaʊnt mə'kɪnlɪ]
Mt. Rainier [ˌmaʊnt reɪ'nɪər]
Museum of the Moving Image [mju:ˌzɪəm‿əv‿ðə ˌmu:vɪŋ‿ɪmɪdʒ]
Neasden ['ni:zdən]
Nebraska [nɪ'bræskə]
The **Netherlands** [ðə 'neðələndz]
⟨New Jersey⟩ [nju: 'dʒɜ:zɪ]
New York [ˌnju: 'jɔ:k]
New York City [ˌnju: 'jɔ:k sɪtɪ]
New Zealand [ˌnju: 'zi:lənd]
Newstead Abbey [ˌnju:stɪd‿'æbɪ]
Nolton Haven [ˌnɒltən 'heɪvn]
North Sea [ˌnɔ:θ 'si:]
Northallerton [nɔ:'θælətən]
Northumberland [nɔ:'θʌmbələnd]
Notting Hill Gate [ˌnɒtɪŋhɪl 'geɪt]
Nottingham ['nɒtɪŋəm]
Pacific Northwest [pəˌsɪfɪk nɔ:θ'west]
Paddington ['pædɪŋtən]
Pakistan [ˌpɑ:kɪ'stɑ:n]
Paris ['pærɪs]
Peak District ['pi:k ˌdɪstrɪkt]
Piccadilly Circus [ˌpɪkə'dɪlɪ 'sɜ:kəs]
The **Piccadilly Line** [ðə ˌpɪkə'dɪlɪ ˌlaɪn]
Pike [paɪk]
Pittsburgh ['pɪtsbɜ:g]
Poland ['pəʊlənd]
Puerto Rico ['pwɜ:təʊ 'ri:kəʊ]
Queens [kwi:nz]
Regent's Park [ˌri:dʒənts 'pɑ:k]
The **River Thames** [ðə ˌrɪvə 'temz]
Rock Circus [ˌrɒk 'sɜ:kəs]
Roman Wall [ˌrəʊmən 'wɔ:l]
Rotterdam [ˌrɒtə'dæm]
Royal Gorge [ˌrɔɪəl 'gɔ:dʒ]
Russia ['rʌʃə]
Scarborough ['skɑ:brə]
Scotland ['skɒtlənd]
Seattle [sɪ'ætl]
Sequoia [sɪ'kwɔɪə]
Shadwell ['ʃædwəl]
Shenandoah [ˌʃenən'dəʊə]
Sherwood ['ʃɜ:wʊd]
Siberia [saɪ'bɪərɪə]
Skegness [skeg'nes]
Snoqualmie Falls [snəʊˌkwɑ:lmɪ 'fɔ:lz]
Snowdon ['snəʊdn]
Snowdonia [snəʊ'dəʊnjə]
South Africa [ˌsaʊθ‿'æfrɪkə]
Spain [speɪn]
Speaker's Corner [ˌspi:kəz 'kɔ:nə]
Spokane [spɒ'kæn]
Staten Island [ˌstætn‿'aɪlənd]
Stratford ['strætfəd]
Suquamish [sʊ'kwɑ:mɪʃ]
Swansea ['swɒnzɪ]
Switzerland ['swɪtsələnd]
Tenby ['tenbɪ]
Times Square [ˌtaɪmz 'skweə]
Tonga ['tɒŋgə]
The **Tower of London** [ðə ˌtaʊər‿əv 'lʌndən]
Tower Bridge [ˌtaʊə 'brɪdʒ]
Tower Hill [ˌtaʊə 'hɪl]
Trafalgar Square [trə'fælgə 'skweə]
Trinidad ['trɪnɪdæd]
Truro ['trʊərəʊ]
Turkey ['tɜ:kɪ]
The **UK** (= **The United Kingdom**) [ju: 'keɪ = ju:'naɪtɪd 'kɪŋdəm]

USA (= **United States of America, US**) [ˌju:es'eɪ = ju:'naɪtɪd steɪts‿əv‿ə'merɪkə, ˌju: 'es]
Virginia [və'dʒɪnjə]
WA (= **Washington**) ['dʌblju: eɪ = 'wɒʃɪŋtən]
Wales [weɪlz]
Waterloo Bridge [ˌwɔ:təlu: 'brɪdʒ]
Waterloo Station [ˌwɔ:təlu: 'steɪʃn]
The **West Indies** [ðə ˌwest‿'ɪndɪz]
Westminster Abbey [ˌwestmɪnstər‿'æbɪ]
York [jɔ:k]
Yorkshire ['jɔ:kʃə]
Yorkshire Dales [ˌjɔ:kʃə 'deɪlz]
Yorkshire Moors [ˌjɔ:kʃə 'mɔ:z]
Yorkshire Wolds [ˌjɔ:kʃə 'wəʊldz]
Yosemite [jəʊ'semɪtɪ]

Other names

Alton Towers [ˌɔ:ltən 'taʊəz]
American Adventure Centre [ə'merɪkən əd'ventʃə 'sentə]
⟨Americano⟩ [əˌmerɪ'kɑ:nəʊ]
the **Angles and Saxons** [ˌðɪ ˌæŋglz‿ən 'sæksnz]
Apple Tours [æpl 'tɔ:z]
Arty ['ɑ:tɪ]
Asterix ['æstərɪks]
Batman ['bætmæn]
Beowulf ['beɪəʊwʊlf]
Big Wheel [ˌbɪg 'wi:l]
All **Blacks** [ˌɔ:l 'blæks]
The **British Library** [ðə ˌbrɪtɪʃ 'laɪbrərɪ]
The **British Museum** [ðə ˌbrɪtɪʃ mju:'zɪəm]
Broadway ['brɔ:dweɪ]
Bugs Bunny [ˌbʌgz 'bʌnɪ]
Camelot ['kæmɪlɒt]
Captain Courage [ˌkæptɪn 'kʌrɪdʒ]
Charlie Brown [tʃɑ:lɪ 'braʊn]
Charlie Chaplin ['tʃɑ:lɪ 'tʃæplɪn]
Chicago Bulls [ʃɪ'kɑ:gəʊ 'bʊlz]
Christopher Columbus ['krɪstəfə kə'lʌmbəs]
° **Commando** [kə'mɑ:ndəʊ]
Dracula ['drækjʊlə]
⟨Dudley Randall⟩ ['dʌdlɪ 'rændl]
Edward I [ˌedwəd ðə 'fɜ:st]
the **Empire State Building** [ˌempaɪə 'steɪt ˌbɪldɪŋ]
Eurostar ['jʊərəʊˌstɑ:]
Factcenter ['fæktˌsentə]
Food Court ['fu:d ˌkɔ:t]
Friar Tuck [ˌfraɪə 'tʌk]
Gala apples ['gɑ:lə]
General Grant Tree [ˌdʒenrl ˌgrɑ:nt 'tri:]
Goose Fair ['gu:s feə]
The **Great Spirit** [ðə greɪt 'spɪrɪt]
Greenwood ['gri:nwʊd]
Guy Fawkes [gaɪ 'fɔ:ks]
the **Hard Rock Café** [ˌhɑ:d rɒk‿'kæfeɪ]
Haywood School ['heɪwʊd 'sku:l]
Hydro [ˌhaɪdrə]
IHS (= **Issaquah High School**) [ˌaɪ‿eɪtʃ‿'es = 'ɪzəˌkwɑ: 'haɪ sku:l]
the **International District** [ˌɪntə'næʃənl 'dɪstrɪkt]
The **Jackals** [ðə 'dʒækɔ:lz]
James Bond [ˌdʒeɪmz 'bɒnd]
James Cook [dʒeɪmz kʊk]
Jan Mark ['dʒæn ˌmɑ:k]
John Lennon [dʒɒn 'lenən]
the **Joker** [ðə 'dʒəʊkə]
Kermit ['kɜ:mɪt]
King Arthur [ˌkɪŋ 'ɑ:θə]
King's Park ['kɪŋz ˌpɑ:k]
⟨Kitty-kitty⟩ ['kɪtɪ kɪtɪ]
Lake Sammamish [ˌleɪk sə'mæmɪʃ]
Lance [lɑ:ns]
Lancelot ['lɑ:nsəlɒt]
Lincoln Square [ˌlɪŋkən 'skweə]
Lois Lane [ˌləʊɪs 'leɪn]
Londoner ['lʌndənə]
M6 [ˌem 'sɪks]
Madison Avenue [ˌmædɪsən 'ævənju:]
⟨Magic Kingdom⟩ [ˌmædʒɪk 'kɪŋdəm]
⟨Major Tom⟩ [meɪdʒə 'tɒm]
London **Marathon** ['lʌndən ˌmærəθn]
Miss Piggy [mɪs 'pɪgɪ]
⟨Mother Nature⟩ ['mʌðə 'neɪtʃə]
The **Odeon** [ðɪ 'əʊdjən]
⟨Oreo *(AE)*⟩ ['ɒri:əʊ]
Pablo García [ˌpʌbləʊ gɑ:'si:ə]
⟨Pepsi⟩ ['pepsɪ]
the **Pike Place Market** [paɪk pleɪs 'mɑ:kɪt]
the **Pilgrims** [ðə 'pɪlgrɪmz]
Pioneer Square [paɪəˌnɪə 'skweə]
Plaza Hotel [ˌplɑ:zə həʊ'tel]
Pug [pʌg]
Pugwacket ['pʌgwækɪt]
the **Queen** [ðə 'kwi:n]
Rainier Road [ˌreɪni:ər 'rəʊd]
⟨Richard Milton Hollingshead⟩ [ˌrɪtʃəd ˌmɪltn 'hɒlɪŋzhed]
Ringo Starr [rɪŋəʊ 'stɑ:]
Robin Hood ['rɒbɪn 'hʊd]
The **Romans** [ˌðə 'rəʊmənz]
The **Round Table** [ðə ˌraʊnd 'teɪbl]
Sherlock Holmes [ˌʃɜ:lɒk 'həʊmz]
Sioux [su:]
Skyline Drive [ˌskaɪlaɪn 'draɪv]
⟨Smokey⟩ ['sməʊkɪ]
The **Sonics** (= **The Seattle Supersonics**) [ˌðə 'sɒnɪks]
the **Space Needle** [ðə 'speɪs ˌni:dl]
Spiderman ['spaɪdəmæn]
St Paul's Cathedral [sənt ˌpɔ:lz kə'θi:drəl]
St. John's School [snt 'dʒɒnz ˌsku:l]
⟨Super Youth pill⟩ [sʌpə‿'ju:θ pɪl]
Superbowl ['su:pəbəʊl]
Superman ['su:pəmæn]
The **Taj Mahal Restaurant** [ðə ˌtʌdʒ mə'hɑ:l 'restərɒnt]
Thunder Looper [ˌθʌndə 'lu:pə]
Tricky Situations ['trɪkɪ ˌsɪtjʊ'eɪʃnz]
Trocadero [ˌtrɒkə'dɪərəʊ]
Twycross zoo ['twaɪkrɒs 'zu:]
Walker Colt [ˌwɔ:kə 'kəʊlt]
Walt Disney [wɔ:lt 'dɪznɪ]
Wembley Stadium [ˌwemblɪ 'steɪdjəm]
Wild West [waɪld 'west]
William the Conqueror [ˌwɪljəm ðə 'kɒŋkərə]
Wimbledon ['wɪmbldən]
Winchester ['wɪnʃɪstə]
World Cup [ˌwɜ:ld 'kʌp]
the **World Trade Center** [wɜ:ld 'treɪd ˌsentə]
Worldfest [wɜ:ld'fest]

List of irregular verbs

infinitive	simple past	past participle	German
be [bi:]	was [wɒz]	been [bi:n]	sein
beat [bi:t]	beat [bi:t]	beaten ['bi:tn]	schlagen
become [bɪ'kʌm]	became [bɪ'keɪm]	become [bɪ'kʌm]	werden
begin [bɪ'gɪn]	began [bɪ'gæn]	begun [bɪ'gʌn]	beginnen
bend [bend]	bent [bent]	bent [bent]	(sich) bücken, biegen
blow [bləʊ]	blew [blu:]	blown [bləʊn]	blasen
bring [brɪŋ]	brought [brɔ:t]	brought [brɔ:t]	bringen
build [bɪld]	built [bɪlt]	built [bɪlt]	bauen
burn [bɜ:n]	burnt [bɜ:nt]	burnt [bɜ:nt]	brennen
buy [baɪ]	bought [bɔ:t]	bought [bɔ:t]	kaufen
catch [kætʃ]	caught [kɔ:t]	caught [kɔ:t]	fangen
choose [tʃu:z]	chose [tʃəʊz]	chosen ['tʃəʊzn]	auswählen
come [kʌm]	came [keɪm]	come [kʌm]	kommen
cost [kɒst]	cost [kɒst]	cost [kɒst]	kosten
cut [kʌt]	cut [kʌt]	cut [kʌt]	schneiden
do [du:]	did [dɪd]	done [dʌn]	machen, tun
draw [drɔ:]	drew [dru:]	drawn [drɔ:n]	zeichnen, ziehen
drink [drɪŋk]	drank [dræŋk]	drunk [drʌŋk]	trinken
drive [draɪv]	drove [drəʊv]	driven ['drɪvn]	fahren
eat [i:t]	ate [et]	eaten ['i:tn]	essen
fall [fɔ:l]	fell [fel]	fallen ['fɔ:ln]	fallen
feed [fi:d]	fed [fed]	fed [fed]	füttern
feel [fi:l]	felt [felt]	felt [felt]	fühlen
fight [faɪt]	fought [fɔ:t]	fought [fɔ:t]	kämpfen
find [faɪnd]	found [faʊnd]	found [faʊnd]	finden
fly [flai]	flew [flu:]	flown [fləʊn]	fliegen
forget [fə'get]	forgot [fə'gɒt]	forgotten [fə'gɒtn]	vergessen
get [get]	got [gɒt]	got [gɒt]	holen, bekommen
give [gɪv]	gave [geɪv]	given ['gɪvn]	geben
go [gəʊ]	went [went]	gone [gɒn]	gehen
grow [grəʊ]	grew [gru:]	grown [grəʊn]	(an)pflanzen, wachsen
have [hæv]	had [hæd]	had [hæd]	haben
hear [hɪə]	heard [hɜ:d]	heard [hɜ:d]	hören
hide [haɪd]	hid [hɪd]	hidden ['hɪdn]	(sich) verstecken
hit [hɪt]	hit [hɪt]	hit [hɪt]	schlagen, treffen
hold [həʊld]	held [held]	held [held]	halten
hurt [hɜ:t]	hurt [hɜ:t]	hurt [hɜ:t]	verletzen, weh tun
keep [ki:p]	kept [kept]	kept [kept]	(be)halten
know [nəʊ]	knew [nju:]	known [nəʊn]	wissen, kennen
lay [leɪ]	laid [leɪd]	laid [leɪd]	legen
lead [li:d]	led [led]	led [led]	führen
learn [lɜ:n]	learned [lɜ:nt], learnt [lɜ:nt]	learned [lɜ:nt], learnt [lɜ:nt]	lernen
leave [li:v]	left [left]	left [left]	(ver)lassen

infinitive	simple past	past participle	German
lend [lend]	lent [lent]	lent [lent]	(ver)leihen
let [let]	let [let]	let [let]	lassen
lie [laɪ]	lay [leɪ]	lain [leɪn]	liegen
lose [lu:z]	lost [lɒst]	lost [lɒst]	verlieren
make [meɪk]	made [meɪd]	made [meɪd]	machen
mean [mi:n]	meant [ment]	meant [ment]	bedeuten
meet [mi:t]	met [met]	met [met]	treffen, begegnen
pay [peɪ]	paid [peɪd]	paid [peɪd]	zahlen, bezahlen
put [pʊt]	put [pʊt]	put [pʊt]	setzen, stellen, legen
read [ri:d]	read [red]	read [red]	lesen
ride [raɪd]	rode [rəʊd]	ridden ['rɪdn]	reiten, fahren
ring [rɪŋ]	rang [ræŋ]	rung [rʌŋ]	klingeln, anrufen
rise [raɪz]	rose [rəʊz]	risen ['rɪzn]	aufstehen
run [rʌn]	ran [ræn]	run [rʌn]	laufen, rennen
say [seɪ]	said [sed]	said [sed]	sagen
see [si:]	saw [sɔ:]	seen [si:n]	sehen
sell [sel]	sold [səʊld]	sold [səʊld]	verkaufen
send [send]	sent [sent]	sent [sent]	schicken, senden
shake [ʃeɪk]	shook [ʃʊk]	shaken [ʃeɪkn]	schütteln, zittern
shoot [ʃu:t]	shot [ʃɒt]	shot [ʃɒt]	schießen
show [ʃəʊ]	showed [ʃəʊd]	shown [ʃəʊn]	zeigen
sing [sɪŋ]	sang [sæŋ]	sung [sʌŋ]	singen
sit [sɪt]	sat [sæt]	sat [sæt]	sitzen
sleep [sli:p]	slept [slept]	slept [slept]	schlafen
smell [smel]	smelt [smelt]	smelt [smelt]	riechen
speak [spi:k]	spoke [spəʊk]	spoken ['spəʊkn]	sprechen
spell [spel]	spelled [spelt], spelt [spelt]	spelled [spelt], spelt [spelt]	buchstabieren
spend [spend]	spent [spent]	spent [spent]	ausgeben, verbringen
stand [stænd]	stood [stʊd]	stood [stʊd]	stehen
steal [sti:l]	stole [stəʊl]	stolen ['stəʊlən]	stehlen
swear [sweə]	swore [swɔ:]	sworn [swɔ:n]	schwören, fluchen
swim [swɪm]	swam [swæm]	swum [swʌm]	schwimmen
take [teɪk]	took [tʊk]	taken ['teɪkn]	nehmen, bringen
teach [ti:tʃ]	taught [tɔ:t]	taught [tɔ:t]	lehren
tell [tel]	told [təʊld]	told [təʊld]	erzählen, sagen
think [θɪnk]	thought [θɔ:t]	thought [θɔ:t]	denken
throw [θrəʊ]	threw [θru:]	thrown [θrəʊn]	werfen
understand [ˌʌndə'stænd]	understood [ˌʌndə'stʊd]	understood [ˌʌndə'stʊd]	verstehen
wake [weɪk]	woke [wəʊk]	woken ['wəʊkn]	wecken, aufwachen
wear [weə]	wore [wɔ:]	worn [wɔ:n]	tragen (Kleidung)
win [wɪn]	won [wʌn]	won [wʌn]	gewinnen
write [raɪt]	wrote [rəʊt]	written ['rɪtn]	schreiben

⟨Classroom phrases⟩

Arriving and leaving

I'm sorry I'm late.	Tut mir Leid, dass ich mich verspätet habe.
I've forgotten my exercise book.	Ich habe mein Heft vergessen.
What's for homework?	Was haben wir als Hausaufgabe auf?
See you next time.	Bis zum nächsten Mal.
Have a nice weekend.	Schönes Wochenende!

If there is a problem …

Are you feeling OK?	Ist alles in Ordnung?
I'm fine, thank you.	Gut, danke.
What's the matter with you?	Was fehlt dir denn?
I'm not feeling well.	Ich fühle mich nicht gut.
I've got a headache.	Ich habe Kopfweh.

Asking for help

What do we have to do?	Was müssen wir denn machen?
What's that in English/German?	Was heißt das auf Englisch/Deutsch?
Can I say: …?/What does … mean?	Kann ich sagen: …?/Was bedeutet …?
How do you do this exercise?	Wie macht man diese Übung?
Did you understand what he/she said?	Hast du verstanden, was er/sie sagte?
No, I didn't understand it either.	Nein, ich habe das auch nicht verstanden.
Could you write it on the board, please?	Könnten Sie das bitte an die Tafel schreiben?
Sorry? Can you repeat the question/sentence, please?	Wie bitte? Können Sie die Frage/den Satz bitte wiederholen?
Can you play the cassette again, please?	Können Sie die Kassette bitte nochmal abspielen?
Could you play it with pauses, please?	Könnten Sie sie bitte mit Pausen abspielen?
Can we do another example, please?	Können wir noch ein Beispiel machen?

Working together

Do we do this in groups/with partners?	Machen wir dies in Gruppen-/Partnerarbeit?
Whose turn is it?	Wer ist dran?
What are we going to do first?	Was machen wir als Erstes?
Who is going to write down our results?	Wer schreibt unsere Ergebnisse auf?
I'd like to present our results.	Ich möchte unsere Ergebnisse vorstellen.

Working at a computer

My computer has crashed.	Mein Rechner ist abgestürzt.
I can't understand this message on the screen.	Ich verstehe diese Meldung auf dem Bildschirm nicht.
It won't accept my username/password.	Mein Benutzername/Kennwort wird nicht angenommen.
What's the address of this website?	Wie ist die Internet-Adresse für diese Seite?
Which option shall I click on?	Auf welches Feld soll ich klicken?
What am I supposed to punch in here?	Was soll ich hier eintippen?
I have saved it on disk.	Ich habe es auf Diskette gespeichert.

Talking about stories, poems, songs, ...

I liked/didn't like the story.	Diese Geschichte gefiel mir/gefiel mir nicht.
I thought it was brilliant/interesting/ funny/really exciting.	Ich fand sie toll/interessant/ witzig/wirklich spannend.
I thought it was sad/terrible/boring.	Ich fand sie traurig/schrecklich/langweilig.
It was OK, but I've read better ones.	Sie war OK, aber ich habe schon bessere gelesen.
I enjoyed it very much.	Ich habe sie gern gelesen/gehört/gesehen.
It was hard to follow.	Sie war schwer verständlich.
There wasn't much action in the story.	Es passierte nicht viel in der Geschichte.
The ending was unexpected/predictable.	Der Schluss war unerwartet/vorauszusagen.
The main/minor characters ...	Die Haupt-/Nebenfiguren ...
The plot/setting/theme ...	Die Handlung/der Schauplatz/das Thema ...
What is the writer/poet trying to tell us?	Was will uns der Autor/Dichter damit sagen?
I like the music but the words aren't very original.	Ich finde die Musik gut, aber der Text ist nicht besonders originell.

Having a discussion ...

What do you think?	Was meinst du?
I disagree.	Ich bin anderer Meinung.
In my opinion ...	Meiner Meinung nach .../Meines Erachtens ...
I can see your point, but ...	Ich verstehe dein Argument, aber ...
I think you are right/wrong.	Ich denke, du hast Recht/Unrecht.
That's one way of looking at it.	So kann man's auch sehen.
I don't follow you.	Ich verstehe nicht, was du meinst.
On the one hand ..., on the other hand ...	Einerseits ..., andererseits ...
I don't think that's relevant.	Das finde ich nicht wichtig.

What the teacher might say to you

Let's have a look at the text on page	Schlagt bitte Seite ... auf.
Please turn to page	Bitte blättert auf Seite ... um.
I'd like someone to write the answers on a transparency.	Ich brauche jemanden, der die Lösungen auf eine Folie schreibt.
You're going to hear the recording twice.	Ihr werdet die Aufnahme zweimal hören.
Would you collect the exercise books/ worksheets, please?	Würdest du bitte die Übungshefte/Arbeitsblätter einsammeln?
Do this exercise for homework.	Macht diese Übung als Hausaufgabe.
Try to find some more information about this topic on the internet.	Versuch/Versucht, weitere Informationen über dieses Thema im Internet zu finden.
Please speak up.	Sprich bitte lauter.
No prompting, please.	Nicht vorsagen, bitte.
Please don't interrupt him/her.	Bitte unterbrich ihn/sie nicht.
Let him/her finish.	Lass ihn/sie ausreden.
Excellent!/Spot on!	Prima! Genau richtig!
Not quite. Think again.	Nicht ganz richtig. Denk nochmal nach.
Have another go.	Versuch es noch einmal.

Bildquellen:

Cover: Pictor International Bildagentur GmbH (swimmer);
Inside cover: Focus, Hamburg, International/Science Photo Library; adaptation: Scivos/Klett-Perthes (satellite map of the USA)
p. 7: Ray Jeanotte, Auburn, WA, USA (mountain and lake, Washington State);
p. 8: Ruth Mitchell, Issaquah, WA, USA (the Alburg family);
p. 9: Ray Jeanotte, Auburn, WA, USA (Village Theatre/shop at Gilman Village/Issaquah's main street/at the bowling alley/at a drive-in restaurant); IFA Bilderteam GmbH, München-Taufkirchen (hiking in the forests); Sally and Richard Greenhill Photo Library/Bilderberg, London (on Lake Sammamish);
p. 10: Ray Jeanotte, Auburn, WA, USA (Daniel Alburg/Alex Alburg/Tori Alburg/Cindy Cho); Stockfood, München (stuffed salmon trout);
p. 11: Ray Jeanotte, Auburn, WA, USA (basketball scenes: "high five"/group of kids);
p. 14: Ray Jeanotte, Auburn, WA, USA (Tori's car keys);
p. 19: The Stock Market (white water rafting scene);
p. 20: Ray Jeanotte, Auburn, WA, USA (Soo/Anna/Isi); Klett Archiv (Josh); Mauritius (Daryl);
p. 22: Ray Jeanotte, Auburn, WA, USA (Seattle International District/Pioneer Square/Space Needle/Seattle International Market); Sportimage (basketball game: Seattle Supersonics - Chicago Bulls),
p. 23: Ray Jeanotte, Auburn, WA, USA (Daniel, Cindy, Tori, Alex);
p. 26: Michael Steinle, Stuttgart (fortune cookie);
p. 28: M. Nichols/Aurora/Bilderberg (Cadillac);
p. 32: Ray Jeanotte, Auburn, WA, USA (students pledging allegiance/IHS Indians logo/students by lockers/IHS notice board); M. Hoffmann/Mauritius (cheerleaders);
p. 33: Ruth Mitchell, Issaquah, WA, USA (Daniel, talking on the telephone/Rachel talking on the telephone);
p. 36: Chad Ehlers/Transglobe (Grand Canyon); Foto & Wort Steenmanns (Mesa Verde); Postl/Silvestris (Shenandoah);
p. 37: Hackenberg (Yosemite); Superstock (Everglades);Foto & Wort Steenmanns (Denali);
p. 40: Guido Steenmann/Foto & Wort Steenmanns (coastal buildings in Florida);
p. 42: Silvestris (black bear);
p. 44: Engelmaier/Buena Vista (Balou);
p. 46: Bilderberg (Drive-in movie theater); Bildarchiv Engelmaier (Bugs Bunny);
p. 49: Peter Newark (longhouse); Bildarchiv Preußischer Kulturbesitz (hunting buffaloes);
p. 50: David Hiser/Tony Stone (wagon train);
p. 54: Focus/Vandystadt (bicycle courier);
p. 55: Peter Ginter/Bilderberg (Times Square/Central Park); Jose Azel/Bilderberg (boy); Thomas Laird/Peter Arnold (Empire State Building); Ellerbrock und Schafft/Bilderberg (Chinatown); Frieder Blickle/Bilderberg (Broadway theater);
p. 59: Westlight/Mauritius (the Braddocks); Age/Mauritius (Shelley Grant); Superstock (Anne Ross); Mauritius (Michael O'Reilly); foto-presse timmermann (Manhattan by night);
p. 64: Lutz Bongarts/Bongarts (Superbowl); Photri/Mauritius (fireworks); Superstock (kid in Halloween costume);
p. 65: Hubatka/Mauritius (by the camp fire);
p. 77: Ray Jeanotte, Auburn, WA, USA (supermarket/motel/carrots/apples/Music Express); Rolf W. Roth, Idar-Oberstein (speed limit);
p. 81: AKG photo (gold diggers);
p. 85: Ulrike Lehmberg, Stuttgart (cake);
p. 88: dpa (Rauchwetter) (Grand Canyon);
Inside cover: Joachim Krüger, Korntal (maps of Manhattan/New York City)

Textquellen:

p. 14: *Friday on my mind* by The Easybeats. Text and melody by Vanda - Young. © Line Music GmbH;
p. 17: Extract from PONS Schülerwörterbuch;
p. 24: *The Melting Pot* by Dudley Randall from "Cities Burning", © Broadside Press, Detroit, 1968;
p. 28: *Americanos* by Holly Johnson/Mangowork Ltd., © Neue Welt Musikverlag GmbH, München;
p. 29: *Spider-Man* from Stan Lee (ed.)/Sal Buscema (artist): "The spectacular Spider-Man", No. 164, p. 16, © Marvel Entertainment Group;
p. 34: Extract from *The Sammamish*. Issaquah High School Yearbook 1995;
p. 35: *Claudia and the Middle School Mystery* by Ann M. Martin. (Baby-sitters Club No. 40) © 1991 by Ann M. Martin. Reprinted by permission of the publisher, Scholastic Inc. The Baby-sitters Club is a registered trademark of Scholastic Inc.;
p. 43: *Brochure,* "Don't feed the bears!" American Park Network, 22 Battery St., 4th floor, San Francisco, CA 94111, USA;
p. 44: *The Bare Necessities* by Terry Gilkyson © Neue Welt Musikverlag;
p. 48: Extract from a *Speech of Crazy Horse* from "Touch the Earth - A Self-Portrait of Indian Existence". Compiled by T.C. Mc Luhan. Abacus; *Map* "Indian reservations" from Children's Illustrated Encyclopedia, p.589 © 1991 Dorling Kindersley Ltd, London; dt. Ausgabe „Das Große Ravensburger Lexikon", erschienen beim Ravensburger Buchverlag, Ravensburg 1992; Extract from *Lucky Luke* 61, Delta Verlag, Stuttgart © Morris;
p. 49: *Map* "Oregon Trail" from Children's Encyclopedia, p.520 © 1991 Dorling Kindersley Ltd, London; dt. Ausgabe „Das Große Ravensburger Lexikon", erschienen beim Ravensburger Buchverlag, Ravensburg 1992; Extract from Louis L' Amour: *The Gift of Cochise*, © 1952 Cromwell-Collier Publishing Co. Ltd.;
p. 54: *Home on the Indian Trail.* Extract from "Little House on the Prairie" by Laura Ingalls Wilder, © Puffin Books, 1964;
p. 56: *Brochure* Empire State Building, © Helmsley-Spear Inc., New York, NY 10118;
p. 58: *graffiti* © Fred Meyer http://www.totalny.com/first person/photodiaries/graffiti/
p. 59: *New York, New York* by Fred Ebb/John Kander. Unart Music Corp. © BMI Warner Bros. Corp.;
p. 62: *Cartoon "Cab from Hell".* Ros Chast. © The New Yorker Magazine, Inc., 1983;
p. 63: *Cartoon "The Streets of New York".* Mc Lachlan, © Punch;
p. 64: *Valentine's card,* Accord Cards, Baldwin Terrace, London N1 7RU, © Design by Beverly Guhl;
p. 67: *Fox Trot comic strip* from: Bill Amend. Fox Trot. The Works, p. 95; Andrews and McMeel, © Bill Amend. Reprinted with permission of Universal Press Syndicate. All rights reserved.
p. 74: Extract from *Captain Courage and the Rose Street Gang* by Jan Mark. © Collins 1987;
p. 72: *Space Oddity* by David Bowie, © EMI Records Ltd., 1990;
p. 78: *Claudia and the Middle School Mystery* by Ann M. Martin. (Baby-sitters Club No. 40) © 1991 by Ann M. Martin. Reprinted by permission of the publisher, Scholastic Inc. The Baby-sitters Club is a registered trademark of Scholastic Inc.;
p. 79: *Wendy cartoon* courtesy of "Seventeen Magazine" 1/1987/ Richard Warwick;
p. 80: *Clementine,* trad., Words and Music by Percy Montrose;
p. 81: *Cartoon "Ed's Cafe"* © Mirror Group Newspapers

Manhattan
Lincoln Square
Central Park West
The Lake
West 65th Street
Lincoln Center
Central Park
East 75th St
West 60th St
Avenue
East 70th Street
Columbus Circle
Fifth
Avenue
East 65th Street
Broadway
Madison
Plaza Hotel
East 60th Street
151st Street
Henry Hudson Parkway
Harlem River
Harlem
The Bronx
Hudson River
Riverside Park
Broadway
Columbia University
110th Street
East Harlem
Upper West Side
Central Park
Reservoir
96th Street
Wards Island
Upper East Side
Fifth Ave
Lincoln Center
Broadway
F.D. Roosevelt Drive
Tenth Avenue
Ninth Avenue
United Nations
Lincoln Tunnel
Roosevelt Island
Queens
Museum of Modern Art
East 57th Street
West 42nd Street
Times Square
Rockefeller Center
Railway
Queensboro Bridge
West 34th Street
Midtown
Second Ave
First Avenue
Lower West Side
Madison Square Garden
Empire State Building
Queens Midtown Tunnel
Hudson River
Broadway
East 23rd Street
West 14th Street
West Village
Greenwich Village
East 14th Street
Lower East Side
Westside Highway
Holland Tunnel
East River
Soho
Little Ukraine
Little Italy
Tribeca
Broadway
China town
Battery Park City
World Trade Center
Downtown
South St
Williamsburg Bridge
Wall Street
Manhattan Bridge
Brooklyn Bridge
Ellis Island
Battery Park
Ferry
Brooklyn Battery Tunnel
Brooklyn
Liberty Island
Statue of Liberty
Statue of Liberty